Key Ideas in Educational Research

Related titles
Educational Research Primer – Anthony Picciano
Philosophy of Educational Research 2nd edition – Richard Pring
Educational Research – Jerry Wellington
Quantitative Methods in Educational Research – Stephen Gorard
Doing Qualitative Educational Research – Geoffrey Walford
Educational Research in Practice – Joanna Swann and John Pratt
Theory of Education – David Turner
Philosophy of Education – Richard Pring

Continuum Research Methods Series
Action Research – Patrick Costello
Analysing Media Texts – Andrew Burn and David Parker
Ethics in Research – Ian Gregory
Research Questions – Richard Andrews
Researching Post-compulsory Education – Jill Jameson and
   Yvonne Hillier
Systematic Reviews – Carole Torgerson
Using Focus Groups in Research – Lia Litosseliti

Real World Research Series
Series Editor: Bill Gillham
Case Study in Research Methods – Bill Gillham
Developing a Questionnaire – Bill Gillham
The Research Interview – Bill Gillham

KEY IDEAS IN EDUCATIONAL RESEARCH

David Scott and Marlene Morrison

continuum

Continuum International Publishing Group
The Tower Building   15 East 26th Street
11 York Road   New York, NY 10010
London
SE1 7NX

www.continuumbooks.com

First published 2006

British Library Cataloguing-in-Publication Data
A catalogue record for this book is available from the British Library.

ISBN: 0-8264-7990-1 (hardback)

Library of Congress Cataloging-in-Publication Data
A catalog record for this book is available from the Library of Congress.

Typeset by BookEns Ltd., Royston, Herts.
Printed and bound in Great Britain by
Antony Rowe Ltd, Chippenham, Wiltshire

Contents

Tables and Figures

Acknowledgements

Parts of Chapters 13, 21, 29, 63, 84 and 110 have appeared in Scott (2000), Scott (2003) and Scott et. al. (2004). Permission to use this material has been given by Routledge Falmer Press and The Open University Press.

The book is dedicated to Oliver, Sarah and Ben.

Preface

This book provides concise, but we hope illuminative, essays on 120 major ideas in the field of educational research methodology. These range from key schools of thought such as *phenomenology, positivism, ethnomethodology* and *postmodernism*, through philosophical concepts such as *induction, realism, relativism* and *power*; educational research strategies such as *case study, experiment, survey* and *ethnography*; educational research methods such as *questionnaires, interviews* and *observations*; to infrastructural issues such as *dissemination, publishing* and *referencing*. It is intended to be a resource for readers with an interest in understanding research methodology in the field of education and also for those engaging in research. It can therefore be used in a number of ways. First, the reader can select particular entries that suit their needs and concerns. Second, it can be read as a text on educational research methodology, though some coherence of argument is bound to be lost if read from beginning to end. Third, we provide opportunities for other routes through the book that attempt to make alternative connections between the different entries. These take the form of an author index, a subject index and a cross-referencing index at the end of each item to enable the reader to make different connections between the concepts and ideas than a linear reading of the text would allow.

Inevitably in a field which is as contested as this, a number of choices had to be made, and these choices broadly reflect our philosophical inclinations and perspectives. Indeed, our decision to include philosophical, strategic, instrumental and infrastructural items reflects a belief that educational research cannot be carried out, or even properly understood, without reference to all four of these concerns. All too frequently, educational research is seen as a technical exercise, which can be engaged in by anyone with the ability to follow a prespecified formula. Our understanding of educational research is different from this, as we believe that the researcher has to engage with the difficult and often flawed business of constructing knowledge through and with other people. This at the very least makes it an ethical affair, and moreover one that has to concern itself with the central issue of how we can know the social world.

This engagement with philosophy means that the researcher has also to engage with the contested nature of the field, and it is therefore incumbent on the authors of a book such as this to be transparent about the value positions which have informed the choice of items and the content of each of the short essays. We have already suggested one such framework, that educational researchers need to engage with philosophical questions about the nature of reality and how they can know it. Further to this, we suggested that because its central purpose is to understand human relations, research is an ethical undertaking. The third undergirding principle is that it is impossible to take a neutral position on many of the debates that structure the field. This book is therefore written from a particular perspective on educational research (critical realism), and our contention is that every other book on educational research methodology has to take a similar stance, though many of them fail to acknowledge this. On the other hand, we have also sought at all times to adopt a critical stance towards positions that we ourselves take up and those taken up by others. Whether we have succeeded or not will depend on our skill, as well as the capacity of the reader to engage with a text that seeks to problematize common sense and generally accepted views of research and education.

David Scott and Marlene Morrison

1 Abduction

Abduction is an interpretivist research strategy. Whereas positivists and variable analysts marginalize the meaning-making activities of social actors, interpretivists focus on these activities, and in particular, individuals' intentions, reasons and motives. This is an insider's perspective, and therefore outsider or external accounts of social actors' beliefs and intentions are considered to give a partial view of reality. It is the beliefs and practices of individuals that constitute the subject matter of research.

The abductive process comprises the way educational researchers go beyond the accounts given by social actors about their plans, intentions and actions in the real world. This process is multi-layered, with the first stage being the collection of data that reports how individuals understand reality, using methods such as semi-structured and auto-biographical interviews. At the second stage the researcher moves from reporting lay accounts to constructing social scientific theories about human relations. Some types of interpretivists argue that this constitutes an illegitimate step, and for them, concepts, ideas and constructs have to be embedded in lay accounts, and their task is to report them. There are a number of problems with this approach: the process of collecting data about these accounts is likely to influence them; and analysing and reporting such accounts involves synthesizing and compressing activities, which constitute a going beyond the original account.

Other types of interpretivists have suggested that it is legitimate, and have developed various methods that allow them to construct social scientific accounts. For example, Schutz (1963: 339) argued that movement from first to second-order constructs comprises the development of models of typical social actors, who have typical motives and behave in typical ways:

> Yet these models of actors are not human beings living within their biographical situation in the social world of everyday life. Strictly speaking they do not have any biography or any history, and the situation into which they are placed is not a situation defined by them but defined by their creator, the social scientist.

In a similar fashion, Weber (1964) argued that abstraction, which is present in social scientific accounts but may not be present in lay accounts, is mediated through the development of ideal types. Though there are some problems with the designation of these typifications, and for Weber, second-order accounts do not necessarily grow out of first-order accounts, most abductive researchers subscribe to Giddens' (1984: 2) admonition that 'all social actors, no matter how lowly, have some degree of penetration of the social forms which oppress them', and therefore address the issue of second-order constructs, or social scientific explanations, in terms of first-order constructs. That is, the latter is prior to the former. The adoption of such an abductive approach also commits the educational researcher to the use of certain types of methods and instruments, for example, semi-structured interviews, rather than standardized tests. Abduction is an alternative to retroductive, inductive and deductive strategies in educational research.

See also:
Biography/Autobiography (8); Deduction (27); Induction (55); Interpretivism (56); Interview (57); Positivism (75); Retroduction (97); Tests (109); Variable Analysis (116).

2   Access

Issues of access, power and ethics are closely intertwined in research projects. This is because educational settings are stratified in various ways; for example, schools are horizontally structured so that individuals within the organization have different amounts of power. Educational institutions are also vertically structured in so far as social markers such as gender and ethnicity confer different amounts of power on members. Furthermore, some institutional members have greater knowledge of, and consequently a greater capacity to manipulate, those power relations than others. Gaining access to an educational institution is therefore a complicated matter, requiring of the researcher strategies to minimize failure.

Obtaining consent to conduct research projects, and therefore gaining access to research settings, requires researchers to give as much information to participants as they can about the purposes of their enquiry, their methodological approach and their dissemination and reporting strategies. However, many educational research projects have emergent features. For example, grounded theory includes a stage of re-evaluation of data-collection methods in response to initial data that are collected. This re-evaluation may entail new methods being employed; and those new methods may not have been anticipated by the researcher and certainly could not have been specified at the initial access meeting. So, the concept of emergence immediately compromises the principle of informed consent. Gaining access in its initial phase therefore demands not complete informed consent, but consent based on as much information as is available at the time.

Consent still has to be obtained by the researcher from potential participants in the research project. Again, this has to be understood in terms of whether it is reasonably given and whether that person is able to give it, even if about matters that directly concern them. In the first case, the issue is whether, given full information about the project, the researcher is entitled to overturn that consent if they feel that it may harm the participant. An example of this might be where a headteacher grants access to their school for the purposes of researching an aspect of its practice, and then does not insist on anonymity in relation to the school because they do not fully appreciate the potential way the press and other interested parties may misrepresent the findings of the report. In the second case, especially with educational research involving children, it might be thought necessary to not just seek permission from the child to interview them, but also from their parents, because it is argued that the child is not able to make a reasonable judgement about their own best interests.

The final issue with obtaining access to research sites relates to the stratified nature of institutions. Though researchers cannot gain access legally to educational institutions without permission being given by the headteacher, sometimes permission is given in relation to every aspect of the life of the school. As a result, teachers, ancillary workers and the like are required to cooperate with the researcher on the grounds that the headteacher gave permission to the researcher. Access however, in its purest form, implies a process of negotiating and renegotiating with all respondents at different levels of the institutional hierarchy and at different times in the project, especially if the emergent nature of the design means that major changes are being made to the methods and procedures. The final principle being invoked here is that of the right of participants not to take part in the project if they do not wish to. Seeking and gaining access to educational sites is frequently difficult and involves the researcher in making judgements about how much information should be given to participants, in what way, and at which point in the lifetime of the project.

See also:
Anti-racism (6); Ethics (39); Gender (49); Grounded Theory (51); Media (63); Method (64); Power (77).

3 Action Research

Eclecticism is a key feature of action research. Described variously as action research, action-research, and action inquiry, various writers have also prefaced the term with words such as collaborative, participative, critical, technical, emancipatory and practical, as if to offer readers a specific type or category of action research. Not surprisingly it has been understood (and misunderstood) in a number of ways. Fundamentally, action research is a research strategy which sets out to change the situation being researched. Its commitment to change does not preclude the use of familiar and 'traditional' research methods, frequently but not always orientated towards qualitative approaches. Its aims and purposes, however, can be seen in contrast to more traditional forms of research in which the intention (indeed requirement) is not to change or influence the situation being studied. Action research developed partly from a dissatisfaction with more orthodox, positivistic approaches to the study of educational phenomena and partly from a desire to use the immediate experiences of educational practitioners to understand and effect change in professional practice.

Important though practicality is, if practical application was all there was to action research then there would be little to distinguish it from other forms of applied research. Lomax (2002: 122) adapts a definition from Carr and Kemmis (1986) to describe action research as:

a self-reflective, self-critical and critical inquiry undertaken by professionals to improve the rationality and justices of their own practices, their understanding of those practices and the wider contexts of practice.

The above definition also suggests that action research is more than practitioner research although the terms are sometimes used interchangeably. All action research involves practitioners; it becomes action research when the researcher includes the investigation of his/her own practice with a view to improving it. As Edwards and Talbot (1994: 52) note:

Practitioner research can only be designated action research if it is actively carried out by professionals who are engaged in researching, through structured self-reflection, aspects of their own practice as they engage in that practice.

The use of terms is more than a question of semantics; it goes to the heart of the aims and purposes of research in education and the value stances that researchers bring to and encompass as part of their research inquiries. As Somekh (1995: 343) points out, action research rejects the concept of a two-stage process in which research is first carried out by researchers and then in a second separate stage the knowledge created by researchers is then applied by practitioners. Instead the two processes of research and action are integrated.

However, even the keenest proponents of action research differ about where the main emphasis in action research should lie. For Elliott (1991) the main emphasis is upon improving practice rather than creating knowledge. Writers like Whitehead (1993) argue that 'action research is a means of creating "living educational theories" that contribute individual epistemologies of knowledge that together contribute to knowledge more generally' (cited in Lomax, 2002: 122). More general agreement lies in acknowledging that action research is more than about *reflective* practice in the sense that Schon (1983) first applied it. Rather the emphasis is upon rigorous and systematic adherence to research techniques and practices (however eclectic) to inform that practice, and a requisite for *reflexivity* not always apparent in all forms of inquiry that are described as 'action research'.

Research rigour is variously understood in action research. As Brown and Dowling (1998) argue, a key issue is the extent to which action researchers are able to disentangle the pursuit of improvements in professional practice from the key skills needed to engage in activity which can be described as educational research. At worse, it is argued, action research plunders the field of educational research for techniques that will facilitate the action. At best, 'the professional practitioner intending to engage in educational research in the interrogation of their own practices, will need to apply the principles and not merely the trappings of these research practices' (ibid.: 167).

So far we have identified at least three fundamental aspects of action research: its *practicality*; its commitment to *change* through improvements in professional practice; and the involvement of *practitioners* in specific and self-reflexive ways. A fourth aspect of action research tends to be its cyclical nature based on a research programme that is a plan for social action. A commitment to the processes of action research is one of stepped engagement in which a feedback loop from initial findings that are implemented and evaluated generates further research in the next cycle(s). Early proponents like Kemmis (in Ebbutt, 1985) describe this in terms of the action research spiral; further elaboration is found in Coghlan and Branick (2001). If two features of the spiral predominate, namely the direct feedback of research into practice and the processual and ongoing nature of action research, the latter is sometimes honoured more in the breach than in practice. For small-scale researchers engaged in Masters and even Doctoral research, finite resources often mean that action research rarely extends beyond the first and/or second stage. Whether and how much this matters may be more an aspect of the way 'academic' work is assessed rather than about its importance to professionals engaging with it. Nonetheless, action research presents challenges for researchers and readers, and it is to a summary of those challenges that we now turn.

The intensely practical nature of action research is both its *raison d'etre* and, some might argue, its Achilles heel. Action research should have professional benefit for those who engage in it since it offers the promise of informed action (praxis) based on the interdependence of educational purposes and means but, by its nature, it is necessarily restricted in scope and scale, and those who engage in it as stakeholder/ actors do not necessarily do so with equal opportunity, commitment or scope. Action research is overwhelmingly concerned with the specific circumstances of changing the activities and the approaches of one or a few practitioners, in one setting or one set of circumstances. How then is it possible to make generalizable comments as a result of action research; or, as Whitehead (1993) would argue, combine and cohere individual epistemologies as contributions to knowledge more generally? In other contexts, for example, Bassey (1999: Chapter 1) regrets an overall lack of coherence in the outcomes of much educational research that remains individualistic and small-scale. In practice, action research is, therefore, often evoked to draw on existing theories and test them, using rigorous methods and a careful evaluation of existing knowledge and its relevance for the particular research setting. Meanwhile, Lomax (2002: 135–6) insists upon an action research frame that is 'practical' and 'authentic' with 'my emphasis on the importance of co-researching rather than treating others as respondents or informants as related to my wish to empower others in the research relationship'.

The word empowerment is used a lot in action research, especially by its keenest advocates, though its meanings and interpretations can vary quite widely. At one level, it tends to refer to the potential for action research to democratize the research process, fully engage practitioners and those with whom they work, like students, for example, and to instil greater respect for practitioner knowledge (frequently in contrast to the expert 'outsider' researcher). However, even at this micro-level, this may depend on the nature of the partnership between the actors involved and the ethical and practical constraints about which kinds of knowledge and actions might be shared in individual educational settings. Moreover, action research is most likely to be carried out in receptive settings with receptive and flexible professionals. As Morrison and Watling (2002: 4) point out, 'these are not necessarily typical of other schools or settings. Perhaps the ones who really need to change are not the receptive, forward looking individuals or institutions. Action research is, therefore, not easily replicable.[1]

At a deeper level, some advocates like Zuber-Skerritt (1996: 5), for example, have aligned empowerment with the emancipatory potential of action research for those who engage in it. In this sense, action research is:

emancipatory when it aims not only at technical and practical improvement in the participant's better understanding, along with the transformation and change within the existing boundaries and conditions, but also at changing the system itself of those conditions which impede desired improvement in the system/organization.

A feature of action research is that the voices of practitioners researching their own practices and of others, for the purposes of improved action, should be prioritized over and above the voice and expertise of external researcher/advisers (though it does not necessarily exclude them as research 'partners'). There are key benefits to such a strategy. It can be claimed that insiders 'know the way we do things round here', as an important starting point for improvements in that culture of 'doing'. But this also presents challenges. In order 'to make the familiar strange', outsiders may be better placed to 'see' what insiders cannot. Denscombe (1998: 63–4) puts this succinctly:

Because the practitioner cannot escape the web of meanings that the insider knows, he or she is constrained by the web of meanings. The 'outsider' may not have the right answer but can possibly offer an alternative perspective which can help the practitioner gain new insights into the problem.

It is not unusual, therefore, for action researchers to draw upon outsiders – such as a consultant or a critical friend – as sounding boards for the progression and understanding of action. Diaries and reflective journals are often used to record subjective opinions on the issues at the heart of action research.

Ethical concerns are paramount in action research particularly because the research gaze is intense and focused upon specific situations, and because researching with fellow colleagues in this intense manner may cause collaborators to 'forget' the bases for their collaboration and the uses to which data collected, in a number of formal and informal settings, might be put. Concerns magnify in single institution settings where power and authority issues may be invasive. This reinforces the requirement upon action researchers to follow recognized standards of research ethics, that include rights to confidentiality, informed consent and an openness about the uses to which the research are to be put.

Finally, we return to the central tenet of action research, namely that the researcher should be both the innovator (the one who poses the key research question(s)) and the implementer (the one who investigates the solutions). While agreeing with Lomax and Whitehead (1998) about the potentially empowering capacity of action research, there is, in some action research writing, a sense of epistemological and methodological naïvety that tends to be ignored. An alternative viewpoint would be to insist that action research is the main route through which the voice of educators will become more and more influential. Advocates like Lomax (2002: 136) are convinced of this: 'I want educators' voices to be heard and I want them to share their values and persuade others about the significance of their work.'

Lomax (2002: 137) provides a useful list of criteria for judging action research; elsewhere, Denscombe (1998: 66) provides a helpful checklist for researchers intending to engage in action research.

See also:

Agency (4); Diaries (30); Empowerment (37); Ethics (39); Evaluation (42); Mixed Methods (66); Power (77); Qualitative Research (80); Reflexivity (87); Research Community (95).

4 Agency

Agency is a term used by educational researchers to describe the active and intentional role of the individual in the construction and reconstruction of social life. It is frequently aligned with, and even contrasted with, structure(s). Furthermore, some research methodologies, strategies and methods prioritize agency, whereas others prioritize structures. If educational research is understood as the examination of persistent relational patterns of human conduct, which are sometimes institutionalized, then the methodology, strategy or method that is adopted is likely to marginalize individual human intention or agency. On the other hand, if educational researchers are concerned with human intentions and the reasons individuals give for their actions, then they are more likely to focus on methods and strategies that allow those individuals to give expression to these inner states.

What is being suggested here is that methodologies that prioritize agency and do not seek to reduce the individual to a mere appendage of external structures require the application of certain types of data-collection processes, such as semi-structured interviews, because only these are appropriate in the circumstances. However, there is a danger with some of these approaches, i.e. phenomenology or ethnomethodology. First, persistent patterns of human relations or structures, whether institutional or discursive, are ignored; and second, descriptions of educational activities are reduced to individual actions with social influences being marginalized.

Various attempts have been made to integrate both types of perspective, and in the process make sense of the agency–structure dualism. Giddens (1984), for example, understands structure as both constraining and enabling of human agency; agency cannot be understood as separate from structure, and equally neither can structure be understood as separate from agency. Bourdieu (1977) distinguishes between habitus and field, where the former is the cognitive map acquired by the individual to allow them to proceed in life, and the latter is the network of social relations that serves to constrain agents. The field conditions the habitus; but at the same time the habitus constitutes the field. Various other attempts have been made to understand the relationship between human agency and objective structures. All, however, have sought to preserve agency in the face of determinist and structuralist forms of knowledge.

It is tempting for educational researchers to ignore agency and human intention as they build theories about how educational institutions and processes work. This is because of the difficulties of making sense of an abstract notion such as agency. Those methodologists who attempt to model human life mathematically, and build into those models predictive tendencies, further exacerbate the problem. Here, the emphasis is inevitably focused on persistent relations between human beings rather than on decision-making and action by individual human beings in the context of enabling and constraining structural influences.

See also:
Critical Realism (21); Ethnomethodology (41); Interview (57); Mathematical Modelling (62); Phenomenology (73); Structure (103).

5 Alignment

Alignment is a way of combining qualitative and quantitative methods within the same research design. An example might be the combined use of a closed-ended questionnaire delivered to a large number of respondents and a focus group or groups, members of which conform to the sampling procedures used for the questionnaire. The procedure is asynchronous, with the former preceding the latter. Methods are aligned so that similar questions are asked of each set of respondents (questionnaire and focus group), but those questions demand more in-depth answers at the second stage than at the first. The purpose is to minimize the weaknesses in the different data-sets; these being in the case of the questionnaire, a lack of depth of question leading to a lack of depth in the answers due to the necessary standardization implied by a closed-ended approach; and in the case of the focus group an inability to generalize to a larger population and the perceived danger that reactivity, and therefore bias, is bound to be present in any loosely structured activity such as this.

Reverse alignment is where the quantitative part of the design is aligned to the qualitative part. An example would be where a loosely framed instrument such as an interview schedule (it is loosely framed because no closed-ended questions are included) is used as the first part of a sequence of research activities. Data that are subsequently collected are then analysed in a quantitative way using a form of discourse analysis that specifies proportions of recorded speech. Subsequent to this a closed-ended instrument is devised which allows access to a larger population of respondents than would be possible using interview techniques.

Both of these processes, alignment and reverse alignment, need to be distinguished from other ways of mixing paradigms, strategies, methodologies and methods such as:

- *Triangulation* (Denzin (1970) identifies four types: data, investi-gator, theoretical, methodological), where the use of different methods allows greater confidence in the validity and reliability of the conclusions of a research project.
- *Expansion*, where the use of mixed methods add scope and depth to a study.
- *Sequencing*, where quantitative work is used to identify cases for deeper investigation; and *reverse sequencing*, where qualitative work is used to determine constructs that are then sequentially used in a quantitative way.
- *Cyclical mix*, where quantitative and qualitative methods are used in a cyclical fashion so there is a qualitative dimension to the first cycle of research in order to map out the setting. In the second cycle this qualitative dimension is reconstructed as a quantitative dimension to allow generalizability to wider populations. In the third cycle, the quantitative dimension is tested on a small number of representative cases to confirm its validity.

- *Data collection mix*, where quantitative and qualitative data-collection instruments are used to collect data, not to compare one against the other for reliability and validity, but because circumstances dictate that for practical reasons the one cannot be used in some circumstances and the other can, and vice versa.
- *Data analysis mix*, where quantitative and qualitative data-collection instruments are used and then analysed by the opposite method. So qualitative data is collected and then analysed in a quantitative way; or quantitative data is collected and then analysed in a qualitative way.
- *Data presentation mix*, where qualitative data/analysis is presented in a quantitative way or quantitative data/analysis is presented in a qualitative way.
- *Paradigm mix*, where the mix is at the paradigm level and the epistemological differences between paradigms are reconciled. The argument is rejected that quantitative methods are paradigmatically different from qualitative methods.

See also:
Discourse (31); Epistemology/Ontology (38); Focus Groups (48); Generalization (50); Interview (57); Method (64); Mixed Methods (66); Paradigm (72); Qualitative Research (80); Quantitative Research (81); Questionnaire (82); Reliability (91); Sampling (98); Triangulation (112); Validity (113).

6 Anti-racism

For researchers of education, anti-racism signifies an ideological and political as well as an epistemological position. While the history of 'race' and its study is at least two centuries old, the starting points of specifically anti-racist approaches in education date back to the late 1970s, and signify a break from a liberal consensus that the study of 'race'* in education is *either* about the ideological and moral as well as practical importance of having good 'race' relations in schools *or* that research about 'race' is primarily about marginalized groups that are most often defined as ethnic minorities/black and ethnic minorities, *or* both. Central to anti-racist approaches is the assertion *first* that 'races' are not biological givens but are constructed politically, socially, geographically and temporally. It follows, therefore, that *second*, 'race', and in particular racialized thoughts and actions, applies to everyone and not just to marginalized groups, however defined. *Third*, and with important methodological implications, the application of an anti-racist research agenda conveys a commitment to political action, primarily to challenge racism in a range of forms that is sometimes also dependent upon the particular disciplinary (for example, psychological, sociological, economic) focus of researchers. It includes research into the existence and ramifications of institutional racism, and the potential, through research, of researcher and research participant empowerment.

Essentialist approaches to 'race' emphasize fundamental differences between races based on a mix of biology and culture, that is mediated by tradition and other cultural mores linked to linguistics, dress and religion. (Similar essentialist positions pertain in relation to gender, discussed elsewhere in this book.) In contrast, for social constructionists, 'race' can only exist as a construction of its time and history; in which case, the construct of 'race' itself is variable, and is supportive of the interests of those who advance them. This is not to argue that there is or has been a linear progressive movement from essentialism to social constructionism among educational researchers; the two approaches can and do coexist among a range of research outputs, and are increasingly interwoven with other constructions of 'similarity' and 'difference' relating to age, disability, sexual orientation and, of course, gender.

More fundamentally, Hall (1981: 69) identifies 'the issue of race' as a central focus for 'understanding how this society actually works and how it has arrived at where it is'. Configured socially, economically and politically, racism changes shape and form according to the historical period rather than in terms of visible biological identities possessed by groups; 'asylum seekers' provide a recent example of a 'group' defined as the 'other' in specific ways. There is, therefore, a distinction here from Miles' (1982: 78) early definition of racism (cited in Jackson, 2000: 49) as an 'ideology that ascribes negatively characteristics ... in a deterministic manner to a group who are additionally identified as being in some way *biologically distinct*' (our emphasis).

A key driver for anti-racist researchers has been to question educational research, most notably in relation to 'race' relations-type research that has sought to maintain an objective or neutral position, yet which, in its conduct and outcomes, it is argued, remains value-laden (Connolly, 1998; Bourne, 1980; Gilroy, 1980). Educational studies of the later 1970s and early 1980s are singled out for particular criticism in reinforcing stereotypical assumptions about the groups of children and young people, usually black and ethnic minority groups, whom researchers conducted research 'on' rather than 'with'. According to critics like Connolly (1998: 2), research attention on specific 'problem' groups at the level of the school not only displaced attention away from 'state racism' at a national level, but also provided additional 'evidence' to reinforce the assumptions of policy-makers.

An alternative position is provided by Hammersley (1998: 32) who argues that the anti-racist research backlash against the 'race' relations approach reflects a 'partisan' approach, which is given the name 'critical' but is 'partial' and, according to Hammersley, ultimately undermining of educational research so long as 'political considerations override intellectual ones'. A counter position has been to argue that 'neutrality in social justice research' continues to constitute a powerful 'myth, whether or not one declares one's value system' (Blair, 1998: 20).

More recently, anti-racist research has turned its attention to current substantive debates which, according to Connolly (1998: 2), reflect the more general influences of poststructuralism, specifically as they relate to theories of 'race' and 'ethnicity'. Among the substantive areas of interest have been the need to further our understandings about 'whiteness' and its various dimensions; to contest notions that all minority ethnic groups experience similar disadvantage and/or experience it similarly; and to contest that all white people are racist (ibid.). In combination, such interests reflect ongoing concerns about the status of identity and multiple identities in globalized and Europeanized societies. Methodological debates and discussions have included those which relate to white and black researchers' perspectives on 'race' and 'ethnicity' (for example, Morrison, 1999); the relative importance of large-scale statistical analyses as well as small-scale ethnographic approaches to researching 'race' and racism in education institutions, in particular the claims that it should and can make; and the need to avoid 'crude stereotypes' (Connolly, 1998: 5). In part, such debates replicate wider discussions about the role of qualitative and quantitative approaches to educational research, and about mixed methods.

Anti-racist research can unleash powerful critiques, as occurred in Osler and Morrison's (2000) study of school inspection and race equality, later reported by Klein (2000). Elsewhere, powerful forces, including those enshrined in funding mechanisms for research on diversity and ethnicity, constrain the kinds and focus of research that can be attempted. In such ways, critical research can lose ground to technicist models of research as problem-solving, and of 'race' as a 'problem'. Scott (2004) argues as much in a recent paper on anti-racist or critical approaches to pedagogy and the curriculum, where in schools, it is argued, conventional forms of knowledge have acted to oppress and discriminate. Yet, following Lankshear et al. (1996: 10), critical pedagogy 'has had to wrestle with a number of serious problems'. Perhaps the most striking of these have been the structural constraints that make it challenging to enact an anti-racist curriculum within the confines, for example, of a national curriculum and specific assessment and evaluation arrangements. A concentration on 'race', gender and/or class might also be considered to lead to reductionist forms of research about identity formation. In summary, research interest in critical pedagogy appears to have lost some ground, on the one hand, to technicist interests in school curricula, and on the other, to the postmodern (ibid.:11).

* 'Race' occurs in inverted commas throughout to signify the contested nature and use of the word.

See also:
Critical Theory (22); Empowerment (37); Epistemology/Ontology (38); Gender (49); Method (64); Methodology (65); Objectivity (70); Postmodernism (76); Power (77); Qualitative Research (80); Quantitative Research (81); Research Community (95); Social Constructionism (99); Structuralism/Poststructuralism (102); Values (115).

7 Assessment

Though assessment is a separate area of study from research methodology, it is also a key term for educational researchers. Assessment should be distinguished from evaluation where the former is understood as the making of judgements about the performance or capability of individuals within an education system, and the latter refers to the making of judgements about individual institutions or systems. These two words are sometimes used interchangeably, as researchers may talk about evaluating the capabilities of the child, or even assessing the quality of a programme. However, generally, they are distinguished by reference to the individual in the case of assessment and the institution in the case of evaluation.

Children are assessed naturally at different stages of their development for formative or summative purposes; and the data that is subsequently collected may be used in a variety of ways by educational researchers, teachers or policy-makers. On the other hand, researchers may assess children outside of naturally occurring testing and assessment regimes. The purpose is to collect data about their performance. Usually, such assessments are made in controlled conditions, and a distinction is drawn between competence and performance. Children are tested and their performance reflects their actual competence.

However, there may be a number of cases where the child either under-performs so that their test score is not an accurate representation of their capability, or over-performs so that the recorded score on the test is an over-estimate of their capability.

Psychometric frameworks may be contrasted with more holistic forms of assessment. Notions of reliability and validity that have informed most of the traditional theories about assessment are now being reformulated in response to a number of criticisms (Gipps, 1994). The first criticism is that formal assessments focus on the performance of the individual at a set point in time and in controlled conditions, and not to the levels of competence reached by the learner. The second criticism focuses on the social dimension of formal assessment. Formal assessments are designed to produce accurate representations of what learners can do and what they know. On the other hand, it has been suggested that the information collected about an individual is always context- and culture-bound. Items in a formal test are chosen by examiners and this process of choosing reflects their own understanding of the world and the set of constructs they possess to order it. The individual taking the test or being assessed may not share this set of constructs.

The third problem with formal assessments is that they do not, and cannot, act formatively. Learning, whether formal or informal, is closely related to assessment. Learners want and need to know what they have learnt in order to make a judgement about what and how they need to learn next. Learning is therefore always self-reflective, and indeed self-reflexive, in that learning transforms the individual's sense of how they understand themselves and the world. This is why the word *formative* is used to describe assessments that are useful to the formation of the individual through learning. The relationship between learning and assessment of that learning is complicated and depends in part on the way summative and comparative assessments – that is, imposed descriptions by other people on the individual concerned – impact on the learning situation. If these are given priority, then formative assessment processes are marginalized.

See also:
Evaluation (42); Reliability (91); Tests (109); Validity (113).

8   Biography/Autobiography

This approach to the study of the social world focuses on trajectories or life patterns of individuals operating within social and historical contexts. Autobiographical data are collected during the course of lengthy semi-structured interviews and through the analysis of documents. The key themes of this mode of research are that:

• The life has a recursive nature; biographical events in the past are reconceptualized in the present and take on a new form. This is not just because memory fades, but also because the person is repositioned in narratives that are presently constituted and did not exist in this particular form in the past. The life is transformed by reflective work and time, and equally, the narrative discourses in which past and present events are embedded also change over time. For the biographer each text then has this recursive dimension to it, a bending-back on itself, even if always presently constituted.

• The account of the life involves an interweaving of the meaning structures of the individual and the person writing the account *and* the discursive structures through which both of them operate. These discursive structures are sometimes described as narratives, and individuals construct their lives in terms of them. Equally, the biographer locates the life of the individual that they are giving expression to in these narratives, which stretch back and forward through time.

• Constructing a biographical account involves making interpretations from fragments of data provided by the individual. Alternative biographical accounts therefore are likely to differ in the emphasis they place on events and influences in the life of the person. This is because the data they collect from that person represents a reconceptualizing of the life. An account is never static, but involves new interpretations of events and activities that took place in the past. This is one form of the double hermeneutic.

• The public and the private in autobiographical and biographical accounts can never be disentangled. This is so for two reasons. The first is that narrative structures are public, and both biographers and autobiographers frame their understandings within these public forms of discourse. The second is that human beings live their lives within society and therefore their meaning-making activities are public affairs.

• The life is always fragmentary, comprising parts as opposed to wholes, narratives that never quite come to fruition and yet exert a powerful structuring influence, disconnected traces, sudden endings and new beginnings. The biographer in turn has to work with these fragmentary data, and indeed describe a life that is never fully formed.

Some educational researchers specialize in life history or biographical accounts, and the emphasis in their work is always on the individual as opposed to the collective. This does not mean that they subscribe to a form of methodological individualism, but understand the individual as part of the society in which they live or lived.

See also:
Discourse (31); Hermeneutics (52); Interpretivism (56); Interview (57); Life History (58); Narrative (67); Writing (118).

9   Case Study

Case study research is possibly the most popular form of educational research with an appeal particularly to educational practitioners and small-scale researchers. Yet its use presents a number of challenges, not least because the term has not been applied uniformly and because there are overlaps with other terms like participant observation, ethnography, fieldwork and life history. Writers like Gomm *et al.* (2000: 2) note that case study is ubiquitous in the sense that *all* research involves cases: 'there is always some unit, or set of units, in relation to which data are collected and/or analysed.' Moreover, case study has been used as a blanket phrase to describe what other forms of social and educational inquiry are *not*, that is, neither experiment nor social survey (ibid.: 2). However, such a binary is misleading. Case studies do not necessarily exclude the use of survey, for example, as part of a research toolkit to investigate a bounded 'case'.

So perhaps the most useful starting point is to define case study in relation to the amount of detailed information collected, the number of cases pursued, the nature of the data collected, and the purposes for which such detailed data collection is sought. The most common use of the term is research which includes the study of a few cases, sometimes one, in which the intention is to collect large amounts of data and study it in depth. Such data is usually, but not always, in alignment with specific approaches to research, namely qualitative and interpretive, with a frequent and specific emphasis upon the use of narrative. The use of case study further implies that cases are not created 'artificially' for the purposes of the research, as with experiments. The reference to the study of naturally recurring situations in which variables are not, or cannot be controlled is, therefore, a hallmark of case study. The purposes for which data are sought may vary but the primary emphasis is upon giving the people of the case a 'voice' – to the extent that the voice of the researcher as external interpreter may be subdued in favour of the insiders to the case. As Hammersley and Gomm (2000) point out, this is so whether the case study is of an individual, an event, an institution or a society. The extent to which the researcher's voice is 'heard' also depends on the purposes of the case study. Again, as Hammersley and Gomm describe, researchers may apply case study with various aims in mind. These may include 'theoretical inference – the development and testing of theory – or the practical value of an intervention' (Hammersley and Gomm, 2000: 4). Relatedly, case study concerns may vary from interest in studying the case in its own terms or for theoretical inference or a mix of both. Moreover, some researchers use case study data as the basis for conceptual or theoretical generalizations or transferability beyond the actual case, described commonly as 'naturalistic' or 'theoretical' generalizations.

Rather mischievously, Gomm *et al.* (2000) entitle their book *Case Study Method* and then take serious issue about whether case study is an approach, a paradigm even, rather than a method. The implications arising from the paradigm position are not insignificant, since they raise very different questions about

> how the social world can and should be studied ... as a distinct research paradigm ... sometimes ... formulated in terms of a contrast between positivism on the one hand, and naturalism, interpretivism or constructionism, on the other. At one extreme, case study is viewed as more akin to the kind of social world that is characteristic of novelists, short story writers and even poets.
> (ibid., 2000: 5)

There has been a proliferation of case study research in educational settings, although the form taken varies quite widely, and has been described by Bassey (1999: 58). He conceives three main types defined variously as (1) 'theory-seeking' and 'theory-testing', (2) 'story-telling' and 'picture-drawing' or (3) 'evaluative' case studies. A key outcome of the first type would be that case studies lead to 'more' and 'less tentative generalizations'. In the second, the emphasis is upon narrative stories and accounts that have clear timelines running through them and a strong sense of the processual. The third type refers to in-depth inquiries into educational 'programmes, systems, projects or events' in order to ascertain their 'worthwhileness, as judged by analysis by researchers' (ibid.). In combination, each case study has to convey its key messages to interested audiences, however defined.

For Bassey (1999) the 'theory-seeking' or 'testing' case study is one in which the singular is chosen because it is thought to be typical of something more general. Stake (1995) identifies this kind of case study as 'instrumental' in which a particular case is examined to understand or refine a theory. The terms 'theory-seeking' and 'theory-testing' are also akin to Yin's (1994) use of the terms 'exploratory' and 'explanatory' case study research that can lead to 'fuzzy propositions' or 'generalisations' (Bassey, 1999: 51–2). The latter are general statements 'with built-in uncertainties ... an appropriate concept for [case study] research in areas like education where human complexity is paramount' (ibid.: 51–2).

Bassey's 'story-telling' or 'picture-drawing' case studies resemble Stake's description of 'intrinsic' case studies. From the use of such terms, readers get a strong sense of a study that is processual, with clear timelines (as in story-telling). 'Picture-drawing' would tend to be more descriptive, but, in relation to both, the expectation is of outcomes that show theoretical insight. 'Evaluative' case studies examine a case's 'worthwhileness' formatively and/or summatively and can be either predominantly objectives-focused or illuminative (Parlett and Hamilton, 1976). Interestingly, the work of the latter prompted one of the first early critiques of 'case study research' from within qualitative research (Atkinson and Delamont, 1985). This paid particular attention to a lack of perceived rigour and an ill-defined 'umbrella' use of the term case study at that time.

Such demands for rigour continue. Mindful of such concerns, and for purposes of summary, educational case study has been subsequently defined as:

an empirical study which is:

- conducted within a localized boundary of space and time (i.e. a singularity);
- into interesting aspects of an educational activity, or programme, or institution, or system;
- mainly in its natural context and within an ethic of respect for persons;
- in order to inform the judgments and decisions of practitioners or policy-makers;
- or of theoreticians who are working to such ends;
- in such a way that sufficient data are collected for the researcher to be able:
  (a) to explore significant features of a case;
  (b) to create plausible interpretations of what is found;
  (c) to test the trustworthiness of these interpretations;
  (d) to construct a worthwhile argument or story;
  (e) to relate the argument or story to any relevant research in the literature;

(f)   to convey convincingly to an audience this argument or story;

(g)   to provide an audit trail by which researchers may validate or challenge the findings or construct alternative arguments.

(Inevitably the terms 'interesting', significant', 'plausible', 'worthwhile' and 'convincingly' entail value judgments being made by the researcher.) (Bassey, 1999: 58)

In various ways, controversies about case study encapsulate some of the wider debates about the nature and purposes of educational research. Here, we introduce five concerns about case study, adapted mainly from the recent mapping of the field by Gomm *et al.* (2000).

1. Boundedness of the case in its 'natural' setting

In case study, the tendency is to conceive of a case as an independent unit presented in its natural condition, as if in a social world of similarly mutually independent units. Brown and Dowling (1998: 166) argue that 'this is a mythologizing of research and a romanticizing of the world' in which, in reality, researchers 'act selectively and productively, that is to say transformatively on their object environment'. Furthermore, their assertion is that the singularity of the bounded case is equally mythologizing:

The fact of the matter is that even a single actor [selected as a case] participates in a multiplicity of potential research sites. (op. cit.: 166-7)

For these writers, then,

There is no such thing as 'the case study approach' other than as constituted in the curricularizing of research methods. (op. cit.: 166-7)

And it follows that

the use of the term 'case' is probably best interpreted as a way of describing one's sampling procedures. (op. cit.: 166-7)

2. Generalizability

For some case study researchers, the aim is to draw conclusions that may be applied more widely than the case itself. Indeed, some sponsors of educational research demand that this should be so. One argument is that case study draws different kinds of generalizations (logical; theoretical; analytical) in contrast to positivist research that draws from statistical analyses (see Mitchell, 2000). A second position would be that case study does not *have* to make any claims for generalization.

The key issue is how readers of case study make use of case study research outcomes and for varied purposes. Stake (2000) describes 'naturalistic generalisation'. Lincoln and Guba (2000) prefer to concentrate on the transfer of findings from one setting to another on the basis of best fit for purpose. A few writers like Ward Schofield (1993) argue that from multi-site case studies, inferences can be drawn that are similar to survey research.

3. Causal analysis

Of key importance to a number of case study advocates is the view that in-depth and time-lined narrative analysis can offer more insight into cause and effect than other methods. However, a key issue remains. As Hammersley and Gomm (2000) point out, how can readers distinguish between contingent and necessary relationships as aspects of events, especially when explanations flow from the few rather than many respondents?

4. The role of theory

Case study researchers have more than one perspective on the role of theory within their studies. 'For some, it must be a theory that makes sense of the case as a bounded system' (Smith, 1978). For others, the analytical task is to view the case in terms of a wider social context. 'Indeed it is sometimes argued that the analysis of a case always presumes some wider context; so the issue is not whether a macro-theory is involved but rather how explicit this is and whether it is sound' (Hammersley and Gomm, 2000: 6).

5. Authenticity

Advocates of case study will frequently stress the importance of 'capturing' reality by representing the case authentically, by using the participants' own accounts of views and events. In some cases, as we have already suggested, this may involve subduing the voice of the researcher. Such assertions about whose voices are 'real' have been hotly contested not only by those who would prefer to follow the methods of the natural sciences but also by constructivists and some postmodernists who would deny the existence of any 'authentic situation' or case that is independent of investigations of it by the researcher(s). This calls into serious question whether the researcher can ever 'tell it as it is' or, as importantly, intercept on behalf of others to do so.

Given the above concerns and debates, it is hardly surprising that sponsors and funders of educational research have often shown ambivalence towards case study, simultaneously sceptical about the particularity of individual case studies yet keen to promote illustrative case studies, especially where, from the funders' perspective, illustrative case studies of 'effective' or 'good practice' can be highlighted and then hopefully modelled by the less 'good' or less 'effective'. Such issues are of specific ethical importance in case study, where small numbers and an intensive research gaze can magnify risks to individuals. Where the value of the best research is not to outweigh injury to participants, agreed ethical guidelines are essential. On case study reporting, Stake (1995: 240) concludes that 'more will be pursued than volunteered' and 'less will be reported than learned'.

See also:
Causation (11); Ethnography (40); Evaluation (42); Generalization (50); Interpretivism (56); Life History (58); Method (64); Methodology (65); Narrative (67); Observation (71); Paradigm (72); Postmodernism (76); Qualitative Research (80); Sampling (98); Social Constructionism (99); Transferability (111).

10   Categorization

For researchers engaged in quantitative or qualitative approaches to education research, or both, the categorization of data for and as analysis is a key process which will vary according to the purposes of research, whether this is mainly descriptive or mainly explanatory, small or large scale, theory building or theory testing, a study of singularity or a search for generalizability.

For qualitative data analysts, a key task is to use categorization in order to abstract the most important features of the educational phenomena studied from detailed, thick and complex data. Categorization may also provide the means to greater precision in comparing one or a small number of examples of that phenomenon, often case studies, with others. Survey research, on the other hand, is characterized by a structured set of data by means of a variable-by-case data matrix. In this case, surveyists collect data about the same set of predefined characteristics or categories (variables) from at least two sets of cases to produce a data matrix. Applied to questionnaire surveys, the construction of variables not only has a powerful effect on how the data can be analysed but also what statistical tests can be used, how data can be presented and which conclusions formed. The type of and format for the questions asked will also determine the categorization of data on a measurement scale.

Categorization and qualitative data analysis

The strength of qualitative data lies in its richness and complexity. Both create challenges in the creation of categories from data and in the 'splitting and splicing' (Dey, 1993) and 'moving backwards and forwards' (Pole and Morrison, 2003) through a set of categories to reformulate or refine them and the analysis. The issue of the extent to which qualitative researchers begin with a number of predefined categories will reflect the purposes of the research as well as the epistemological and policy-into-practice orientations of the researcher and the researched. This means that some qualitative researchers begin with explicit rather than implicit categories; for example, problem-solving or evaluation-focused researchers will tend to devise categories that derive from the problem or the evaluation task. This is not to argue that categories will not also emerge from the data themselves, but to distinguish such processes from the emergent or grounded categorization frameworks more favoured by proponents of grounded theory.

The categorization of qualitative data also emerges from reflection-as-analysis by the researcher or what Dey (1993: 98) describes as 'the mirror image' to emerge from reflective thought when 'the actor acts' and 'the analyst analyses – this is integral to their roles as subject and researcher'. It is also part of the iterative process of reading, annotating and coding the data and specific data bits. For qualitative data analysts, categorization may be more than a skill; it also constitutes a methodological disposition to cope with the need to discard and reformulate categories, as well as subdivide them, as more precision is sought, and then links and connections are made between data bits. While the use of maps and matrixes may vary (Miles and Huberman (1994) are enthusiastic advocates of both), the key issue remains structured and systematic approaches to data bit retrieval and connections building as well as careful audit trails of evidence gathering and analysis, and of explanations supported or discarded, in order to draw appropriate conclusions that include theoretical and conceptual development.

Categorization and quantitative data analysis

Numerical information, usually known as data, is commonly known as quantitative data or categorical data. The latter refers straightforwardly to the total number of phenomena that a researcher finds in a particular category and is an assignation of kind not degree that can be summarized visually in the form of bar graphs, pie charts or frequency tables. This needs to be distinguished from categorization as a *process* that occurs once numerical information has been collected. De Vaus (1996: 288) has described this as 'ways in which variables can be prepared for analysis and how the first dip into the data might proceed'. This precedes the subsequent stages of clarifying the nature of the relationships between variables (causal or spurious; direct or indirect), accounting for unexpected relationships, checking the robustness of findings, and eliminating alternative explanations (ibid).

Categorization, therefore, refers to several key processes: namely, preparing the variables for analysis by recoding existing variables, creating new ones and by checking for missing data. Recoding is applied in three main ways: first, to rearrange the order of the categories of the variable; second, to change the value of a variable (important when developing scales); and third, to collapse categories of a variable into fewer categories (justified for sound statistical or substantive research reasons) (ibid.: 277–81). New variables can be created either to develop more detailed scales or to create useful data derived from a combination of data collected. For de Vaus (1996), as for Marsh (1982) earlier, the focus of categorization at the point of initial analysis is to look at and for 'the relationship at the kernel of the analysis' and to 'avoid . . . fancy analysis until this has been done' (de Vaus, 1996: 287).

Computers

Computerization has, for many years, assisted the categorization processes typical of statistical and numerical analyses of larger-scale data-sets produced by surveys (commonly through the use of SPSS (Statistical Package for the Social Sciences)). Its use in the management and audit of qualitative data has also developed greatly, especially in the past ten years. Equally, its role in qualitative data analysis has become widespread if contentious (see elsewhere in this book). Following Dey (1993: 268), the key issue may not be whether qualitative software packages *substitute* for researchers' thinking qualitatively about categorization, but how, in application, software packages *shape* such thoughts. This is not so far removed from the exhortations of statistical analysts 'not to simply [look] at a number of frequency distributions and bivariate relationships' but 'to account for the initial [data] set' which compels researchers 'to think, and develop explanations' (de Vaus, 1996: 289).

See also:
Case Study (9); Coding (14); Epistemology/Ontology (38); Ethnography (40); Grounded Theory (51); Interpretivism (56); Methodology (65); Mixed Methods (66); Qualitative Research (80); Quantitative Research (81); Statistics (100); Subjectivity (104); Survey (105); Variable Analysis (116).

11 Causation

There are a number of influential theories of causation in social and educational research. Four stand out: deterministic causation, multi-deterministic causation, probabilistic causation and generative causation.

Determinism

Deterministic causation is a theory of relations between phenomena, where one object impacts on another, and causes a change in the behaviour of the other. The two objects can be said to be in a causal relationship. In every case of the two objects entering into a relationship, the one will cause a reaction in the other. This does not imply symmetry, because, though the assertion being made is that A causes B, there are no grounds for inferring from this that B causes A. However, there are a number of problems with this theory of causation, especially as it relates to the social world. First, the objects that enter into this causal relationship may not be the same objects that are being described, though the observer thinks they are. Bhaskar (1979) refers to this as the ontic fallacy, where the operation of objects in nature is conflated illegitimately with the knowing of them.

Second, if this is correct, then researchers are rarely in a position to ever know these causal relations, but only relations between their manifestations; but an assumption should not be made that this exhausts reality. Third, the educational and social sciences operate in non-deterministic or open systems. What this means is that though objects cause changes in other objects, future causal relations themselves may not replicate these original actions because the constituent nature of the object has changed, and as a result new causal configurations are now in place.

Multi-determinism

Multi-deterministic causation implies at its simplest that the same event may be caused by a number of different actions. This theory has been criticised on a number of grounds. An event may appear to have a number of causes; in reality, the observer has been deceived, and is therefore wrong about what actually caused something to happen. The causal sequence may be so complicated that the means of describing it are not adequate to the task. Lists of causes about, for example, historical events are therefore not helpful in explaining causal relations. Further to this, objects in nature and in social life may lose or change their generative powers, so they no longer have the capacity to produce effects. Multi-deterministic causal theories also sometimes conflate antecedent causes with conditions for action.

Probabilistic

The third model of causation has been more influential, especially among variable analysts and mathematical modellers. This suggests that though researchers are unable to identify deterministic causal mechanisms, they can identify probabilistic relations between objects in the social sciences, and this allows them to make predictions within certain parameters. The claim is made that this form of causality is able to explain imperfect regularities, that is, the existence of counterfactual cases. This is because no claim is being made that in every single instance the two phenomena under investigation will result in the one causing the other to happen. Not all smokers get lung cancer, but there is a probabilistic relation between smoking and lung cancer.

Again, this causal theory has a number of problems. First, it relies on observations of regularities that occur. And yet the existence of spurious regularities would seem to indicate that, even with a probabilistic range, these observations and the relations that are inferred from them can be wrong. A number of examples may illustrate this. A hooter in London signaling the end of the day's work in a factory does not cause workers in Birmingham to pack up and go home, even if the two phenomena correlate perfectly over time. A good correlation has been discovered between human birth rates and the population trend of storks in different regions of Sweden, but the one does not cause the other to happen. The identification of counterfactual cases does not solve the problem of the indeterminacy of human relations; it merely enumerates the degree of uncertainty that the researcher has about these observed regularities. The degree of uncertainty that researchers have is a function of the lack of knowledge they have about the supposed relationship. The problem, however, goes deeper and this is that an assumption is made that regularities in nature constitute the natural and social worlds. Generative theories of causation would suggest otherwise.

Generative

Generative theories of causation, popularized by critical realists, suggest that reality is stratified and emergent. Probabilistic versions of causal relations refer to only one level of reality, and therefore frequently causal relations are cited which turn out to be either misconceived, spurious or not able to predict the future. Pawson and Tilley (1997: 34) argue for a generative understanding of causation:

Causation acts internally as well as externally. Causality describes the transformative potential of phenomena. One happening may well trigger another but only if it is the right condition in the right circumstances. Unless explanation penetrates to these real underlying levels, it is deemed to be incomplete. In pursuing causal explanation via a constant conjunction model, with its stress on that which can be observed and controlled, it has tended to overlook the liabilities, powers and potentialities of the programmes and subjects whose behaviour it seeks to explain.

Deterministic, multi-deterministic and probabilistic theories of causation about relations between educational phenomena all suffer from this deficiency.

See also:
Closed and Open Systems (13); Correlational Research (18); Critical Realism (21); Determinism (29); Epistemology/Ontology (38); Historical Research (53); Mathematical Modelling (62); Prediction (78); Variable Analysis (116).

12 Childhood Research

Given that children as pupils and young people as students are considered to be central to all the activities that constitute compulsory education, it is astonishing that, until recently, they have remained peripheral to core debates underpinning educational research. The reasons for this are at least two-fold: first, classroom research which has explicitly focused on interactions between teacher and pupil has tended implicitly to prioritize the teacher, focusing on pupils mainly in so far as they affect or are affected by the theories and professional practices of teachers. Second, research about children and childhood has tended to be multi-disciplinary and inter-disciplinary, and not surprisingly, multi-paradigmatic. In which case, both epistemological and methodological interests in children and childhood have tended to be splintered rather than considered coherently. Underlying assumptions that researching children is similar to or synonymous with researching adults have not helped. More recently, attention has been given not only to the ways in which existing research approaches require adaptation to meet the needs of childhood research but also that innovatory and distinctive approaches are required.

Such innovation has developed in tandem with, and sometimes been preceded by, new theoretical and conceptual understandings of what constitutes 'being children' and, it follows, meanings of childhood. As Sinclair Taylor (2000: 21) writes, it is 'adults who generally write about children' and have also defined children and childhood (according to the UN Convention (1989) everyone under the age of 18). Despite being key stakeholders, children have had 'diminished opportunities to play their part in raising standards' (ibid.: 32) in education. In recent years, various constructions of childhood have been problematized and contested. If childhood is, in combination, a biological, social, political, legal, economic, as well as educational construct, then it also follows that definitions of childhood will vary according to 'the cultural mores and practised values experienced by the community groupings in which children find themselves' (Lloyd-Smith and Tarr, 2000: 62).

There are corollaries in educational research as some researchers have turned their attention away from research 'about' or 'upon' children in education, and more towards research 'with' children, and a prioritization of children's perspectives (Lewis and Lindsay, 2000; Mac Naughton *et al.*, 2001). In this sense, interpretive approaches to research with children have been developing since the late 1980s, in various forms that have been summarized by France *et al.* (2000: 151), among others:

> Children (O'Brien *et al.*, 1996) and young people are seen as 'creators' and social actors who are active in creating themselves in different social contexts. As James and Prout (1990) suggest, this is a shift away from an emphasis upon structure to that of agency where children are recognized in their 'own right'. Children are, therefore, seen as having a perception and experience of childhood that greatly enhances our understanding, in late modernity, of childhood. This is not to deny that childhood is a negotiated process where children are active in constructing their own social worlds, and reflecting upon and understanding its meaning and significance to their own lives.

The last sentence in this quotation suggests something of a dilemma for those researching with children. From such an interpretivist framework, theory emerges from data in much the same way as for all research that is influenced by grounded theorizing (Glaser and Strauss, 1967). Yet we have already noted that research with children might require, at least, amended approaches, and at best, new and innovatory approaches. A number of methods have been developed such as 'write and draw' (France *et al.*, 2000) as well as specific approaches to focus on discussion groups, interviews and conversations with children, child-centred observations, diaries, photographs and video-recording, and questions that might be addressed to children as a variant on the questionnaire survey approach. The alignment between such approaches and choice of paradigms is described, with examples, by Hughes (2001) in relation to early childhood research.

Ethical issues loom large in research with children. Again, the lack of interest in specific concerns largely mirrors the relative neglect of children's perspectives in education research, although they are more established in medical ethics. While Lindsay (2000: 3–19) points to a number of focal points and levels of interest when it comes to researching children (such as the teacher's employer, local ethics committees, the peer reviews of bodies who fund research with children, professional bodies like the British Medical Association (BMA) or the British Educational Research Association (BERA), or academic review of published research), in combination they have struggled to ascertain ethical principles that might relate to research with children. Two issues predominate. The first relates to informed consent where the emphasis is upon children's vulnerability and the extent to which children might be considered 'informed' as a counter-position to intrusiveness, and, at worse, abuse (ibid.). The second issue relates to anonymity and confidentiality. As France *et al.* (2000: 155–6) report, researchers have taken both absolutist and relativist positions. Where research reveals a child to be 'at risk', for example, some researchers have insisted that 'an adult participant has a moral obligation to assist them in a way that is "protective" '(Fine and Sandstrom, 1988, cited in France *et al.*, 2000: 155). Butler and Williamson (1994: 42) take a more absolutist line, insisting on 'complete confidentiality – meaning that no further action will be taken without the full consent and knowledge of the child' (also cited in France *et al.*, 2000: 156). This, of course, ignores the fact that, as adults, researchers have legal (and ethical) obligations to take action in some circumstances.

Perhaps, above all, research with children in education settings throws into sharp relief the power relations between adults and children, whether this is between adult researchers and children as research participants, or between participants, researchers and other adults, predominantly teachers and also parents, who not only, and in varying degrees, 'control' children's lives but also the 'telling' of those lives by children who experience education in different ways.

See also:
Access (2); Culture (23); Epistemology/Ontology (38); Ethics (39); Focus Groups (48); Grounded Theory (51); Interpretivism (56); Method (64); Methodology (65); Paradigm (72); Power (77); Qualitative Research (80); Quantitative Research (81).

13   Closed and Open Systems

A key question in educational research is whether the methods of the natural sciences can be applied to the social sciences, and in particular to the study of education. One of the difficulties with this is that the natural sciences in general work with closed systems whereas the social world constitutes an open system. Indeed, natural scientists either work within naturally occurring closed systems or deliberately create such systems, i.e. laboratory conditions, where they seek to control those external factors that may contaminate the workings of the system. Social scientists generally have a more difficult task and this is because the objects with which they are dealing – human behaviours, relations between individuals and structural properties of systems – are less amenable to this type of treatment, in part, because human beings are reflexively able to monitor the conditions under which they live and within which they make decisions, and therefore change their beliefs and behaviours.

A closed system operates in two ways. First, the object under investigation, which is the repository of those causal powers that the researcher is interested in, operates in a consistent manner; those causal powers refer to all similar cases and the object does not change its constituent nature. Second, the external conditions for the exercise of the causal mechanism remain constant, allowing the object to continue to operate as it has always operated. If these two relations of a closed system are present, it is possible to infer a causal relationship, in which regularities are produced. In the social world, these two conditions are frequently violated. Objects do not operate consistently, and this is because their essential nature changes, so it becomes impossible to argue that there is no change over time between different cases. Furthermore, the external conditions for the exercise of these causal mechanisms may also change; it is therefore likely that over time and in different places non-equivalent manifestations of those causal powers are in operation.

An example of the way closed systems operate is gendered relations with regards to school performance. Boys outperformed girls in most examination subjects until recently; now girls outperform boys in the same examination subjects. Clearly something has changed. Some of these changes can be identified, for example, the relative degrees of confidence boys and girls have in performing in examinations, the sense of emancipation girls have now acquired, the desire of girls to be equal to boys and so forth. What has changed is the constituent nature of the object. Furthermore, those external conditions may also have been transformed, so learning conditions and experiences in schools are different from what they were before; there is less overt discrimination against girls in the employment market, and this in turn has contributed to greater incentives for girls to stay on at school after the compulsory leaving age. This is clearly an open system, as there is evidence here of internal and external inconsistency.

The consequences of social and educational researchers operating in open systems are that methods have to be chosen and used that take account of this. Sayer (1992: 177) argues that:

Assumptions of linearity, additivity and of the possibility of discovering practically adequate instrumentalist laws of proportional variation all depend for their success on the particular material property to which they refer.

If change is irreducibly qualitative, because of the changing internal and external nature of the object and the way it works, then mathematical modelling of these properties and processes is likely to be unsuccessful.

See also:
Assessment (7); Causation (11); Critical Realism (21); Gender (49); Mathematical Modelling (62); Method (64); Positivism (75); Qualitative Research (80); Reflexivity (87); Structure (103).

14　Coding

How and why education researchers collect evidence is critical. Different methods produce different kinds of information and are premised on various epistemologies about what 'counts' as 'real' data. The collection of information does not produce data automatically. What researchers *do* with information is key. It is through forms of sense making by researchers that 'raw' information becomes research data. Fundamental to data analysis is a two-stage process: the sifting and selecting of information collected into 'data bits' and assigning to them a label or a category that is usually called a 'code'.

There are similarities as well as differences in the coding practices of qualitative and quantitative research, but it is how researchers use the coded material that constitute the main distinctions. Similarities derive from the inclusion of open-ended questions in mainly quantitative questionnaire surveys and structured interviews. These generate qualitative data, which can, in turn, be 'counted'. Even here, however, similarities may be superficial. While 'counting' is a legitimate, if limited means of identifying codes for qualitative data, more significantly, the tendency among surveyists is to 'resolve' the 'problem' of open-endedness by assigning such data to pre-coded categories, often determined in pilot surveys. As Dey (1993: 58) suggests, coding has 'mechanistic connotations' that denote symbols or abbreviations of longer terms. These are often applied in questionnaire surveys, where structured responses can be assigned to predefined categories called *pre-codes*. The latter is less useful in qualitative approaches where coding involves more overlapping sets of initial and follow-up codes.

Coding quantitative data

Before questionnaire and interview survey data are analysed, responses are edited and then coded to allow data to be converted into electronic form usually for statistical manipulation using computer software, and for this reason the codes are usually numerical. Editing allows the identification of incomplete, inaccurate or inconsistent responses. *Codebooks* provide a systemic documentation of the basis used for making coding decisions, especially important when multiple coders are used. For each question, a coding frame is devised to include the question number and wording, the application of numerical codes for each category of answer and a description of what each category covers.

Information provided in a *coding frame* may also be accompanied by a *variable name* that is often an abbreviation, for example, the age at which a respondent started teaching like AAFTP (age at first teaching post). Survey design is also likely to include *column numbers*, indicating which columns in the *data matrix* are occupied by the responses to the question. There is a strong emphasis on the relationship between pre-editing and coding to maximize reliability and the statistical manipulation of data. Thus, if questions generate too many responses that are coded as *other*, then questions will need extending. If questions do not allow for a sufficient range of pre-coded responses, then the researcher may end up with many questions left blank or unanswered. And some forms of questions are more challenging to manipulate statistically, especially when they invite a range of responses, and ask the respondent to rank in order of importance or priority.

It would be wrong to assume that coding for closed or open-ended responses in quantitative analysis is atheoretical. Researchers bring their theoretical perspectives (mostly deductive) to shape both the questions *and* a range of codes for the responses they expect to receive (Pole and Lampard, 2002). How open-ended responses are coded depends upon established statistical procedures in which, for example, questionnaires might form the basis of a trial coding frame that is then applied to a further sample set of questionnaires. To summarize, the application of coding to quantitative data is primarily for analysing the relationship between quantifiable items, whether the intention is to present and summarize numerical data (descriptive statistics) or to determine the significance and level of confidence in the significance of research results (inferential statistics).

Coding qualitative data

Within the field of educational research, qualitative approaches hold considerable sway, mainly because of the emphasis that is placed upon understanding educational activities and processes from respondent self-report that, in combination, are considered to provide holistic accounts of institutions, individuals, or other phenomena. Researchers then go beyond this to offer critical accounts of informants' understandings. Coding is used to sort and 'break down' the data by looking in detail at its characteristics and provide first steps in discovering that the 'whole' is more than the sum of the 'parts' (or data bits). This allows researchers to obtain larger 'pictures' of research evidence. Coding is, therefore, an early phase in the researcher's reinterpretation of other individuals' interpretations, an activity that has been described as the double hermeneutic of educational research.

Creating codes is conceptually as well as methodologically demanding. Researchers apply multiple skills simultaneously. They find meaning in terms of the empirical data collected and meaning in relation to other categories or codes. It is what Dey (1993) describes as the 'internal' and 'external' aspects of making and grouping codes. Its complexity should not underestimate its role as practical activity requiring skills in data reduction and management as well as creativity and reconstruction. Coding has been characterized as a stepped process: from *initial* or *open* to coding that is increasingly differentiated, comparable (*axial*), conceptual and abstract (Miles and Huberman, 1994). The coding challenge is also to demonstrate rigour and transparency in data recording, and is a key aspect of the qualitative researcher's *audit trail*.

Ethnographers, for example, may choose to be entirely dependent upon assigning codes that emerge from the data. Such groundedness cannot, of course, ignore the theoretical predispositions that researchers bring both to data collection (as anticipatory data reduction) and to coding. Yet, coding processes are key to understanding ideas that underpin inductive approaches to theory building such as Grounded Theory (Glaser and Strauss, 1967). Combined with intense reading of the data, these are essential in the 'discovery' of theory from data.

Computer–aided coding

Exponents of computer-aided analysis for qualitative and quantitative data using NUD*IST, The Ethnograph and SPSS, for example, are growing in number. In combination, they enable the analyst to take different coding 'cuts' (Dey, 1993: 58) through the 'data bits' with increasing technological sophistication, and over shorter timescales. Advocacy rests on the computer's ability to store and manage data, its capacity to assist in the process of analysis, and, in relation to qualitative research, its approximation to quantitative approaches. This has fuelled controversy about the role of computers, especially in qualitative analysis, including coding. Proponents (Richards and Richards, 1998) claim that because computers facilitate the exploration of links, they can be used for theory generation. A critique offered by Coffey and Atkinson (2000) on the growth of Computer Assisted Qualitative Data Analysis Software (CAQDAS), for example, takes issue with what they consider to be an over-emphasis upon the mechanics of coding and a reduction in the full potential of grounded theorizing (discussed also in Pole and Morrison, 2003: Chapter 4). In contrast, they advocate an approach to computer use for qualitative analysis that departs from coding and search-and-retrieval processes only and allows more experimentation with the use of text and hypertext.

Note: NUD*IST is the registered trademark of Qualitative Solutions and Research Pty Ltd.; The Ethnograph is a registered trademark of Qualis Research Associates; SPSS is the trademark of SPSS Inc. SPSS Screen Images.

See also:
Data Reduction (25); Deduction (27); Epistemology/Ontology (38); Ethnography (40); Grounded Theory (51); Hermeneutics (52); Induction (55); Interpretivism (56); Interview (57); Method (64); Qualitative Research (80); Quantitative Research (81); Questionnaire (82); Reliability (91); Statistics (100); Survey (105); Values (115); Variable Analysis (116).

15   Comparative Research

In an increasingly globalized yet fragmented world, there has been a burgeoning of comparative educational research. In major part, this relates to an international policy emphasis upon understanding and knowledge about the potential and actual contribution of education to create and sustain the human capital necessary for the prosperity of developing as well as advanced economies. Research methodology is strongly implicated in comparative research much of which is also described as cross-cultural study. International examples abound but perhaps the best known, from a current policy perspective, are European-wide studies that are supported by European Union funding initiatives and conducted by researchers who, while constituting research teams and networks, operate from their own country 'base' and work towards ends which are primarily policy driven.

For example, across Europe, multi- and trans-national studies of vocational education and training (VET) have been conducted since the early 1980s. Krzeslo *et al.* (1996: 71–5) are among writers to have pointed to the methodological challenges of such studies. These are identified as three-fold. *First*, the substantive terms used in research that is conducted in different countries may be understood in diverse ways, and as a product of the history of those countries. With regard to VET, for example, the terms 'skill' and 'apprenticeship' are variously understood in Europe. *Second*, comparative research teams may operate from a range of intellectual traditions and predispositions which may not be fully understood beyond the boundaries of the national research team, and is more than a linguistic issue (important though this may be). In other words, the assumption that the challenges of comparative multinational research can be overcome by representation on the European-wide team by national researcher 'representatives' is problematic. This leads to the *third* important point, namely, that the practicalities of doing comparative research do not necessarily include the development of comparative methodology to challenge 'ethnocentric assumptions' or provide 'a research agenda which can accommodate a range of different conceptions of the research focus and methodology' (ibid.).

Issues of ethnocentricity on the part of researchers who travel to other field sites in order to conduct research have a long history, mainly in the anthropological tradition. Two extreme kinds of methodological challenge have been identified. At one end of the spectrum have been ethnographic tensions in 'going native' if and when ethnographers step beyond the fuzzy boundaries of 'grasp[ing] the native's point of view' (Malinowski, 1922). At the other end of the spectrum are dangers of intellectual 'tourism' where researchers make brief excursions into other countries (whether through brief visits or reviews of the literature of that country, or both). Walker and Dimmock (2004: 275), for example, refer to the dangers of 'perfunctory views of [educational] leadership in different cultures and contexts' in order to highlight the challenges in assuming that research-based understandings of educational leadership can necessarily be imported or exported successfully between countries that vary culturally, politically, socially, economically and/or educationally.

From the above it might be wrongly assumed that, in education research, we are identifying methodological challenges only in terms of distinguishing between research which might be considered as exotic or the geographically distanced 'other' (as understood from early anthropological research) and more recent studies that have focused upon multi-national studies in which the ways of life and outlooks of those nations (key elements of culture for Alasuutari 1995, for example) might be considered similar. This might be especially so where dissimilarity has been dissipated by the internationalization of media and entertainment networks. Yet, importantly, research in education also focuses upon comparative research within nations, and as part of regional, local and institutional frameworks. In this sense, the term comparative refers to cross-cultural understandings about and practices of education in contexts of age, gender, disability, social class, ethnicity and so on. In the ethnographic tradition, such interests have a long history in which the cultural translations and conflicts that arise from the various meanings that schooling has for the actors who participate in it have been foregrounded.

'Comparative' is applied to method as well as to methodology. Hammersley and Gomm (2000: 239) describe comparative method as requiring:

> Data ... from more than one case, perhaps from a substantial number, such as the effects and various candidate causal factors that can be controlled or assessed. The most powerful version of the comparative method is experimentation, which involves creating the cases for testing a causal claim.

Here, the experimental group receives one form of 'treatment' (new class seating arrangements, new reading materials, new method of teaching) while the control or comparison group does not. For many reasons, but primarily ethical, experimental studies are less common in educational research than case studies where the comparative method draws mainly on the techniques of eliminative or analytical induction (Hammersley and Gomm 2000: 239–49). For these writers, there are several challenges relating to the use of comparative method to produce causal explanations, regardless of whether the aim of case study is for description or theoretical development. Counterpoints to this position come from case study advocates like Becker (2000) and Miles and Huberman (1994). And elsewhere, Ward Schofield (1993) examines the prospects for generalizability that derive from the comparability of independent case studies.

Finally, the application of well-known methods, like interviews, observations and surveys in cross-cultural contexts, has also been subject to critical commentary. So, for example, Verhoeven (2000: 17) discusses cross-cultural interviewing not only in terms of the need to understand the various meaning systems that the interviewee and interviewer bring to the interview, but also to those of 'mutual respect' in which both 'have to build up a we-relationship which is hindered by their different stocks of knowledge' (ibid.: 19). Challenging enough when both parties speak the same language, this becomes even more so when both parties speak different forms of the same language (for example children and/or young people) or when both parties speak different languages (occasionally to the extent that a third party or linguistic interpreter enters and mediates the encounter). This reinforces the need for comparative researchers to take different cultural contexts into account at all stages in the research process; this includes instrument design, data collection and, as importantly, at the reporting and dissemination stages (Broadfoot, 1996).

See also:

Culture (23); Dissemination (32); Ethnography (40); Experiment (44); Interview (57); Method (64); Methodology (65); Research Community (95).

16 Content Analysis

Content analysis originated in the USA and in particular was a technique developed by academic researchers interested in analysing the content of newspapers. The technique was essentially a counting exercise, and though ideally suited to newspaper texts was quickly adapted to other types of texts, such as interview transcripts. Descriptive categories are constructed which refer to properties of the text being examined, and the content analysis is designed to identify the number of times that property appears in the text. Examples of properties which are frequently examined in this way are the length of sentences in books commonly read by children in school; or the number of times that certain key words appear in a newspaper article. These are fairly straightforward; however, the category or categories chosen have to be both exhaustive, i.e. they enable full coverage of all the statements in the text being examined; and exclusive, i.e. statements fit into each category and could not fit into any other category. As soon as the category becomes a high-inference as opposed to a low-inference category, as in seriousness of news coverage or degree of racial bias, then because content analysis is essentially a quantitative technique, it is harder to be certain that statements in a text fit with these prespecified categories. Low-inference variables are less likely to prove problematic in content analysis.

Furthermore, all too frequently content analysis is used to make inferences about what the text refers to, as in a transcript of an interview which in turn makes reference to the actions and beliefs of an interviewee. This chain of referencing means that the counting of specific categories in the transcript may subsequently lack referential validity since it refers to the transcript and not the events or activities that are discussed within that transcript. Other forms of analysis, such as critical discourse analysis, linguistic discourse analysis and various forms of conversation analysis are used by educational researchers in preference to content analyses because in their judgement, they are better able to describe and theorize the contents of the research, and because educational researchers tend to focus on high-inference variables.

See also:
Categorization (10); Coding (14); Conversation Analysis (17); Critical Discourse Analysis (19); Documentary Research (34); Historical Research (53); Linguistic Discourse Analysis (59); Qualitative Research (80); Quantitative Research (81); Variable Analysis (116).

17 Conversation Analysis

Educators talk a lot. So do pupils and students, parents and governors. Not surprisingly, education researchers are interested in such talk. At its most fundamental, conversation analysis is the rigorous and systematic analysis of talk (Hutchby and Wooffitt, 1998). But not just 'any' talk. In the sense used here, talk refers mainly to that which is 'produced in everyday situations of human interaction: *talk-in-interaction*' (ibid.: 1, their emphasis). The development of conversation analysis (CA) owes much to ethnomethodology and Garfinkel's (1967) analysis of 'folk' ('ethno') knowledge. A key assumption underpinning CA is that talk is highly organized; research interest lies in the investigation of how and why individuals make sense of what the other says, primarily in terms of how people take turns and respond to one another, frequently in relation to sequences of interactions. A distinctive aspect of CA is in the natural occurrence of talk and not in the artificial manipulation of conversation in experiments or under laboratory conditions. This means that the most common instrumental device for engaging in CA is the audio (and video) recorder and the analysis of transcripts that derive from naturally occurring 'talk-in-interaction'. Such transcriptions are always precise. This is because of CA's intense interest in paying detailed attention to that which others might see as trivial or commonsensical, such as length of pauses and overlap between interactions that occur as conversations.

While CA has relevance for branches of linguistics such as sociolinguistics, it is argued that 'the questions CA addresses arise more from a sociological basis than from a linguistic basis' (Hutchby and Wooffitt, 1998: 23). Contrasting CA with linguistic discourse analysis (described elsewhere in our text), Hutchby and Wooffitt draw upon Montgomery's (1986: 51) distinction between CA as being 'more concerned with verbal interaction as instances of the situated social order' and the primary focus of linguistic discourse analysis that is upon 'verbal interaction as a manifestation of the linguistic order' (Montgomery, 1986: 51). From a sociological perspective, a key aspect of CA's relevance and import is its methodological contribution to describing the methods that people use to account 'for their own actions and those of others. These are the "ethno-methods" that are the subject of ethnomethodological inquiry' (ibid.). Such interests emerge in Garfinkel's work, for example, in part, as a critique of more conventional social science which, in the 1960s, was closely aligned to the more positivist approaches of survey research. His insistence was upon all forms of social interaction as interpretive processes, and of a social science centred in phenomenology and hermeneutics.

Several fundamental assumptions underpin CA. Adapted from Silverman (2001: 167), specifically his summary of Heritage's (1984) account of CA, these relate: *first*, to the structural organization of talk which is independent of the talkers or their characteristics. From this perspective, talk-in-interaction, in contrast to Garfinkel's early perspectives, is a structural configuration in its own right 'to be treated as on a par with the structural organization of any social institution, i.e. as a "social fact" in Durkheim's terms' (Silverman, 2001: 167); *second*, to its sequential organization, and *third*, to its empirical grounding in the data. 'The empirical conduct of speakers is treated as the central resource out of which the analysis may develop' (Heritage, 1984: 242, cited in Silverman, 2001).

Given the data-driven nature of CA, it is clear that data and transcription techniques are core to CA, in particular its attention to:

- conversational turns-taking;
- conversation openings and adjacency pairs, i.e. the ways in which

different kinds of talk, like questions and answers, greetings and return greetings, invitations and acceptances or declinations, come in pairs;

- how and to what extent institutional talk is similar to, or differs from, the structures of 'ordinary' conversation, for example, as might occur in 'formal' or less formal conversations that occur between teachers and students in educational settings, and the various ways in which each are recorded.

In CA, the transcript is used in conjunction with the tape. The resulting text draws upon a wide range of standardized CA conventions in order to signify and unpack the 'messiness' of talk that include 'the duration of pauses, audible sounds which are not words ... stresses, extensions and truncations that are found in individual words and syllables' (Hutchby and Wooffitt, 1998: 75).

Since its inception, CA has evolved as an inter-disciplinary method. The complexity of its analytical techniques has led some commentators to query its relevance beyond socio-linguistic or ethnomethodological academies. Hutchby and Wooffitt (1998) draw our attention to its practical relevance in relation to three areas, namely, the production of political rhetoric, the design of information technology and the treatment of speech disorders. All have potential relevance for educators and education researchers. For example, if researchers wish to understand more about the potential of e-learning, then in order to design computer systems that will enhance such learning, and further our understanding of the nature of the engagement between the computer, the communicator, and the receiver or mediator of the same, then CA may assist researchers in understanding how such engagement occurs in other 'every-day' learning interactions. Similarly, the study of talk-as-interaction between teachers and learners, and through formal and informal conversations, may assist in the further understanding of teaching and learning with those who, for various reasons, experience speech difficulties as a special education need. Lastly, education researchers 'hear' the political rhetoric of politicians as it relates to educational matters. CA has the capacity to reveal 'the systematic interactional properties of persuasive and effective political discourse' (ibid.: 230), thus assisting researchers to understand prevailing as well as past educational discourses.

Elsewhere, critics of CA extend beyond those who question its methodological techniques or practical relevance to include critics from within sociology who continue to question its 'limiting' and micro-focus upon talk-as-interaction rather than upon the macro issues of power and dominance into which such interaction is embedded (MacLure, 2003: 190).

See also:
Critical Discourse Analysis (19); Empiricism (36); Ethnomethodology (41); Hermeneutics (52); Interpretivism (56); Linguistic Discourse Analysis (59); Phenomenology (73); Positivism (75); Relevance (90).

18 Correlational Research

Correlational research needs to be carefully distinguished from experimental research where variables and conditions are manipulated and controlled, so that the effects of one variable on the other variable can be identified. Experimental treatments have been criticized on a number of grounds: they have weak external validity; there are ethical and procedural difficulties with their practical application; and though more sophisticated designs have been developed, in most cases they are concerned with the manipulation of a single variable, whereas in educational research, it is usually the case that a number of variables contribute to a specified outcome. For these reasons, correlational researchers deal with data that refer to events and activities that have already occurred, and would have occurred without any intervention from the researcher.

Correlational researchers examine relationships between variables. A distinction is sometimes made between a correlation and an association, where the former is concerned with continuous variables (the scale of value has more than two points on it), and the latter is concerned with dichotomous variables (the scale of values only has two points on it). Table 1 is an example of a continuous variable: social class.

An example of a dichotomous variable is sex, because there are only two points on the scale, male and female. A third type of variable is

Table 1: ABC Scale

Group A:	Professional workers (lawyers, doctors, etc.), scientists, managers of large-scale organizations.
Group B:	Shopkeepers, farmers, teachers, white-collar workers.
Group C1:	Skilled manual (i.e. hand) workers – high grade, e.g. master builders, carpenters, shop assistants, nurses.
Group C2:	Skilled manual workers – low grade, e.g. electricians, plumbers.
Group D:	Semi-skilled manual workers, e.g. bus drivers, lorry drivers, fitters.
Group E:	Unskilled manual workers, e.g. general labourers, barmen, porters.

called a discrete variable, where it only incorporates a number of specific points on the scale and values refer to those points and not to positions in between them.

Common forms of associational and correlational relationships between different types of variables can be determined using some well-known measures. Some examples are displayed in Table 2.

Table 2: Associational and Correlational Relationships and their Measures

Measure	Nature of Variables
Pearson product moment	Two continuous variables; interval or ratio scale, linear relationship.
Rank Order or Kendall's tau	Two continuous variables; ordinal scale.
Phi coefficient	Two true dichotomies; nominal or ordinal series.
Kendall's coefficient of Concordance	Three or more continuous variables; ordinal series.

These research techniques can also be divided into four types: exploratory relational studies (examining the relationship between two or more variables); exploratory partial correlational techniques (controlling the effect of one variable to allow examination of the relationship between two others); multivariate techniques (examining the association between dependent and independent variables); and prediction studies (correlational techniques that allow the prediction of the operation of one variable from the operation of another).

See also:
Causation (11); Ethics (39); Experiment (44); Generalization (50); Mathematical Modelling (62); Prediction (78); Variable Analysis (116).

19   Critical Discourse Analysis

Critical discourse analysis (CDA) describes a wide range of educational research that is focused upon the analysis of language (commonly used in interviews or in conversations) as well as written texts from documents. Central to the use of the term 'critical' is the notion that the ideas and knowledge that form the content of such texts reflect a form of power which may be used by one group to control (an)other group(s).

Unlike conversation analysis, CDA is eclectic in the sense that the texts and talk that are researched do not *have* to be naturally occurring. Following Austin (1962), Potter (1997) describes three key elements of CDA. *First,* CDA is anti-realist in the sense of denying that there is ever one 'true' description of reality. *Second,* a key interest of CDA is in the ways in which research participants 'construct' realities. *Third,* CDA is concerned with the way in which talk and texts construct coherence, sometimes through telling convincing stories to constitute an 'objective, out-there reality' (Potter, 1997: 179).

In the CDA of documents, for example, texts are also seen as

> vehicles for ideologies which present society from the viewpoint of particular social groupings; the discourses contained within official documents can thus be seen as an attempt by the state to maintain the status quo. (Pole and Lampard, 2002: 163)

CDA may take a number of forms, as it investigates the structures and rules of discourse which, as Pole and Lampard point out, both shape and are shaped by socio-cultural contexts (ibid.) in which different discourses may be conflicting (Wetherell and Potter, 1994). One form is where

> semiotics focuses on the relationship between the *signifier*, such as word, picture, or object, and the *signified*, which is the mental image or meaning associated with that thing. The signifier and the signified together constitute a *sign* ... and a collection of signs can convey a complex system of communication. (Pole and Lampard, 2002: 163, their emphases)

Another form is derived from feminist literary criticism, for example, in which the ideology is 'seen as inscribed in the discourse, and produced and reproduced within literature specifically and in cultural practice generally' (ibid.).

According to Kress (1990: 84), what binds an otherwise eclectic range of theories drawn from linguistics and from social and critical theory, is its 'overtly political agenda' and purposive intentions to bring about social change, predominantly of the emancipatory kind. Elsewhere, Luke (1995: 13) describes 'CDA as a political act in itself' in its attempt to interrupt and deconstruct 'everyday common sense' features in talk and texts.

A number of concepts feature strongly in CDA. Silverman (2001), for example, discusses 'interpretive repertoires' like 'science' and 'motherhood' as ways in which talk and texts enable their producers to define their identities and moral status. 'Stake' and 'scripts' are other focal points of CDA in examining ways in which talkers and writers 'attend to the normative character of their actions' (ibid.: 179–80).

CDA has been used widely in education research since, as MacLure

(2003: 187) points out, 'education is one of the key sites for the "disciplining" of subjects and the inequitable distribution of symbolic and material assets', especially education which comes to constitute 'real' or formal knowledge, or the only knowledge worth knowing. Whether the educational researcher's focus of interest lies in gender, ethnicity, class or other inequalities that are part of the structural fabric of education, CDA provides a range of 'other' readings, first through the process of deconstructing the knowledge elements contained in the text or talk and then reconstructing them to demonstrate its origins and/or 'oppressive nature' (ibid.).

Eclecticism in approach, as well as underpinning theories, have brought a number of criticisms. These range from the methodological (Hammersely, 1997) to the theoretical, and from a critique that highlights conceptual confusion and/or incoherence. Pennycook (1994) questions whether CDA is fundamentally about 'unmasking' ideology in order to reveal an underpinning 'truth'. If this is the case, he argues, there is a basic contradiction between this position and a recourse to Foucault, for whom 'revelations' of an 'external' truth or discourse would have been an anathema. For Pennycook and others (like Poynton, 2000), perhaps the most serious intellectual problem confronting CDA lies in trying to marry the orientations of linguistics with social and critical theory, an endpoint similarly shared by MacLure (2003: 190–1) who concludes that 'whilst connections remain between the fine grain of language and action ("what people say and do")', an 'integrated discourse theory' to 'seamlessly accommodate linguistics and poststructuralism would ... appear impossible'.

See also:
Conversation Analysis (17); Critical Theory (22); Documentary Research (34); Empowerment (37); Feminist Research (47); Interpretivism (56); Linguistic Discourse Analysis (59); Power (77); Structuralism/Poststructuralism (102).

20 Critical Incidents

The narrative themes that underpin biography, autobiography and ethnography are frequently explored as a series of sequences and patterns of events and actions that are known as critical incidents. What makes the event critical or significant varies and, in education, can range from episodes in a teacher's career history or a description of a classroom event, school-based meeting or encounter. Critical incidents, therefore, straddle both the processes of detailed data collection that constitutes qualitative research, and its analysis. This is unsurprising, given the iterative engagement between data collection and analysis that is central to such research. Critical incidents are part of a story-telling genre; whether the teller is the researcher or research participant, or both, such incidents provide important frames in which to sequence and narrate the key events of such stories. In biography and autobiography, they might also be described as 'the narrative props' upon which to tell the biographer's story, that is also frequently confessional (Coffey, 1999: 128–9). Critical incidents draw variously upon field and observation notes, interview and diary data as well as a range of relevant documents.

They have been described in a number of ways, but frequently the emphasis is upon the typicality of an incident, action or episode in relation to other incidents, actions and episodes. However, typicality may not always be the key feature. Focusing on the educational significance of a dramatic event, for example, Woods (1993a: 56–9) describes the criticality of an incident in terms of a number of key aspects which included an event that produced change (notably radical and significant); had a distinctive structure and sequence (described as conceptualization, explosive, convergence, and celebration stages); produced important developments in learning; and a particular momentum in staff relations. Readers get a sense of the dramatic and momentous. Whether such incidents are seen as dramatic for all readers and actors are matters of interpretation and reinterpretation. Perhaps the key issue lies in the extent to which such events are seen as significant by the key actors in the story (see also Tripp, 1993).

The strengths of critical incident analysis are similar to those applied to narrative analysis overall. In addition to exploring events as stories (that includes research activity stories), critical incidents focus research attention upon actors' 'meanings' and 'voice' (Cortazzi, 2002: 200) and upon what Coffey (1999: 129) describes as restoring the 'polyvocality to the text – suggesting multiple versions of multiple realities; an understanding of lives and selves shaped by different and varied voices'.

See also:
Design (28); Diaries (30); Documentary Research (34); Ethnography (40); Life History (58); Narrative (67); Qualitative Research (80); Textuality (110).

21 Critical Realism

Critical realism is a social theory, which attempts to reconcile positivist and post-positivist views of the world. There have been a number of prominent theorists in this field; however, the progenitor of the theory is usually considered to be Roy Bhaskar. Critical realism is based on a critique and rejection of empiricism. For empiricists, what is given to the senses constitutes the world as it is. It is possible to accurately describe that world, a world of sense impressions, if the correct procedures are followed, and these correct procedures comprise the observer or researcher bracketing out their own preconceptions of the world and making an objective assessment of it. Language can therefore act as a neutral medium for describing the world. For Bhaskar (1979), there are two major problems. The first of these concerns the way cause and effect are treated as 'the constant conjunction of atomistic events or states of affairs, interpreted as the objects of actual or possible experience' (Bhaskar, 1979: 158). What is being conflated here is epistemology (how we can know reality) and ontology (reality itself). He describes this as the ontic fallacy. Second, this means that a successionist rather then generative view of causation is being proposed. Bhaskar (1979) distinguishes between structures that generate and have the potential to generate occurrences and the atomistic viewpoint adopted by empiricists, where reality consists of these constant conjunctions of experiences.

On the other hand, critical realism also seeks to distance itself from radical relativism. Whereas with empiricism, descriptions of the world are collapsed into sense data, radical relativists working from a different perspective sever the link between text and reality so that only texts have epistemological significance, and these only make reference to other texts and not to any underlying reality. In short, radical relativists are anti-realist. Bhaskar (1979), as a realist, though not of a naïve kind, identifies three domains: the real, consisting of mechanisms; the actual, consisting of events; and the empirical, consisting of experiences. Events can happen in the world without them being observed. Mechanisms can neutralize other mechanisms so that nothing changes in life that can be directly observed; indeed, mechanisms can retain their potentiality for influencing the world, without them actually doing so. What this suggests is that these mechanisms are relatively enduring, whereas our capacity and our procedures for knowing them changes and is determined by social and political arrangements, in the present and stretching back in time.

Underpinning this theory is a strong belief in realism and what

Bhaskar (1979) means by this is as follows: there are objects in the world whether they are known or not; knowledge is fallible because any claims to knowledge that are made are open to refutation; there are trans-social truths where the observer can only access appearances, but these appearances refer to underlying mechanisms which are not easily apprehended; finally, those deep structures or mechanisms may actually contradict or be in conflict with their appearances. Critical realism is therefore able to explain emergent structures, whereas empiricist and radical relativist descriptions of reality always lag behind the way society is presently constituted, which is understood as an ongoing process.

Critical realism has certain implications for educational research. For example, educational researchers frequently collect data in mathematical form that allows them to identify associations or correlations between variables. It is assumed that these associations or correlations correctly describe reality and that cause–effect relations can be inferred from them. Critical realists would suggest that the identification of causal relations is a much more complex affair and that conflating associations or correlations with causes may lead to a mistaken view of reality. Critical realism is not without problems itself, and these focus on the existence of these mechanisms which cannot be known in any straightforward sense, and the difficulty of knowing them when any description of them is relative to ways of understanding embedded within particular societies. Critical realism is, however, an attempt to overcome the antagonism between empiricist and interpretivist viewpoints about reality and how it can be known.

See also:
Causation (11); Correlational Research (18); Empiricism (36); Epistemology/Ontology (38); Fallibility (46); Positivism (75); Realism (83); Relativism (89); Social Constructionism (99); Structure (103); Variable Analysis (116).

22 Critical Theory

Critical theory is a research perspective that foregrounds the notion of emancipation, so that it not only describes the world or generates knowledge about it, but also seeks to change it by detecting and unmasking beliefs and practices that limit human freedom, justice and democracy. As Scott and Usher (1999: 24) argue:

The 'critical' can therefore be said to be marked by a disengagement from the 'scientific' as conventionally conceived, with an accompanying critique of its distinguishing features such as 'objectivity', value neutrality and the strict separation between knowing subjects and objects to be known, or, to put it another way, the self and the world.

Most feminist and anti-racist researchers locate themselves within the bounds of critical theory, because they understand the world and the way knowledge is constructed about that world, in the first case as male-centric and in the second case as racist. Jurgen Habermas is the best-known critical theorist, and he has argued that it involves both ideology critique and the taking of rational action on the basis of knowledge. It is therefore both an epistemological and an ethical theory.

As a theory of research, its principal characteristic is an acknowledgement that the researchers are unable to maintain a disinterested stance when collecting, organizing or analysing data, but their belief systems, and more importantly their political projects, are implicated in their work as researchers. They cannot step outside these frameworks and political projects, so decisions they make about what constitutes knowledge, which data to collect and how certain types of data should be interpreted are always made from a particular perspective. Values are therefore central to research. Indeed, Habermas (1972) identifies three types of knowledge (see Table 3), the third of which, the critical, is central to critical theory.

Researchers, therefore, have to choose between these three types of knowledge, and the implication of making such a choice is that their initial decision about research methods not only reflects the truth, but also commits that researcher to certain educational values as well (cf. Carr, 1995).

These forms of knowledge, and indeed critical theory itself, have been criticized on a number of grounds. It has already been suggested that the underpinning principle of critical theory is that the researcher operates with and through a particular political project and a particular set of values. This commits the critical theorist to a view that positivist/empiricist forms of knowledge, even if expressed as objective, disinterested and truthful, conceal their value base. Critical theory is therefore not only an alternative *but also* a more truthful epistemology. Two problems with critical approaches are immediately obvious. The first is that if research is always based on, indeed driven by, a set of political aspirations, these in turn have to be justified, and though it may be generally accepted that anti-racist and feminist projects are inherently worthwhile, it is more difficult to provide absolute justifications for

Table 3: Forms of Knowledge (adapted from Carr, 1995)

	Empirical Analytic	Historical Hermeneutic	Critical
Research Methods	Natural; scientific; Experimental; Quantitative.	Historical; Interpretive; Illuminative.	Critical social science, Emancipatory action research.
Form of Research Knowledge	Objective; Nomological; Explanation.	Subjective; Ideographic; Interpretive.	Dialectical; Reflexive; Praxis.
Human Interest	Technical.	Practical.	Emancipatory.
Practical Purpose	Instrumental.	Deliberative.	Critical action.
Human Nature	Deterministic.	Humanistic.	Historical.
Educational Philosophy	Neo-classical.	Liberal progressive.	Socially critical.
Educational Values	Preparation for given form of life.	Self-actualization; Meritocratic form of life.	Empowerment; Transformative form of life.

them. The second problem is more serious still, and this is that if critical approaches are essentially political programmes, the researcher may be justified in ignoring the strict evidential bases of the claims they are making. In terms of emphasis, the political project takes precedence over the careful citing and collecting of evidence or data.

See also:
Action Research (3); Anti-racism (6); Determinism (29); Empowerment (37); Epistemology/Ontology (38); Ethics (39); Experiment (44); Feminist Research (47); Historical Research (53); Interpretivism (56); Nomothetic Statements (69); Objectivity (70); Positivism (75); Quantitative Research (81); Reflexivity (87); Subjectivity (104); Values (115).

23   Culture

When educational researchers use the term *culture* they draw upon a range of meanings that derive from the social sciences and, in particular, sociology, social psychology and anthropology. Most definitions are derived in some form or another from anthropology which refers to culture as all that is learned in a social group, and includes knowledge, beliefs, art, morals, law and customs. For Goudenough (1981: 110), culture provides 'systems of standards for perceiving, believing, evaluation and acting'. In earlier German and Northern American usage, a further distinction was made between adaptive culture, namely, ideas, values and customs, and material culture which refers to the artefacts of that culture including buildings, tangible manufactured goods, and so on. Traditionally, then, the latter were the province of archaeologists and the former of sociologists, psychologists and anthropologists, with historians and historical researchers straddling both. What remains of that distinction is encapsulated by the term 'cultural lag', first developed by the early Chicago School of sociologists; this suggests that when there is a gap between the technological development of a society and its moral and legal institutions, the potential is for there to be an increase in social conflict and problems.

The term *political culture* refers to the norms, values and symbols that help to legitimize the distribution of power and authority, and education has been used in various ways to socialize young citizens into the forms of citizenship that are deemed appropriate to that society. In recent years, such socialization has become more complex as society has become more diverse, where citizens may have multiple identities, and the forces of ethnicity and nationalism may 'pull' and 'push' citizens in various directions. Sociologists of education have used the term *cultural relativism* to discuss and research the cultural forces that affect the way knowledge as well as educational practices are produced through educational experiences, which afford superiority to some forms of knowledge and practices, and disadvantage those whose knowledge and practices are considered inferior.

The term 'culture' is operationalized at a number of research levels. In education, and particularly in the fields of educational leadership and management and school effectiveness and improvement, a search for the kind of organizational culture most likely to maximize pupil achievement and attainment, effective leadership and management and teacher/learner relations has been rather akin to the search for the 'holy grail', made more complex by the need to make researchable the phenomena of school 'ethos', 'mission', and 'leadership' and its relation to any or all of the above. Sergiovanni (2003: 23), for example, draws upon the work of Habermas (1987) to define culture as 'the knowledge, beliefs, and norms from which we derive significance'. For Sergiovanni, 'if culture wanes in a school, meaning is lost, traditions are ruptured, and parents, teachers, and students are likely to drift in a sea of apathy and indifference' (ibid.: 23).

In education leadership and management, reference is made to culture management in terms of 'the ability of leaders to know and understand what the organizational culture is, modifying that culture to meet the needs of the organization as it develops' (Horner, 2003: 30). Here, we begin to get a sense of organizational cultures in which formal and informal rules and norms coexist that are mediated and contested in educational settings (Ball, 1987). This has led some researchers to investigate the existence of and prospects for cultures of collaboration (Leithwood *et al.*, 2003), collegiality or collectivity, as well as finding evidence of 'contrived' forms of any or all of these. Fullan (2003) has written extensively about the need for a 'culture of change' and of a 'reculturing' of schooling that foregrounds effective pedagogy and a focus upon teaching and learning in the classroom. There is much in research about culture that has strong ideological and school-based predispositions towards school improvement and the role of leaders/ managers in effecting cultural change to achieve this. Counterpoints are provided, in the main by a range of critical rather than problem-solving theorists (see Ozga, 2000) and discussed elsewhere in this volume, with Stephen Ball (1987), among others, having made seminal contributions to debates that make links between power, culture and 'managerialism' in education.

This does not exhaust the list of researchers' interests in the cultures and sub-cultures of educational experience, often epitomized by ethnographic engagement in specific settings, and as teacher or pupil cultures. Finally, Coffey and Atkinson (2000: 21–3) are among writers to have reminded us that educational research is itself a cultural exercise with many competing traditions within, as well as between, best-known approaches that are also mediated through academic and disciplinary cultures. The example drawn is from ethnography, which, they argue, is at a 'cultural cross-roads' characterized by 'a clamour of styles and justifications' and 'subversive and transgressive tendencies'. This draws our attention as much to the changing and slippery concept that is called culture as a topic for research investigation, as it does to the culture of research, which is also changing, and lacks homogeneity in any fixed sense.

See also:
Comparative Research (15); Ethnography (40); Historical Research (53); Power (77); Values (115).

24 Data Display

Information can be translated into and displayed as data in a number of ways and near the beginning, during and at the end of an education research study. Both translation and display are inextricably linked. Variations in data display relate to the epistemological as well as methodological underpinnings that guide the research being undertaken. Display involves a visual format for presenting data, so that the reader and user can draw valid conclusions from it. Sometimes distinctions are made in terms of distinctiveness in display between research that focuses upon numbers and that which does not, or between qualitative or quantitative approaches. This is simplistic. However, key areas of differences in display relate to the coherence of statistical calculation and analysis to inform display in the latter, and a focus upon thick description in the former. Quantification is not only amenable to mathematical manipulation but also to the representation of that manipulation in well-established forms of display, such as distribution curves, rank order lists, frequency tables, pie charts and bar graphs, each made more straightforward for display purposes by developments in computing packages for statistical measures such as the mean and frequency distribution, the chi square test, the Mann–Whitney test and Spearman's rho, for example, and in a variety of presentational forms.

More recently, the focus has been upon the use of data display for qualitative data analysis, an area thought formerly to be more amenable to dense textual representation than to visual display. Miles and Huberman (1994: 90) are among researchers to have pioneered new approaches to qualitative data display, arguing that data display can be used to draw initial and interim *descriptive* conclusions about the bounded 'case' and later, when more data is available, to aid and present *explanation* or 'plausible reasons for why things are the way they are'. The advocacy of qualitative display is, in part, a regaling against extended, poorly framed texts that make it difficult to look at the whole rather than the parts (often written sequentially), and in formats that are increasingly rejected, it is argued, by policy-makers (ibid.: 91). Display formats can be various but two forms predominate in qualitative studies: the use of matrices and the use of networks with a series of nodes to link them (sometimes known as spidergrams). Data is also presented as short text, quotes, abbreviations, symbols, lines, arrows, and so on. In recent years, the speed, quality and formats for data entry, usually comprising coded data segments, has been increasingly affected by and reflected in computer software packages such as

NUD*IST, NVivo and also in hypertext, which have been used to develop a 'picture' of themes and patterns or to look for chains of evidence. Moreover, such maps and pictures are also used for various analytical purposes, to assist researchers as they construct conceptual maps and pathways through the data or as an aid to longitudinal events analyses. And Miles and Huberman (1994: 153) provide examples used in the construction of causal networks that 'display ... the most important independent and dependent variables in a field study ... and of the relationships among them' in which 'the plot of these relationships are directional rather than solely correlational'.

From a range of starting points, data display is used increasingly in qualitative and quantitative research. A less than sophisticated use of visual display might lead the inexperienced researcher to 'hide behind' the display, assuming wrongly that the display is, of itself, a substitute for textual explication, a tendency even more appealing given the colourful and impressive forms of representation now available on computer. A best position, therefore, would be to engage in data display as part of a skilful descriptive and explanatory exposition of the visual and the written, and in terms of best fit for the purposes of the research study (see also Brown and Dowling, 1998: 108–9).

See also:
Categorization (10); Coding (14); Correlational Research (18); Dissemination (32); Qualitative Research (80); Quantitative Research (81); Statistics (100); Writing for Academic Purposes (119); Writing as Representation (120).

25   Data Reduction

The term data reduction is associated primarily with qualitative data analysis. While the iterative link between data collection and analysis is a key aspect of all qualitative study, not all researchers are in agreement about the precise point at which analysis begins. As Bryman and Burgess (1994: 218) comment: 'sometimes, analysis seems to begin more or less upon entering the field ... whereas others appear to delay analysis pending the accumulation of a substantial body of data.' Bogden and Biklen (1982) draw a distinction between analysis that begins in the field, and analysis that occurs after data collection. Whichever the starting point, all processes begin with a sorting and making sense of the data collected, and this inevitably involves some element of data reduction as data is coded and summarized. For Miles and Huberman

(1994: 10), data reduction is a key process in 'three concurrent flows of activity' that constitute data analysis. Such activities are: data reduction, data display and conclusion drawing/verification. Data reduction is further subdivided into two components – anticipatory data reduction and data reduction. 'Even before the data are actually collected, anticipatory data reduction is occurring as the researcher decides (often without full awareness) which conceptual framework, which research questions, and which data collection approaches to study' (ibid.). And as Pole and Morrison (2003: 74) point out, for qualitative researchers 'working in tightly applied frameworks of educational policy and practice, "anticipatory data reduction" may take on a specific nuance, although the processes involved preclude neither novel nor emergent concepts or outcomes'.

Data reduction is, then, 'a process of selecting, focusing, abstracting, simplifying, and transforming the notes that appear in written-up notes or transcriptions' that is part of analysis and simultaneously requires the researcher to 'make analytic choices' (Miles and Huberman, 1994: 10–11). Yet, the relationship between data reduction and the kind of qualitative research being produced is also important. Miles and Huberman epitomize what Brewer (2000) and Pole and Morrison (2003) describe as 'positivist' qualitative research (in their case, referring to ethnography). Here, tightly structured organizational frameworks for data analysis are typified in the three-fold model, that uses matrices and display. Such an approach is compared with 'humanistic' research, where the emphasis is upon the researcher's 'disappearance from the research account ... to write the insiders' words and actions as if unaffected by the researcher's presence' (Pole and Morrison, 2003: 77), an approach that has been strongly contested, less on technical grounds as 'un-reduced' data, but more on epistemological grounds that such a reality *cannot exist*:

> Once we abandon the idea that the social character of research can be 'standardised out' or avoided by becoming 'a fly on the wall' or 'full participant', the role of the researcher as active participant in the research process becomes clear. He or she is the research participant *par excellence*. (Hammersley and Atkinson, 1995: 19)

For 'postmodern' and 'post-postmodern' advocates of qualitative research, including ethnography, there 'will always be competing versions of reality and multiple perspectives that the analysis must address' (Brewer, 2000: 108), and, therefore, data which concerns relationships developed in the field, and the characteristics of the researcher, would always need to be included in the final account, along with context, the methodology and fieldwork practices used (ibid.).

Whichever the epistemological nuance, the underpinning rationale for data reduction is as an early-stage process, sometimes used synonymously with initial coding procedures, and then later in the search for higher and higher levels of understanding – first, as a signpost to further data collection and second, for emergent theoretical frameworks that are drawn from connections made between the coding, categorization and conceptualization of data.

See also:
Categorization (10); Coding (14); Data Display (24); Epistemology/ Ontology (38); Ethnography (40); Methodology (65); Postmodernism (76); Qualitative Research (80); Reflexivity (87); Subjectivity (104); Writing (118).

26 Deconstruction

Deconstruction has its roots in the philosophy of Jacques Derrida; however, it has now become a commonly used method in other disciplines, with education being one of these. Derrida in his voluminous writings has sought to dispel the illusion that words, phrases and statements, indeed language itself, can adequately capture the nature of the world itself. Though the language user might refer to a referent that he or she is describing, for Derrida, meaning and reference are always absent. This creates certain problems for Derrida because he has chosen to communicate ideas, which he then argues cannot be communicated or at least cannot be fully explained. So, one of his favourite devices is to place an idea or concept or construct 'under erasure'. Whatever meaning is being attached to those ideas, concepts and constructs, it never adequately captures them, because meaning is elsewhere.

Derrida (1978) offers a general critique of Western philosophy by emphasizing the deficiencies of phonocentrism and logocentrism. Phonocentrism gives priority to the spoken word at the expense of the written word, and therefore exaggerates the extent to which that thought originates from an individual with a fixed identity. Logocentrism is the belief that language has a referent in reality, and though there are ideological disputes and misunderstandings, it is still possible to anchor description of the world in that world itself. This is a search for epistemological foundations. For Derrida, language comprises the endless play of metaphor and inter-textuality, so that reference can only be to other metaphors, and has no external location. Deconstruction is the method chosen to do this. It involves a constant dismantling of the underlying notions of presence and external reference that characterize writing and a focusing on the way metaphors are used and related to each other.

Postmodernists have been greatly influenced by Derrida's notion of deconstruction; it has however, come to be used in a number of ways. One way would seek to deconstruct these linguistic forms (the use of binary oppositions which marginalize some forms of life at the expense of others; the attachment of evaluative connotations to particular words or phrases; the alignment of some ideas with others; the construction of boundaries around forms of thinking which act to exclude and marginalize) without at the same time putting in their place reified alternatives. Burbules (1995) suggests that the postmodern story may best be understood in relation to three narrative tropes: the ironic, the tragic and the parodic. The ironic trope is an attempt to indicate to the reader that meaning is never fixed or essentialized, and that the position one can take up can never be definitive or natural. The tragic trope is an acknowledgement that any attempt to speak as it were outside the comforting modernist assumptions enshrined in everyday and commonsense discourses is bound to be ambiguous, unsettling and incomplete. The third narrative trope identified by Burbules is the parodic where the only option open is to play the game without at any time taking up foundationalist or fixed positions.

A second way might be to understand the way power constructs are embedded in linguistic and epistemological forms without taking an extreme anti-realist position. And yet a third position might be to understand the way bias is present in educational research with the purpose of eliminating or accounting for it. This last would appropriate the use of a notion such as deconstruction for a different purpose than was originally intended, as Derrida uses it as a way of countering phonocentrism and logocentrism. Deconstruction has, however, become a commonly used term in educational research.

See also:
Determinism (29); Epistemology/Ontology (38); Narrative (67); Postmodernism (76); Power (77); Realism (83); Textuality (110).

27   Deduction

A typical deductive process comprises the following:

1. A research hypothesis is developed, and a number of discrete variables are identified, which the hypothesis suggests coexist in a specified way.
2. The hypothesis is operationalized, so that the relations between the variables and the operation of the variables themselves can be construed as observational data and can be measured.
3. Data are collected and a strategy, whether it is experimental, survey or case study, is chosen. In addition, a sample of cases is made, and the relationship between this sample and its parent population is established.
4. The empirical data is then used to confirm, disconfirm or partially confirm the original hypothesis or hypotheses.
5. This process may be replicated, and if this further process of testing is successful, the hypothesis becomes accepted as theory.

A number of assumptions underpin the deductive process. The first of these is that discrete and measurable variables can be identified. So, for example, each individual human being can be racially classified, and that classification is not determined in any way by context, self-reporting or history; or at least, that measure of race and consequent gradations in the classificatory system are agreed and generally accepted in society. The second assumption concerns the place and role of values in research. Though values are accepted as a necessary part of the act of identifying the variable and its consequent gradations, they do not subsequently act as distorting or biasing moments in the deductive process. A consequence of accepting this is that the researcher is engaged in a process of imposing a set of constructs, and various relations between them, on the reality that they are investigating. They are not therefore responsive to emergent structures, or to disputed definitions implicit in variables, as structures and definitions are predetermined. This may lead to a process whereby constructs and ways of ordering the world are reified, and do not reflect the world as it has now become. The method lacks predictive power as it is wholly based on events and ways of construing those events that occurred in the past.

Deductive modes of thought and experimental approaches have therefore generally not been popular among educational researchers, as educational precepts that persist over time are few and far between. Most research designs build in an inductive element, so that the conclusions educational researchers come to are responsive to the setting that they are investigating; and though values play a part in deductive strategies, the reflexive element of research is relatively neglected, as it is assumed that the values of the researcher and the way they construct reality do not play any further part in the proceedings after the prespecification of the problem and the predetermination of the conceptual framework.

The best-known deductivist is Karl Popper (1976), though his method is more akin to a process of critical rationalism. His approach consisted of a number of explicit steps:

1. Method consists of trying out tentative solutions to problems that occur and these are tested and criticized. If a proposed solution is not open to reasonable criticism, then it is excluded as unscientific, although perhaps only temporarily.
2. If the solution to the problem can be criticized, then it is subject to a process of refutation.
3. If the refutation is successful, a new solution is proposed, and this is accepted temporarily until a new refutation is successful.
4. The method of science is one of tentative attempts to solve problems, by conjectures, which are controlled by severe criticism. No final solution is possible.

Because neither inductive nor deductive research strategies have provided convincing explanations of how social scientists develop knowledge of society, other strategies have been developed. Two of these are retroduction and abduction.

See also:
Abduction (1); Anti-racism (6); Case Study (9); Experiment (44); Induction (55); Power (77); Prediction (78); Reductionism (84); Reflexivity (87); Replication (92); Retroduction (97); Sampling (98); Survey (105); Values (115); Variable Analysis (116).

28 Design

Research design refers to the schema or plan that constitutes the entire research study. It includes a summary of the intended research topic and distinguishes between the research problem and the research questions that are derived from the problem. Research design will give due attention to why the research study is worth investigating and pays specific attention to its potential significance. Research designs need to demonstrate that the problem for investigation is doable, given available resources, and may often (but not always) suggest a relationship to be investigated. The topic for research refers precisely to what the researcher seeks to find, investigate, know or refute. From some, but not all, research perspectives the term 'problem' implies a search for a 'solution'.

Morrison and Watling (2002) draw upon Denscombe's (2002) 'ground rules for social research' in order both to suggest a framework for research design and to identify criteria against which a research design might be judged. Ten areas are identified as follows.

Purpose

Research designs include statements of aims and objectives. The former refers to the purposes of the research and signals its intentions. Effective design also captures the essence of the study, and provides the reader with an overall sense of direction. Research objectives constitute clear refinements to the general aims that are specifically geared towards research direction and research outcomes. One key aspect of that refinement involves the articulation of research questions which indicate what information or data is being sought. Qualitative researchers commonly start off with a large question that may be subdivided into a number of sub-questions. Quantitative researchers normally start with questions that derive from a particular theory and use the language of relationships between variables and hypotheses.

Relevance

Research design gives specific attention to the originality of the intended study and the 'gaps' that the research is designed to 'fill'. This requires clear explication of the indicative literature already reviewed and that which remains to be reviewed. There may be something of a paradox here, in the sense that researchers cannot complete their literature review until they have formulated their research problem, and yet the indicative literature will help to formulate and develop the same, and in the case of emergent data from grounded theory, there will, in particular, be an ongoing dialogic link between the data and the literature, which needs to be designed 'in' to the research.

Resources

Effective research design matches research intentions with resources available and constructs a full explanation of what it is realistic (or not) to achieve given opportunities and constraints. This also requires full attention to publishing and dissemination opportunities, resources for which need to be allocated as part of the planning process. Of key importance is the need to build in time for access negotiation and research processes like data collection, as well as for analysis, writing up and preparation for dissemination.

Originality

The potential scope and scale of the research as it relates to originality (substantive, theoretical and/or methodological) is integral to the research design.

Accuracy

Clear statements about how the data is to be collected, managed and analysed are integral aspects, linked to which are issues of accountability.

Accountability

There is a need for a clear demonstration that the data has been collected in ways and formats that are justifiable.

Generalizability

Because not all research is intended to be generalizable beyond the boundaries of a specific entity or locale, then the research design needs to signal the relationship (if any) between the research and its usefulness in terms of generalizibility and/or justify other grounds for its relevance.

Objectivity and subjectivity

A key issue in research design is the need for researchers to signal very early on where they will 'stand' in relation to the research they are conducting. Of specific interest here is the need to signal the paradigm(s) in which researchers are working and the philosophical, as well as value, judgments upon which the research is predicated. Cresswell (1994: 15) draws attention to a range of assumptions that need to be made explicit; these relate not only to issues of epistemology and ontology but also to methodology, the use and style of language and also to issues of ethics.

Ethics

In research design, clear statements are necessary in relation to the ethical and legal implications of the research.

Proof

A clear articulation of how researchers will make claims about the veracity of their research are start- rather than endpoints in all research designs.

As Morrison and Watling (2002) comment, not all researchers will give equal weighting to the above points. Yet, a key concern is that attention to emphasis and weighting is built into the research design.

There are a number of formats that are commonly used to present research findings, and notwithstanding attendant dangers of rigidity and over-simplification, Cresswell (1994: 13) is among research methodologists to have signalled the formats most commonly used for presenting research that is based mainly on quantitative or qualitative work, or both. A key matter with regard to the latter is the ability to justify, as part of research design, researchers' intentions to be methodological 'purists' or 'pragmatists'. Also acknowledged is a more widespread variation in the formats for qualitative than for quantitative work.

Finally, it is perhaps worth noting Meloy's (1994: 44–5) articulation of 'quality' as it relates to research as this provides potentially powerful clues as to what needs to be demonstrated through design. Here, progress, process and outcomes might be related to issues of verité (intellectual honesty and authenticity); integrity (structurally sound); rigour (depth of intellect); utility (contribution to the field); vitality (important, meaningful, exciting); and aesthetics (whether writing is pleasing to anticipate and experience).

See also:
Access (2); Discourse (31); Epistemology/Ontology (38); Ethics (39); Generalization (50); Method (64); Methodology (65); Mixed Methods (66); Publishing (79); Qualitative Research (80); Quantitative Research (81); Variable Analysis (116); Writing (118); Writing for Academic Purposes (119).

29 Determinism

If determinism is understood as what will inevitably happen given a particular set of antecedent conditions, then x determines y. However, a distinction is usually drawn between strong determinist explanations where the individual is understood as incapable of intervening in the flow of cause and effect due to a genetic predisposition to act in a certain way, and weak determinist explanations where the individual is conceived of as a product of social forces over which they have no control. Furthermore, a belief in genetic or institutional determinism does not imply that human beings are in a position to predict what will happen. This is because they are unlikely to have complete knowledge of events and activities in the world.

With determinist explanations, individuals are thought of as the possessors of certain attributes or essences that compel them to behave in certain ways and not others, whether they know it or not. Determinism implies that actors' descriptions of their behaviours, projects and desires may not just be mistaken, but are irrelevant to any proper description of, or theorizing about, human activity. Human behaviours that do not fit the normal pattern are pathologized, with the individual deemed to have acted in a perverse manner. Furthermore, these compelling mechanisms are universal in that they transcend place and time; or at least, though genetic modification can occur, this occurs very slowly and therefore the natural can be identified in a secure way.

Determinist explanations may take an institutional form. Here the body is not programmed to reproduce those predetermined behaviours. However, social arrangements are deemed to be so compelling that individual human behaviour is determined by them. For example, structuralist explanations may position individuals as immersed in social discourses, which means that they behave in conformity with their hidden codings. Societies in time and place may be structured so that individuals are positioned within different discursive frameworks, and it is these frameworks that determine individual human behaviour. Social forms therefore may be constructed, in that they are the end product of a series of decisions made by individuals and groups of individuals stretching back in time, but still work in determinist ways.

Either of these two forms of determinism may be incorporated into educational research methodologies, and indeed those approaches that marginalize self-reported descriptions of intentions and beliefs have a tendency to adopt a view of society as all-constraining, or of biology as a set of codes that determine how individuals behave. The reasons individuals give for the way they behave are therefore considered to be irrelevant to the conduct of everyday life and consequently do not play a significant part in descriptions that educational researchers make of social settings. Forces that are external to human consciousness cause human behaviours, and in order to understand these forces, the researcher needs to explain those persistent patterns of human conduct which can be adequately expressed in mathematical form. Archer (1990) suggests here that these methodological approaches prioritize structure at the expense of agency so that action is neglected. Ethnomethodological and symbolic interactionist perspectives are underpinned by a rejection of either genetic or institutional determinist structures.

See also:
Agency (4); Causation (11); Discourse (31); Ethnomethodology (41);
Reductionism (84); Statistics (100); Structuralism/Poststructuralism
(102); Structure (103); Symbolic Interactionism (106).

30 Diaries

Diaries are among a wide and often complex array of documentary
materials of interest to educational researchers. Diary-focused research
is also a distinctive research genre that straddles qualitative and
quantitative research. Diary keepers are either researchers or research
participants, or both. While most attention is given here to diary use by
research informants, initial attention is drawn to diary use by
researchers, and to diaries that are solicited accounts for the purposes
of research rather than unsolicited accounts. (For the latter, Scott (1990)
provides a useful account.) Moreover, for our purposes, diary keeping is
also seen as an essentially social act, even though historic or romantic
associations with the term might be to view diaries as intimate or
personal (Morrison and Galloway, 1996).

Researchers' diaries
For researchers, and in particular, qualitative researchers, action
researchers and ethnographers, diaries are more than procedural tools
for managing and documenting research stages that are sometimes
referred to as 'audit trails'. Important though these are, diaries are also
integral to the production of the data record 'that underpins the
conceptual development and density' (Strauss, 1987: 5) that is featured
in all qualitative accounts of educational experience. The potential
contribution of diaries, however, will always need to be seen as
complex; differences in meaning and use, for example, may depend
on a range of cultural contexts and situations.

In earlier accounts of use by researchers, distinctions are made
between logs, diaries and journals (Holly, 1984; 1989). A log might be
seen as a truncated record or *aide-mémoire*, while a diary might be
viewed as containing more personal and detailed information. As
Burgess (1994) suggests, these distinctions are probably more useful
analytically than in practice, since the umbrella term 'diary' can
comprise substantive, methodological and analytic elements. Diaries
can be used to serve a range of critical purposes for the researcher.
They offer tools for plotting research progress and critical research
moments that can be charted alongside agreed tasks and targets for the

research, as agreed among the research team or with the research supervisor.

Diaries raise issues about the recording and categorizing of data, especially how much to record and their purposes and/or extent of inclusion in the final research account. Morrison (2002a) gives a clear rationale for the purposes of diaries for the researcher and summarizes their role in her own research as a daily record, as a reservoir of analytical memos and as a record for ongoing retrospection and introspection, warning readers that their various uses by researchers should not imply that a diary ever presents a complete record or neutral medium of production, or that it will remain unaffected by other writing and reading that is part of the qualitative research process (see also Atkinson, 1992). Miles and Huberman (1994: Chapter 4) also caution new researchers, arguing strongly against allowing diary data to accumulate for weeks or months without engaging in early analysis of the data.

Researchers' diaries are important elements of action research, being used as tools for reflection and the provocation of personal and professional change and are also used as part of ethnographers' accounts of educational experience. Rarely are diaries used as stand-alone research instruments. In combination with interviews, photographs and videos, diary data can make important contributions to research, especially qualitative research.

Research informants' diaries

As for all personal accounts, diaries exhibit the strengths and weaknesses of information that is solicited from research informants. Yet in educational research, where there may have been a tendency to privilege the oral and the observed – what people say they do and what they are observed doing – diaries provide an interesting counterpoint. Whether this is because, as Hammersley and Atkinson (1995: 165) suggest, we tend to assume that the spoken account is more authentic or spontaneous, diaries have specific uses in picking up the minutiae of educational experience. This is not to suggest that all diaries are of the traditional, paper-bound kind. Diary research links to newer literary styles of research account, electronic diaries as well as schema for coding more sensitive information. Diaries are used in a wide variety of contexts and can also be both large scale and highly structured (Gershuny et al., 1986).

Whichever form taken, four key assumptions need to be borne in mind. *First*, diaries rest on the view that research informants are in a particularly advantageous position to record aspects of their lives and experiences. This is to do more than extol the value of self-report;

rather, diarists are social actors who can make 'visible', through diary writing, 'inside' information that might not be visible or available to the researcher. *Second,* diaries allow researchers access to evidence that might not otherwise be available on logistical (researchers cannot be everywhere) or ethical (researchers ought not to be everywhere) or pragmatic grounds (researchers need to be elsewhere). *Third,* combined with other forms of data collection and analysis, diaries are based on a premise that the researcher can collect, collate, aggregate and analyse diary data in order to produce a wider and/or deeper picture of what educational experience means to individuals and to groups. *Fourth,* diary accounts have the potential to produce large amounts of data. Researchers need to convince themselves, as well as the diarists, that such pursuits are worthwhile, and to reach agreement with diarists about which aspects can be open to public scrutiny, and how such data will be analysed.

Diary designs

For interpretive as well as action researchers, the notion of designing a diary might seem like a contradiction in terms. Yet, researchers will need to design booklets or proformas that suit the contexts of their research and their relation to other kinds of data to be collected. Instructions for use, both oral and written, need to be reinforced over the data collection period, often supported by progress calls to ascertain stages reached (see also Morrison, 2002a: 219–20; and Bell, 1999: 148–9).

One of the challenges in designing diaries may be to make their format and appearance sufficiently appealing to encourage what is, for diarists, a time-consuming activity that can become onerous. Non-completion is an ever-present problem that is only ever partially overcome by attention to cosmetic detail. For this reason, large-scale use of diaries is rarely to cover extended time periods (Gershuny *et al.*, 1986). Instead, periods can be either one or seven consecutive days, but two-to-four non-consecutive day diaries and part-day diaries are also possible. Large-scale designs are clearly not possible for the small-scale educational researcher but similar challenges pertain. Objections to diaries of longer duration is that agreement to participate may becomes difficult to secure, and that the quality and rate of response may vary and/or decline. This can mean that the gap between the event and its recording and interpretation by the diarist may also decline.

Diary data analysis

Theoretical emphases may affect how diaries are analysed. Diarists are creators of written texts that are open to descriptive or perspective analysis (Purvis, 1984). In the case of descriptive analysis, the diarist is witness to the educational phenomena of interest to the researcher. But diary data can also be used as representative indicators of the perspectives of the group to which the diarist belongs. Like any document, diaries can be considered in terms of 'authenticity, representativeness, credibility and meaning' (May, 1993: 144). As with data collection, data analysis can take quantitative and qualitative forms. The essential components remain the text, the audience and the diarist.

Content analysis can be quantitative or qualitative with computer analysis becoming more commonplace. Quantitative analysts derive categories from the data in order to compare and count them. Qualitative data analysis draws upon diary writing as a process or construct in which diarists address potential and actual readers. 'Reading' of the text accompanies consideration of data from other sources and methods, and some research accounts draw upon the use of both qualitative and quantitative approaches.

Diary design must take account of how diaries will feature in the final research account. Platt's (1981) advice on the presentation of findings from documents is instructive, especially her suggestion for a clear enunciation of the role of diaries from the outset, and the use of diary extracts as illustrative data for general themes emerging from the overall research.

Diary interviews

Diaries are rarely used alone. Pre- and post-diary interviews are often used. Pre-diary interviews set the research scene, explain the purposes of the exercise, and reinforce agreement by diarists to participate (see, for example, Morrison and Galloway, 1996). Post-diary interviews allow matters recorded briefly, as they happen, to be discussed retrospectively in detail (Burgess, 1994). More reflective styles of recording can also be followed up in interview and may stimulate additional information and data, bearing in mind, of course, that post-diary interviews also exacerbate the time-consuming nature of the method. In such ways, interviews after diary completion allow reinterpretation of data as an interactive process, help verify facts, contribute to triangulation procedures and/or provide a means for informal feedback. Above all, the diary interview sets side-by-side the written word and the oral evidence of one person.

In summary, diaries can be used qualitatively and quantitatively to illuminate a range of issues. An interactive genre, writing, reading and interpreting are complex processes involving several parties. Diary writing has, to date, prioritized certain groups of research informants. Diarists need adequate writing skills, to feel at ease in reflecting on paper, to possess sufficient resources and feel stable and secure enough to express themselves coherently in written accounts. Diaries have been used traditionally with women, children and young people, who possibly see diary keeping as an empowering process or see themselves as insufficiently powerful to resist researchers' requests to participate. In certain respects, we might consider that research which is focused upon more senior or statused educators might be ideally suited to diary keeping. Another interpretation would be that potential research informants who have power and status might be more likely to resist this potentially intrusive and revealing research genre.

Morrison (2002a) provides a wide range of illustrative examples of diary use in educational research.

See also:
Action Research (3); Documentary Research (34); Empowerment (37); Ethnography (40); Interview (57); Narrative (67); Qualitative Research (80); Quantitative Research (81); Writing (118).

31 Discourse

The word *discourse* is used in a number of different ways by educational researchers.

- It may be used as a synonym for speech; what a person says is therefore their discourse. Discourse analysis refers to the way researchers try to make sense of the thought processes of individuals, through an analysis of how they express themselves.
- A more extensive meaning given to the term is sometimes referred to as *situated discursive practice*. Here, the language of social actors is analysed in terms of the way it is used in the social setting being investigated. Discourse is therefore a joint production between a number of individuals. An example might be classroom talk, where what is being examined is how the teacher and the children in his or her class share a common language or discourse. It is the shared discourse that is the prime focus of the investigation, and it does not refer to any underlying reality.
- Structuralist and postmodern thinkers use the idea of discourse in a different way. For them, meaning resides not in the way language is used in commonplace ways, but in the underpinning structures of language or discourses. What this means is that the language-speaker is embedded in particular formations of lan-

guage, which allow him or her to think in specific ways and not in others. Discourse therefore has this restricting capacity. For Foucault (1972) these discursive formations have no absolute value in reason and cannot be thought of as being better or worse than any other discursive formation; however, they do have powerful effects. The researcher therefore has the task of identifying these discursive formations, and understanding how individual actions and behaviours result from them. Further to this, discourses change, and become more or less influential. Foucault has coined the term *genealogy* to describe the process by which these discursive formations can be examined in history.

• Some structuralist and postmodern thinkers want to go beyond this and talk about grand or overarching discursive formations. Foucault describes these as epistemes, whereas the philosopher, Alistair MacIntyre (1988), calls them traditions. They refer to the way knowledge is constructed in particular societies and the rules that allow new knowledge construction. People living in the fifteenth century in England thought, talked, behaved and lived their lives differently than people in the twentieth century in England, and this is because they lived their lives through and within different discursive formations. The danger of accepting such a notion in its entirety is that trans-epistemic knowledge becomes unfeasible. Human beings are locked into particular and specific epistemes and any judgements that they make are always made from within the bounds of that episteme.

Educational researchers may use any of these definitions, and since they are conceptual frameworks, this will influence the methods and strategies that they use to try to understand them.

See also:
Conversation Analysis (17); Critical Discourse Analysis (19); Historical Research (53); Postmodernism (76); Power (77); Structuralism/Post-structuralism (102).

32 Dissemination

Dissemination is about communicating the results of education research to an audience. Different audiences may have different expectations and, in the 'writing up' of research, primacy is usually given to those who are the target audience for evaluating the research.

For doctoral students this will be supervisors and examiners. In sponsored research, the emphasis may be upon its import and relevance for policy-makers and/or practitioners, however defined (but see below). Research reports, whether for sponsors or for examiners or for the academy, tend to be bound by certain well-known conventions. Commonly, research reports will be published for dissemination according to those conventions. But increasingly, dissemination requires a re-working of the findings, whether by the authors of the research or by interested others. This is less likely to occur when dissemination by the research author(s) is to the readers of specialist education periodicals and journals and to audiences at education conferences attended by the like-minded and the similarly occupied. More recently, however, the term is increasingly applied to a sextet of potentially interested audience groups namely: participants in the research, the wider education academy, the academy beyond education, policy-makers and takers, education practitioners, and the wider public. This range of audiences is further 'layered' by variety in dissemination levels – institutional, local, regional, national and international. The complexity of dissemination is greatest when the need or requirement is to communicate with different audiences, sometimes simultaneously, and over defined timescales. Complexity is further compounded by the constraints faced by educational researchers at the research contract agreement phase, when dissemination might be restricted or circum-scribed by research sponsors.

It is, perhaps, the dissemination of specialist work for public consumption that requires the greatest skill (and risks associated with misinterpretation). The output of education researchers often produces new knowledge or refinements to existing knowledge. What most (but not all) researchers share is an intention to make their findings available to a wider audience. A key task, therefore, is to translate authoritative findings into accessible expositions for a variety of audiences. This demands much of the researcher in terms of writing styles, exposition formats and presentational strategies and techniques, and can bring researchers into relations with various sections of the media. Some researchers have been unprepared for unexpected challenges in the interpretation of findings by others, instead preferring to expect that authoritative commentary, namely their own, will 'speak for itself'. Such tendencies are in decline, not least because sponsors of education research, in particular research councils, require applicants to elucidate a dissemination strategy as a key aspect for determining whether the research is worth funding. Walker (nd), in a paper for the Economic and Social Research Council, draws on comments from so-called 'heroes of dissemination' who are skilled in 'communicating the fruits of social and economic research to a wider audience'. Here, Sir Peter Hall refers to tendencies for academics to talk to each other, rather than anyone else, in 'hermetically sealed languages' (Walker, nd.: 6). John Curtice (ibid.: 4) describes the relation between the academy and the media as 'an interactive exchange' in which 'you cannot say that your truth is more important than theirs. You need to understand, even sympathise with the journalists' "news" values.' Furthermore, for Patrick Minford, 'dissemination is itself a discipline. To write for lay readers of newspapers [for example] is to be forced to put things in a different way' (ibid.: 11). Meanwhile, each 'hero' points to the costs and benefits of time and energies devoted to 'public' dissemination especially when the academy demands increasingly that more energy is devoted to communication through peer-reviewed journals, crucially as part of the Research Assessment Exercise (RAE), for example. Walker extracts a number of themes from such comments:

1. The media and the academy work with different timescales and language codes. This requires an awareness of the differences between the two and what this entails in terms of mediations between them and the time that can be allocated by each.
2. Skilled disseminators are secure in their knowledge base before they disseminate.
3. Dissemination can be intellectually stimulating. The need to be 'succinct' emphasizes further the importance of point 2.
4. 'Talking' to a wider audience gives a breadth of useful feedback.
5. The media is not a unified or homogeneous entity. A range of dissemination strategies and skills are required for different kinds of media.
6. This suggests that dissemination training is important.
7. Finally, dissemination is an 'act of faith'. Often a long-term task, the belief is that it can have an indirect rather than a direct effect on the contexts in which policy-makers as well as educators work and make decisions for action. (Adapted from Walker, nd.: 15–16.)

So far, while dissemination is seen as complex practice, the relationship between dissemination and different kinds of education research and their underpinning epistemologies are not revealed; neither are the ethical considerations that constrain the forms and manner in which education research is communicated. Rather, in the above descriptions, there is a tendency to view dissemination as a kind of neutral 'skill' to be nurtured and learnt rather than as a contested, limited and mediated activity.

For most education researchers, a dissemination 'career' begins with postgraduate and importantly, doctoral study, and, commonly, dissemination of research is firstly at departmental seminars and then at academic conferences. Issues of writing are discussed elsewhere in this volume, and are accompanied by the need to develop presentational skills for specific audiences. These are summarized, for example, by Watts and White (2000) where helpful advice is given about research papers (including poster presentations), delivery, the use of illustrative materials, handling questions and discussions (or lack of either or both), controlling nerves, and so on. All of these issues remain pertinent for most researchers throughout their careers, although the nature of engagement as well as the range of audiences will change. 'Getting published', usually in education and education-focused journals, has a dual purpose: it is the bedrock upon which the careers of most academics depend and, in the past, it has also been the main vehicle for the dissemination of research. Synergy between such aims has not always been apparent and this has fuelled debates about the 'usefulness' of education research (discussed, for example, by Bassey, 1999) and about what Gage (1991: 10) discusses and debates as the 'obviousness' of social and educational research by posing the question: 'Are the results of such [social and educational] research mere truisms that any intelligent person might know without going to the trouble of doing ... research?' As noted earlier, such debates have raised questions about the relevance of academic engagement for 'wider' dissemination purposes.

It has also been suggested that specific methodological approaches to research bring distinctive dissemination and ethical challenges. Ethics is discussed elsewhere in this volume. While the relation between research approach, ethical principles and dissemination is implicated in *all* research, ethnographic research can be cited as one example where there may be particular issues (see Pole and Morrison, 2003; Brewer, 2000; and elsewhere in this text). Researching few cases qualitatively raises issues of identifiability as well as generalizability. Moreover, it is asserted that 'the publication of results is perhaps more problematic in ethnographic research because of the emotional engagement it involves and because, occasionally, it reveals publicly to respondents that they have been duped' (Brewer, 2000: 102). Brewer continues:

> The effects of both these circumstances are the same; ethics should constrain the form and content of data dissemination and publication ... This involves being mindful of the use and misuse people make of the findings especially where the research is sensitive or political ... and recognizing that people's bigotry may be inflamed by what they read and that the results can be interpreted by members of the public. (ibid.: 102)

In specific circumstances this may mean:

> that agonizing over prose is also necessary to avoid revealing information that might be used to threaten the physical safety of informants, or threaten the continued enjoyment of their life or behaviour. (ibid.: 102)

All this suggests that frequently espoused commitments by disseminators to the anonymity and confidentiality of research informants and the data provided by them can be of limited value, and that promises of either or both during dissemination cannot be guaranteed.

With an increased emphasis upon applied research, both in terms of problem-solving and evaluation, dissemination features strongly. If, as Clarke and Dawson (1999) suggest, such research should meet the basic criteria of *utility*, *propriety*, *feasibility* and *accuracy*, the links between any and all of these to dissemination practices are critical. Politics is implicated in all forms of education research; in applied and evaluative research its 'political nature' (Patton, 1988) is central, and at a range of dissemination levels and contexts. Such concerns also draw our attention to the ways in which dissemination can be framed with specific intentions in mind. Thus, drawing upon Rossi and Freeman's (1993) discussions about evaluation research, for example, dissemination might be directed to research utility in terms of *first*, its direct or instrumental effect(s), *second*, its conceptual elements, and *third*, its persuasive features. Among the challenges of such a typology is, of course, that those to whom dissemination is directed may not only select specific aspects of potential and actual utility but also understand the term differently. Understandings are, in turn, informed and affected by the knowledge and experience that various interpreters bring to dissemination, by partial and selective choice of dissemination outputs to effect decisions and actions, and by the power of some interpreters more than others to act or not upon the findings reported.

Rossi and Freeman (1993) have listed a number of strategies to maximize the effectiveness of dissemination. While they apply these specifically to evaluation research, some, if not all, strategies are generally relevant to education research:

1. Dissemination is not a one-off end 'product' or activity but often consists of a number and range of interactive engagements with sponsors, supervisors, research participants and/or other researchers at a number of stages during the research process.
2. This necessitates different forms of formative and summative writing and presentation for various audiences.
3. While such forms of feedback are subject to the same ethical

principles and procedures that pertain to all forms of research made 'public', both sponsors and participants can benefit from such forms of interactive engagement.

4. The utility of research is enhanced when researchers are sensitive to the views and aspirations of various stakeholders through the lifetime of the research, and, as appropriate, engage with potential users about interpretation and dissemination as the research progresses. (Adapted from Rossi and Freeman, 1993.)

In combination, points 1–4 point to a dissemination strategy as central to research design and, furthermore, they emphasize the importance of interim and formative dissemination. As Clarke and Dawson (1999: 182) comment, at minimum, this prepares 'stake-holders' for what the final dissemination 'might contain and thus spares them any unpleasant surprises'. Such factors also emphasize the need for 'primary' and 'secondary' dissemination strategies, in which Rossi and Freeman (1993: 452) position full 'technical' research reports as 'primary' and mass media outputs, like websites, press releases, oral presentations and videotapes, as 'secondary' dissemination activities and outputs.

All this suggests that dissemination is an essential and integral feature of education research and its design. Increasingly, communicating research findings to potential users outside the research and/or the education community has become a key part of researchers' lives and work. Practical guidance is burgeoning (Gaber (nd); McGrath (nd); Vaitlingam (nd)). Yet, none of this, we suggest, should detract from critically important arguments in favour of independent and critical research on educational policy and practice that does not limit the dissemination of education research *only* to that which is immediately useful for policy-makers or designated by the same as a problem-to-be-solved. Here, dissemination challenges may be of a different order, and the argument is for practitioners and the academic community to work together to constitute both a research and a dissemination community that provides an evidence base from which, following Ozga (2000) and Scott (2000), so-called 'evidence-based' policy-making in education might continue to be assessed and challenged.

See also:

Epistemology/Ontology (38); Ethics (39); Ethnography (40); Evaluation (42); Evidence-based Practice (43); Qualitative Research (80); Quantitative Research (81); Research Community (95); Writing (118).

33 Distribution

Distribution refers to the different ways that mathematical data collected from tests or questionnaires can be displayed so that relations between the cases are made explicit. The most basic form of distribution is a *simple frequency* type, where scores are listed along with the number of times that they appear. This type of distribution is mostly used when the scale is a nominal one, no rank order is implied and there is no known interval level between points on the scale. However, if the variable comprises a large number of scaled points, as in the income of teachers in the UK, then a *grouped frequency distribution* approach is usually adopted, where class intervals are used, and the various scores that fit within these class intervals are recorded in terms of how frequently they occur. A variant on this is a *cumulative frequency distribution*. Here, frequencies are recorded as they accumulate up the scale. So, for example, scores in a mathematical test can be displayed in the following way (see Table 4).

Table 4: Cumulative Frequency of Mathematics Test Scores

Class Interval	Frequency	Cumulative Frequency
90–99	6	86
80–89	9	80
70–79	11	71
60–69	9	60
50–59	8	51
40–49	13	43
30–39	15	30
20–29	6	15
10–19	9	9

Relative frequency distributions report the proportions or percentages of scores falling into each category, and again a *cumulative relative frequency distribution* table can be formulated, where cumulative percentage totals are included. With large sample sizes, *percentile distributions* are sometimes displayed, where each raw score has attached to it a corresponding percentile rank.

Frequency distributions are counts of instances of a variable and these may be expressed as *tables* (usually expressed as number and percentage), *bar charts* (the height of each bar shows its value or frequency), *pie charts* (the angle from the centre is proportional to the frequency), *histograms* (these express continuous data in bar form and are useful for expressing relative frequencies of the data-set), *frequency polygons* (joining together the mid-points of the bars of a histogram) and *scatter plots* (these express on a graph the relationship between two different variables or their co-variance). The scale used may be *nominal* (counting), *ordinal* (ranking), *interval* (measuring differences) or *ratio* (equally spaced with a true zero point).

The distribution relationship may be *unimodal* (single variable), *bimodal* (involving two variables) or *multimodal* (more than two variables). Those forms of distribution modelling that use parametric probability calculations depend on their relation to a notional idea of a normal curve or bell-shape. Distributions however, may be *skewed to the right* (positive), or *to the left* (negative), and either *flat* or *thin* (kurtosis). Various non-parametric tests can be applied in cases such as these. More complicated forms of mathematical modelling, such as regression and multi-level modelling, build on a notion of score distribution.

See also:
Mathematical Modelling (62); Prediction (78); Questionnaire (82); Regression Analysis (88); Statistics (100); Tests (109); Variable Analysis (116).

34   Documentary Research

Documentary research draws upon materials that already exist and are, or may become, available to the researcher in education. In other words, they are not the outcome of first-hand or primary research investigation. A neglected genre other than by historical researchers, documentary research came to the attention of most social scientists in the early 1980s in an article by Jennifer Platt (1981) entitled 'Evidence and proof in documentary research'. Much of the commentary that followed subsequently, notably from Scott (1990), draws upon such starting points. Documents are used mainly for four purposes in educational research:

- *First*, to provide a starting point in the early stages of research, including the formulation of researchable problems and research design.
- *Second*, to contribute to the development of key concepts and the construction of research instruments.
- *Third*, to provide a source of data in its own right, as an alternative

to primary data sources, and in the case of multiple sources, to provide a means of comparing similarities and differences among those sources or to draw from a larger data-set.

- *Fourth*, in conjunction with the collection of primary data, to assist in the evaluation, assessment and/or analysis of that 'new' data, often in terms of providing the wider picture or context.

Central to Scott's interest in documentary research, is to insist that its fundamental principles are no different than for any other kind of evidence used by researchers in the education and social sciences, but that because different kinds of documents have particular features, then there is a need for specific techniques to analyse them. The quality of evidence from documents is underpinned by four criteria:

1. *Authenticity*. Is the evidence genuine and of unquestionable origin?
2. *Credibility*. Is the evidence free from bias and distortion?
3. *Representativeness*. Is the evidence typical of its kind, and if not, is the extent of its untypicality known?
4. *Meaning*. Is the evidence clear and comprehensible? (ibid.: 6)

Authenticity raises issues of 'known provenance', such as whether the researcher knows that the document has been stored untouched and unedited since it was first produced. *Credibility* refers to the extent to which documents produced in the past are 'believable' in terms of the period or the events which led to their production. *Representativeness* refers to typicality or not. This is not to say that secondary sources necessarily have to be typical or atypical of a wider event, group or setting but that the researcher needs to be aware of the extent of either. The criterion *meaning* refers to whether the researcher can understand and can make sense of the data. Again, using the findings from a large-scale survey in education is only sense-making if the researcher is also aware of the questions asked, the contexts in which they were asked, and the forms of coding and analysis deployed. And as Scott (1990: 10) also argues, this can only be ascertainable from secondary sources if researchers are aware of the 'theories of meaning' that the original researchers brought to their coding and analysis of the data.

In educational research, it is issues of *representativeness* and *meaning* that have tended to feature most prominently when documents are the main source of the researcher's interest. Considering representativeness first, documents need to be sampled as systematically as possible. As Pole and Lampard (2002) comment, the unavailability of some documents may be something akin to what happens when assessing survey non-responses. If researchers wish to generalize from a sample of documents, the key issues may relate to whether the sampling is for theoretical or statistical purposes, and Pole and Lampard (2002: 158) also point to Plummer's (1983) comment that 'a handful of good life histories may give adequate coverage of a cultural world'.

When our attention turns to the meaning of documents, then a number of interlinked strategies are necessary. These include an examination of the document's context and circumstances of production, including the 'norms' of presentation. As importantly, however, there are issues relating to the subjectivity of the reader and the intended as well as unintended meanings of the author. In this regard, Scott (1990: 31) uses the term 'hermeneutic circle' to explain how the researcher 'reads' a document initially from his or her own frame of reference, then tries to understand what the author means, which is, in turn, reconciled with the framework of meanings that the researcher brings to the document, thus allowing the researcher to extract both meanings. This still begs the question of how the researcher gets 'inside' the author's meanings. Different analytical approaches (see below) relate to a range of methodological and epistemological stances. In which case, for example, some researchers will follow the tenets of semiotics and meanings that are mainly internal to the text. Commonly, in education research, attention is given to broader contexts of external structure and agency with regard to the perspectives of audiences and author(s) (Giddens, 1982).

To define what a document is or is not has been a subject of debate, especially with regard to the status of ephemera like advertisements, pictures, maps or coins, for example. Again, following Scott (1990: 12–13), the definition referred to here is 'a physically embodied written text, where the containment of the text is the primary purposes of the physical medium' and where a wide rather than a narrow definition of text is applied. Part of the researcher's role is to establish what the purpose of the document is/was in order to make it useful/usable in relation to the researcher's own project. Scott also uses the dimensions of *authorship* and *access* to classify documents. In relation to the former, it then becomes possible to distinguish between the 'personal' and the 'public' or 'official spheres', and in relation to the latter to the 'availability of documents to people other than their authors' and to issues of 'closed', 'restricted' or 'open' access. (ibid.: 14–18).

Pole and Lampard (2002: 152) have produced a helpful typology of documents:

Documents can be:

- written (e.g. books and webpages);
- visual (e.g. photographs and films);

- physical artifacts (e.g. buildings and clothes);
- primary (e.g. witness accounts of events);
- secondary (e.g. second-hand accounts of events);
- tertiary (e.g. abstracts, indices);
- private (e.g. letters and diaries).

Documents may be produced by:

- the state (e.g. political and legal documents);
- organizations (e.g. university prospectuses, car advertisements);
- the mass media (e.g. newspapers);
- artists (e.g. paintings and sculptures);
- anyone (e.g. personal address books).

Documents may be:

- published;
- publicly available via archives;
- in private archives;
- unarchived and located within households and organizations.

Diaries and journals are described in other entries for this volume, so will not be discussed here. We will consider official statistics here since, it might be argued, discussions of their potential usefulness as well as challenges encapsulate many of the arguments relating to the advocacy of documentary research in education. Official statistics, whether from the DfES, Ofsted or from other official sources, have a specific appeal precisely because they might be considered objective (and therefore impartial), authoritative (and therefore credible) and factual (and therefore unambiguous in meaning). Yet there is a plethora of evidence (Bulmer, 1980; Scott, 1990) to suggest that official statistics are both a *topic for* investigation by education researchers as well as a resource, that with due scepticism, might be used to enhance and develop the research topic. In this regard, Denscombe (1998: 164–5) points to three factors:

1. The extent to which what is being measured is clear-cut.
2. Whether there are vested interests in the statistics being produced.
3. The extent to which the statistics are the outcomes of a series of decisions made by people (the argument being that where decisions are based on a series of judgments and discretions at various stages of counting, the more open to challenge are the resulting statistics).

As Scott (1990: 95) also points out, the researcher's task may then be three-fold: *first*, to interpret what the statistics actually mean; *second*, to consider the match between official interpretations of the statistics and the researcher's; before *finally*, the researcher uses them to further inform his or her research.

How documents are analysed depends upon the epistemological and methodological frameworks that researchers bring to the process. Broadly, analysis can be seen on a continuum from positivist approaches, in which content analysis applies a mainly quantitative technique, to qualitative forms of content analysis which resemble the methods used by qualitative researchers to analyse data from interviews and naturalistic observations. Other approaches draw upon the field of semiotics and structured linguistics in which the meanings of documents are decoded using 'systems of rules' or 'signs' that are embedded in the text (Barthes, 1967).

Feminist literary criticism examines the ways in which ideology is inscribed in discourses and reproduced within documents, especially published literature. In critical discourse analysis, documents are analysed and meanings deconstructed in ways that focus specifically upon the notion that the ideas and knowledge 'read' and 'written' in documents reflect or constitute forms of power which are used by one group to control another. From such perspectives, the researcher's task is to reconstruct documents so as to make transparent their structures and oppressive essence(s).

Finally, multiple documentary research as the basis for secondary or meta-analyses, frequently from different survey documents, for example, should also be noted. Analyses can provide single researchers with the opportunity of tackling research topics that would otherwise be impossible through first-hand research.

See also:
Deconstruction (26); Diaries (30); Epistemology/Ontology (38), Hermeneutics (52); Historical Research (53); Linguistic Discourse Analysis (59); Power (77); Representativeness (93); Writing (118).

35 Emotionalism

The term 'emotionalism' derives from attempts to distinguish between different kinds of qualitative research and stems mainly from the work of Gubrium and Holstein (1997). Emotionalism is one of four 'idioms' used to construct and then criticize analytical preferences, particular kinds of discourses, investigatory approaches and ways of writing (the other three being naturalism, ethnomethodology and postmodernism). In the idiom of emotionalism, researchers, it is argued, prioritize the need for prolonged and 'intimate' research engagement with participants and hence its association with ethnography, especially of the humanist kind. A key research tool is the interview, especially unstructured interviews and frequently life history engagement. For Gubrium and Holstein, emotionalism provides a gateway to understanding about people's experiences of and in education but they would argue this privileges 'common sense' understandings and under-emphasizes the extent to which qualitative researchers work at 'the lived border between reality and representation' (ibid.: 102).

Interviews are the preferred tool to obtain authentic accounts of subjective or 'lived experience'. Interviewers may actually encourage the interviewee to raise questions or tell their own stories. The approach has been favoured in feminist research where subjects have been encouraged to give their own accounts, in part as a means to break down or at least disrupt the power relations between interviewer and interviewee and also to challenge earlier, and, in their view, patriarchal separations between facts and values. Increasingly, such disruptions are also a feature of research about children's perspectives of their experiences in pre-school and compulsory schooling, although the research may draw upon different kinds of interview tools such as drawings, photographs and videos to enable children to tell their stories. (Feminist and childhood research perspectives are discussed elsewhere in this volume.) Such approaches have specific implications; these include a rejection of the need for 'distance' between researcher and research participant and an emphasis upon deep, rich and dense accounts.

Such accounts of interviewing have been open to criticism, among which, perhaps, the best known is Hammersley and Atkinson's (1983: 110–11) argument about the naïvety of assuming that unstructured or non-directive interviewing might not, in itself, be a form of social control, in which interviewees either feel compelled to talk (see also Morrison and Galloway, 1996) or reluctant to tell-it-as-it-is. More fundamentally, telling-it-as-it-is is subject to researchers' powerful interpretations of the interviewee's story, which is, in turn, open to reinterpretation as a range of truth(s). Silverman (2001) adds two more challenges. The first relates to whether individual stories are actually 'authentic' and 'meaningful' or whether, instead, they reflect interviewees' cultural assumptions (sometimes unconscious) about how they ought to recount and represent their experiences (ibid.: 93). The second relates to issues of 'distortions' (following Denzin, 1970) which might, and sometimes do, get in the way of the interview account, not least of which are difficulties in 'penetrating the private worlds of individuals' when the relationship between interviewer and interviewee is relatively fleeting (Silverman, 2001: 93–4), and where there is potential for mismatch in expectations and understanding of the interview by interviewer and interviewee. Perhaps, most fundamentally, Silverman raises important questions about the sense in which emotionalism aligns or misaligns the 'romantic' with 'politically correct' approaches to interviewing in order to 'access authentic reality' (ibid.). This is not to negate its value, but rather to treat its findings as interpretations in need of further investigation.

See also:
Childhood Research (12); Ethnography (40); Feminist Research (47); Interview (57); Life History (58); Method (64); Power (77); Qualitative Research (80); Realism (83); Textuality (110); Writing as Representation (120).

36   Empiricism

The classical form that empiricism usually takes is that all knowledge is derived from experience. There are two variants of this. The first is that all knowledge causally originates from experience, and the second is less dogmatic and suggests only that all knowledge is justified by experience. In the first case, an assumption is made that the human psyche has a *tabula rasa* form on which experience leaves its mark. There are, therefore, no innate ideas. This view is problematic, in that it is unable to explain notions such as time and necessity as these cannot be directly observed; indeed, it is hard to understand how these could be construed as observable phenomena. Thus the second and weaker variant – knowledge that can be believed is justified only through experience – is considered to be more credible.

Positivism has its origins in the classical theory of empiricism, and indeed borrowed from empiricism the idea that knowledge has its foundation in sense data. The principal problem that it encountered relates to the impossibility of accessing data through the senses without some prior theory to make sense of it. In short, observations are concept-dependent. This has to be distinguished from concept-determination, because this implies that theories developed about reality are observation-neutral. There would be no need to make observations if theory development was always prior to the making of observations.

However, concept-dependency does have implications for the strategies and methods adopted by educational researchers. These are that any empirical data-set has a theory attached to it, and a theory implies a system of values when the data refers to the social world. Facts can be collected about human relations but those facts are always theory-impregnated. This would cast doubt on the possibility of a positivist/empiricist science of educational activities, where:

> observation is theory-neutral and a-theoretical; experience is given; a univocal and transparent language is possible; data are independent of these interpretations; and there are universal conditions of knowledge and criteria for deciding between theories. (Usher, 1996: 15)

The rejection of the radical separation of facts from values has led to the development of alternative methodologies, such as critical theory and postmodernism, where assumptions are made that theory, and indeed a system of value, is prior to and underpins the collection of data. However, this does not necessarily lead to the conclusion that since data, and therefore facts, are inevitably informed by values of one type or another, there is no point in empirically examining the world. Observations may be concept-dependent but they are not concept-determined. This would imply a reversion back to an anti-realist or radical relativist position where a clear separation is made between reality and the description that is made of it. Thus, in educational research, empiricism cannot be conflated with empirical research, though it frequently is, and this is because other more convincing accounts of the relation between ontology and epistemology have been developed.

See also:
Critical Theory (22); Epistemology/Ontology (38); Observation (71); Positivism (75); Postmodernism (76); Realism (83); Relativism (89); Values (115).

37 Empowerment

Empowerment is interpreted in a range of ways in education research and the labels attached to, or substituted for, the term are multiple. At its core is the notion that the processes and outcomes of educational research will, for researchers or research participants (or for both), generate degrees of self-understanding, self-awareness and knowledge that will lead to action to ameliorate or improve the situation of participants in educational settings and/or those with whom they work and study. For large-scale change to occur at the level of the social system, the words 'enlightenment' and 'emancipation' need to be added. Enlightenment is underpinned by a move from a situation of (following Marx) 'false consciousness' whereby research participants (often defined as the oppressed) come to 'see themselves in a radically different way from their current self-conception' (Fay 1993: 34) and 'act upon their situation to radically alter their social arrangements and alleviate their suffering' (ibid.: 36).

In education, empowerment-focused research has been described variously as 'critical' research (Fay, 1993); 'conviction' research (Smith 1993); 'empowerment' research (Troyna, 1995; Fetterman, 1994a; 1994b); practitioner or action research (Guba and Lincoln, 1981; 1989); 'advocacy' research (Cameron *et al.*, 1992); and by its dissenters as 'partisan' research (Hammersley, 1998). Critically, empowerment has a key place in both anti-racist and feminist research though the means to empowerment might sometimes be seen to fragment along specific methodological lines. The key role of such research is in enabling disadvantaged or marginalized groups to become aware of their collective power to create knowledge and effect action. An early exponent of empowerment research, for example, was Paulo Freire who used various methods to make Brazilian rural peasants aware of their oppressed conditions in order that they might challenge them.

Readers gain a view of research that is more collectively based and action-orientated than research that is vested in the hierarchical research structures and practices of the academy, an 'unequal world', according to Troyna (1995: 397, our emphasis), in which 'researchers have potential to exacerbate and reinforce inequalities both *within* and beyond the research process'. What underpins empowerment research, then, is a 'conviction that research takes place in social settings where power relations are stratified by class, race, gender, age and other structural characteristics' (ibid).

The perspectival and action-orientated dimensions of empowerment research have been applied to all research participants including children, and to research with a range of purposes, including evaluation. So, for example, increasing numbers of researchers with children do so using frameworks that prioritize concerns not only to alter the power balance between themselves and children but also to empower children to be action-takers in education settings (for example, Davis *et al.*, 2000; Mayall, 1994). In evaluation research, empowerment evaluation is defined as 'a democratic approach designed to promote self-determination' (Clarke and Dawson 1999: 25). Drawing on Fetterman's (1994b: 305) work, evaluation is 'to help others help themselves ... .[and] ... focuses on improvement, is collaborative, and requires both qualitative and quantitative methodologies'. There are important corollaries here with action research to provide empowerment though learning that occurs when research participants move from learning as insight to learning in and as action (Carr and Kemmis, 1986).

Empowerment research has not been without its dissenters and concerns are methodological, political as well as practical. There are methodological objections that 'partisan' research is methodologically 'impure' in the sense that 'political considerations' so override 'intellectual ones' to produce 'biased' research that casts doubt on the integrity and credibility of research, based 'on a simplistic sociological theory in which there are only two sides – the oppressors and the oppressed' (Hammersley, 1998: 32). There are also concerns that empowerment ideals become circumvented in practice as a consequence of major structural constraints, including the power of a dominant discourse, to prevent empowerment research from being seen as anything other than an ideology that, stripped of context, is of limited application (Scott, 2000: 11). In feminist research, there have been objections that feminist politics, especially in its most activist forms, have detracted from the development of women's studies (Patai, 1994) by an over-emphasis on methodological debates about empowerment in which, it is argued, feminist academics appear to be speaking to one another rather than to other women (or men), with attendant dangers in constraining rather than affecting action. At a more basic level, there are concerns about whether empowerment research or empowerment evaluation research:

> actually gives programme participants a real and influential voice in the evaluation [or research] process. As Mark and Shotland (1985) assert, stakeholder participation can lead to pseudo-empowerment. (Clarke and Dawson, 1999: 29)

Two reasons are given: first, that ultimately, the power of the researcher is based on his or her own judgements of the evidence base and not those of the research informants; second, that while research participants may have a say in the research, they have very limited opportunities to affect change action other than in the short-term or as situation specific.

Rejoinders to such critiques have been many and are ongoing. Issues of power and powerlessness in education both as a research concern, and in relation to research methodologies and tools to investigate such experiences, are central to improving those experiences. Critical empowerment research retains its importance in stripping away some of the facades of 'objective' 'scientistic' research. As Gillborn (1998: 53) concludes in relation to anti-racism, it also confronts postmodern preoccupations with multiple realities and differences that seem to do little to challenge the structural inequalities of 'race', class, gender, disability or sexual orientation, by focusing instead upon research that is predicated upon emancipatory action.

See also:
Action Research (3); Anti-racism (6); Childhood Research (12); Critical Realism (21); Critical Theory (22); Evaluation (42); Feminist Research (47); Gender (49); Postmodernism (76); Power (77).

38   Epistemology/Ontology

Epistemology refers to how educational researchers can know the reality that they wish to describe. This needs to be distinguished from ontology, which refers to the nature of this reality. Clearly, there are relations between the two, in that the belief they have about the nature of reality has an influence on the way they can know it. This does not exhaust the levels at which the educational researcher needs to operate. Researchers also adopt strategies which in turn rely on methods that allow the researcher to collect the appropriate data and analyse it. It is therefore possible to illustrate these four levels and indicate a set of possible relations between them in the way shown in Figure 1.

What this allows the educational researcher to do is argue that there are some philosophical questions to be answered that are prior to the decisions they have to make about the strategy and methods that they adopt. Empiricists believe that there is mind-independent reality waiting to be discovered, and that social reality consists of the constant conjunction of atomistic events or state of affairs (ontology). They further believe that that these atomistic events can be known through observations made by researchers, who can behave in an objective fashion and not bring their own conceptions and preconceptions to the act of observation (epistemology); indeed, that to entangle them with the values of the researcher would not allow a clear picture to emerge. The next level is the strategic level, and a further argument is made to the effect that these constant conjunctions of events or objects are

Ontology

Epistemology

Strategy

Method

Figure 1: Methodological Levels

similar enough to allow precise quantification of them, and indeed demand this type of treatment because relations between them can only be known in this way. Finally, at the level of method, an instrument is chosen which conforms to the researcher's ontological, epistemological and strategic beliefs to allow data to be collected and analysed.

However, it is likely that, if a different decision had been made at the ontological level, then this would have led to different decisions being made at the other levels. So, for example, if a depth ontology is subscribed to, where reality is understood as stratified along the lines of the empirical consisting of experiences, the actual consisting of events and the real consisting of underlying mechanisms, and furthermore, that this last level cannot be directly observed and does not influence events and experiences in a mechanical way, then this has implications for the decisions that the researcher makes at the levels of epistemology, strategy and method.

Another way of examining this dilemma is to argue that decisions made at the epistemological level may also affect decisions made at the two lower levels. Thus, if the researcher believes that knowledge is multi-perspectival, strategies and methods that do not allow access to this multi-perspectival viewpoint are likely to be rejected. Another example might be a decision by the researcher to use precise and quantifiable data-collection methods to collect data about matters that cannot be described in this way. This would be a perverse decision; and the mistake that the researcher is making relates to their inability to think through these methodological issues at the ontological and epistemological levels. Thus, issues to do with how we can know reality, such as the place and role of values in the research act, or the types of relationships that one should enter into with research subjects, or the degree of detachment that the researcher adopts in the collection of their data, have implications at the other three levels, and these questions are prior to strategic and instrumental questions. There are three principal epistemological frameworks: *objectivism*, *subjectivism*, and *constructionism*, usually known as *social constructionism*.

See also:
Critical Realism (21); Empiricism (36); Ethics (39); Method (64); Methodology (65); Objectivity (70); Quantitative Research (81); Realism (83); Social Constructionism (99); Strategy (101); Subjectivity (104); Values (115).

39   Ethics

Ethical approaches to educational research take three forms: covert, open autocratic and open democratic. If researchers operate covertly, then they are concealing from participants the nature and purpose of their activities. An example of this approach is Hockey (1991), where the researcher, having gained permission from the commanding officer of the battalion to conduct his research, then took on the role of a squaddie in order to understand fully what is was like to be inducted into the British Army. Likewise, Fielding (1981) pretended to be a member of the National Front in the UK to gain access to the research setting, when this would have been denied to him if he had been open and honest about his purposes. In these two cases, the need for naturally generated and authentic data was balanced against the resulting deception that it was thought necessary to employ. Experimentalists, furthermore, build into their research designs an element of deception, in that their control and experimental groups are not told which is which. Again, the reason for this is to avoid reactivity by participants, so that both groups are not aware of the experimental design of which they are a part.

However, most educational research studies seek, if at all possible, to abide by the principle of informed consent, and therefore can be described as either open autocratic or open democratic. Even here, the principle of informed consent can never be absolute, as the researcher is rarely in a position to provide respondents with a full account of what they are going to do because most research designs have an emergent dimension to them. Given this caveat, the researcher usually informs participants about the nature of their research, and this may involve negotiating and renegotiating access at various points in the lifetime of the research project. So, if the research is to be conducted in a school setting, careful attention is paid to the various levels of power within the organization, with the initial negotiation to gain access being conducted with the headteacher and/or the governing body, and subsequent negotiations conducted with teachers and students (perhaps through their parents) to allow access to specific settings within the institution itself.

A further principle is invoked by educational researchers in the conduct of the research, and this is that they will protect the interests of participants in their research, as they may be involved in collecting information which is sensitive or has the potential to do harm to that participant or group of participants. In order to meet this requirement, various anonymity devices are used in the writing of the report, or its subsequent reporting, either to members of the organization being researched or to other bodies interested in the results of the research. Again, this might involve minor deceptions, so, for example, contextual information is provided which deliberately misinforms the reader about the setting or people within the setting. Furthermore, participants in the research setting may not be aware of the potential risks when information is released to the general public, and in this case, the researcher may make a decision to protect their interests even if those interests are not fully understood by the participants themselves.

In this sense, a distinction is being drawn between an autocratic and a democratic approach to educational research ethics. In the former case, the researcher takes responsibility for the collection and subsequent reporting of data, whereas in the latter case, the researcher allows participants in their research project a veto over what is included and what is not included in the research report. This may involve lengthy processes of negotiation and renegotiation with participants, and highlights how with case study research, epistemological and ethical issues are frequently intertwined. If transcribed data collected from participants in an interview study are then subsequently returned to respondents, with the injunction that they should agree to its release and that they should check that this is really what they wanted to say, both epistemological and ethical dimensions are being invoked. With democratic researchers or evaluators, there is a sense in which this

process of negotiation and renegotiation can have no natural resolution, and an arbitrary decision is made to close down these processes.
Furthermore, it is not always clear that research participants have an
equal standing with researchers when they engage in these processes of
negotiating the release of data. There is, therefore, always an autocratic
dimension to this process, and this enjoins the researcher to take
responsibility to protect the interests of participants in their research.

See also:
Access (2); Case Study (9); Dissemination (32); Empowerment (37);
Epistemology/Ontology (38); Evaluation (42); Experiment (44); Power
(77); Respondent Validation (96); Validity (113).

40 Ethnography

Many definitions of ethnography have emerged in recent years and the
term has been used almost synonymously with qualitative approaches
to research, primarily observation but also case study and life history,
and occasionally even to represent qualitative research itself. Brewer
(2000) refers to the dichotomy between ethnography as a method and
as a methodology, in the former to refer to ethnography as a collection
of methods and in the latter to signal a specific theoretical and
epistemological orientation to research. As Pole and Morrison (2003: 2)
point out, to make matters more complex, ethnography is used as a
noun and a verb, in that it is discussed as the product of a specific kind
of research as well as the activity of doing ethnography.

While its origins lie in the work of nineteenth-century anthropologists who journeyed primarily to observe different and 'other' cultures,
in the last 30 years educational settings have been fertile grounds for
ethnography. In response to some of the ambiguities and complexities
concerning ethnography, Silverman (2001: 45) posits 'a common
terminological solution' which is to say that what education and social
science researchers do with their observations is 'something extra'. He
continues:

> *Ethnography* puts together two different words: 'ethno' meaning
> folks, while 'graph' derives from 'writing'. Ethnography refers,
> then, to social scientific writing about particular folks (ibid, his
> emphasis).

What then are the characteristics of ethnography or the 'something
extra' that researchers in education do with their data? Following Pole

and Morrison (2003: 3), the principal common characteristics of ethnography are:

1. A focus on a discrete location, event(s) or setting.
2. A concern with the full range of social behaviour in that location, event(s) or setting.
3. The use of a range of different research methods which may combine qualitative and quantitative approaches but where the emphasis is upon understanding social behaviour from inside the discrete location, event or setting in order to produce what is often described as 'thick' or 'rich' data (Geertz, 1973).
4. An emphasis on data and analysis which moves from detailed description to the identification of concepts and theories which are grounded in the data collected within the location, event or setting.
5. An emphasis upon rigorous or thorough research, where the complexities of the singular are of greater significance than overarching trends or generalities.

It may be the case that such features are also aspects of other kinds of research. This suggests that further detail about what ethnographers expect to achieve by doing ethnography and producing ethnographies is needed. Brewer's (2000) description of ethnography as a method and as a methodology is helpful. Methods refer to the tools used by ethnographers to gather data and Pole and Morrison (2003) provide and describe an extensive array of methods derived from both first-hand experience (observation and participant observation, interviewing, life history, focus groups, drama and fiction) and secondary sources of data (surveys, official statistics, diaries, photographs, art and artifacts). Methods are selected in relation to fitness for ethnographic purpose and act to limit and delimit the data collection process, how ethnography can be done and the procedural rules to be followed. Brewer (2000: 2) also describes the methodology that constitutes ethnography in terms of 'the broad theoretical and philosophical framework into which these procedural rules fit'. In a general sense, ethnographers are interested in everyday events and situations with an emphasis upon insiders' accounts. In such ways, their interests lie primarily in the subjective realities that constitute individuals' experiences. Primacy is given to the importance of situated meaning and contextualized experience.

The concern with contextualised meaning ensures that the structures which shape, limit and in some cases define social action are central to the understanding of that action ... The common theme to emerge is that ethnography is located within the approach of naturalism. (Pole and Morrison, 2003: 5)

This locates the approach within the tradition of Verstehen and interpretative analysis. While naturalism is concerned with the setting and location in which social action is created and experienced, ethnography draws upon the sociological and philosophical approaches of social interactionism, hermeneutics, phenomenology, linguistic philosophy and ethnomethodology. The intention to collect data from 'real-life' situations enhances the sense in which ethnography draws upon observation. Recently, technological advances have widened the scope of the ethnographer's observations to include photography, video and other visual media. Developing still is a range of virtual approaches to ethnography in which the Internet and other forms of information technology may be used (Hine, 2000).

In privileging the insider's view as ethnography's *raison d'etre*, Pole and Morrison (2003: 8) argue a case 'for pluralism of methods rather than methodological pluralism' when they write about 'inclusive ethnography' in order to arrive at a position where methods more commonly associated with positivist approaches to research *can* be usefully deployed 'as long as the quantitative methods adhere to the epistemological principles of naturalism, in seeking to gather data with as little disturbance to the everyday rhythms of the location as possible' and where quantitative data might be used to provide 'a picture of the wider context in which the specific location and the social action therein takes place' (ibid.: 8–9).

In response to the issue of whether there is a *distinctive* ethnographic method, Pole and Morrison also draw on Brewer's (2000) descriptions of 'big ethnography' and 'little ethnography' in which 'big' refers to the whole enterprise that includes methodology and method, and 'little' refers to the discrete locations, events and settings upon which ethnography finds focus. They also distinguish between 'field work' and 'field research' as key components of ethnography in which 'field work' refers to the immersion of self into the ethnographic inquiry and 'field research' is designated as 'a less specific approach based on a discrete location, but not exclusively inside it' (Pole and Morrison, 2003: 10). In which case, it is argued, quantitative method can contribute to 'little ethnography' but its 'lack of engagement with the interior world of actors within the specific location does not qualify [it] as "big ethnography"' (ibid.: 10). The key point at issue is not that ethnography is based on a philosophy of 'anything goes' but that ethnography is a distinct approach 'in which there is no meaningful method [qualitative or quantitative] without methodology' (ibid.).

Ethnography is not without its critics and challenges. Not all topics for research in education lend themselves to this approach. More fundamentally, ethnography has been challenged on the grounds of its imprecision, and its emphasis upon rich description which, to critics, signals a lack of rigour and/or subjectivity. Moreover, the ethnographer's interest in the singular, and in specific interpretations of social actions, has also led to accusations of anecdotalism and an inability to generalize in ways that might contribute to the wider interpretation of educational issues and/or to practical application, being bounded by both time and space.

At one level, such challenges are difficult to counter; at another level, they are not. To challenge ethnography on the technical grounds that it fails to match the characteristics more generally associated with quantitative and positivist approaches to education research might be considered to miss the point. Ethnography does not set out to produce precise, objective and generalizable findings. This does not mean that ethnographic data is not systematically and rigorously grounded, but its emphasis is upon clearly enunciated organizational frameworks for its data collection and analysis of discrete social action. Such concerns link ethnography directly to the importance of *reflexivity* in research. Again, following Brewer (2000: 108) the emphasis is upon the:

- relationships developed in the field;
- characteristics of the researcher and how these relate to the people in the field;
- time and circumstances in which the research was carried out;
- methodological and fieldwork practices used;
- broader educational, socio-economic and political contexts in which the research took place.

Ethnography is notable for applying the essences of grounded theory (Glaser and Strauss, 1967) to analyses. While it cannot apply the same procedures to determine reliability and validity as other research, concentrating instead on issues of authenticity, meaning, plausibility and credibility (Hammersley, 1992b), it remains essential that its analytical procedures and audit trails of evidence are transparent, systematic and open to public scrutiny.

For its proponents, ethnography is both a process and a product. Its strength lies in its capacity to offer conceptual and theoretical accounts of social action. While the argument is not made that ethnography produces generalizable findings, this is not the same as arguing that ethnography cannot engage with issues that go beyond the discrete. This it does with confidence, and:

in such a way that there is a connection with wider social behaviour, social processes, and broader structural issues. Ethnography enables us to view education not in isolation but as part of the wider social and economic context of which it is a part, whilst at the same time holding on to the detail of the specific location, event, or setting. (Pole and Morrison, 2003: 160)

For some writers, like Scott (2000: 74), its strength is also its Achilles heel, for while 'it is accepted in the academy' where 'its organs of dissemination are now well enough established to sustain it as a serious activity', it may be 'less acceptable within wider policy-making forums'. In which case, ethnographers may be 'weakened by their inability to participate in macro-political processes'. Such concerns may need to be reconsidered in relation to recent and changing forms of ethnography that are variously described by Eisenhart (2001), Pink (2001) and Hine (2000), who, in combination, link recent conceptualizations to changing technological forms and globalization issues. In such ways, novel forms of representation present exciting prospects for ethnography to capture vicarious educational experience.

See also:
Case Study (9); Epistemology/Ontology (38); Focus Groups (48); Generalization (50); Grounded Theory (51); Interview (57); Life History (58); Method (64); Methodology (65); Phenomenology (73); Qualitative Research (80); Quantitative Research (81); Realism (83); Reflexivity (87); Subjectivity (104); Symbolic Interactionism (106).

41   Ethnomethodology

Ethnomethodology is a research perspective that foregrounds the intentional activity of human beings. It can therefore be located within those theories that Archer (1990) describes as upward conflationary, where structural dimensions of human action are reduced to a series of inter-subjective negotiations between individuals. It has some affinities with phenomenology, though perhaps its distinctive feature is the methodological approach that its adherents adopt, and this is different from those methodological approaches adopted by phenomenologists. A leading ethnomethodologist, Heritage (1984: 4), offers this definition:

It is the study of the body of common-sense knowledge and the range of procedures and considerations by means of which the ordinary members of society make sense of, find their way about in, and act on the circumstances in which they find themselves.

It is opposed to downward conflationary viewpoints in which individual agency is marginalized, so that society simply exists of structures that act to constrain or determine the life of the individual. However, implicit within the writings of Harold Garfinkel (1988), considered by many to be the founding father of ethnomethodology, is an acknowledgement that external structures do exist and are then used by individuals to accomplish their tasks and fulfil their desires. Institutions are therefore the creation of human agency and are always being reformed in the light of new decisions made by individuals and collectivities of individuals. Individuals for Garfinkel, however, are not endlessly creative or even persistently reflexive; and he acknowledges that most human action is routine and delivered without much prior thought. Even then, structures, whether small- or large-scale, are the artful products of individuals. It is easy to see from the discussion so far how ethnomethodologists are concerned above all else with the way individuals create meanings for themselves, and ethnomethodologists themselves are not exempt from this process.

One way in which human beings create meaning is by offering accounts of their lives, and they do this when asked by researchers, but more importantly in their everyday actions. Ethnomethodologists are interested in both these accounts and the accounting procedures that they go through. So a pupil in a school, if asked to explain poor behaviour in class, offers an account of why they behaved as they did. Furthermore, if that same pupil was then asked by a researcher why they behaved as they did, they might give a different account, and this is because accounts and the resources that individuals draw on to construct their accounts are influenced by context. This description of human action has one further consequence, which is that researchers in studying and reporting on human actors become inevitably a part of what they are researching, and thus their interventions in naturally occurring social settings change the nature of what they are studying. Even asking a simple question of a respondent in an interview situation may result in new reflexive work by the individual, which they would not have done unless they were being interviewed. This introduces an added complexity to the research act.

Ethnomethodologists have adopted two principal methodological strategies: conversation analysis and breaching experiments. In the former case, they are interested in the taken-for-granted way conversations are organized and in particular the relationships between utterances. In the latter case, and they initially became notorious for this, they sought to artificially violate common and everyday actions in order to shed light on how people construct reality. So, for example, Garfinkel asked his students to behave as though they were boarders in their own homes and then record how other members of their family responded to this new set of behaviours. Such experiments showed how individuals normally act in accord with commonsense assumptions about how they are supposed to behave.

Ethnomethodologists argue that without account being taken of the way individuals work to construct meaning in and about their lives, a distorted view of reality becomes the norm. In particular, they take exception to descriptions of reality that rely on scientific techniques and statistical analyses, which allow causal or associational explanations to be formulated about social life. They are more interested in how members of society go about their self-appointed task of seeing, describing and then acting on the world in which they live.

See also:
Agency (4); Causation (11); Conversation Analysis (17); Determinism (29); Interpretivism (56); Interview (57); Methodology (65); Phenomenology (73); Positivism (75); Reflexivity (87); Structure (103).

42   Evaluation

All research purports to make a contribution to our understanding of the many and various matters that are thought to comprise education. Researchers also place implicit and explicit emphases upon assessing the value or worth of the phenomena investigated by them. Once we introduce the terms 'value' or 'worth', it is not difficult to appreciate that our judgments and evaluation of worth are intrinsically political and philosophical, and made more complex by the predilections of researchers and sponsors about what counts as 'useful' research, for whom and which purposes. One exemplar of such debates pertains to the distinctions between critical and problem-solving theory in education and the relationship between either or both to research that is focused upon the formal and informal practices of education.

While evaluation is not a new concept, it has become an undertaking increasingly performed by specialist or professional evaluators within and beyond the education academy. This is hardly surprising given a globally pressing need, obsession even, in policy and practice to make judgments about what works best and least in education, in order to maximize the value-added dimensions of education and minimize or eradicate its 'costly' and 'failing' elements.

As 'an elastic word that stretches to cover judgments of many kinds' (Weiss, 1972: 1), evaluation to greater and lesser degrees retains the emphasis placed upon it by its originators, mainly from the USA, namely that it is both possible and appropriate for researchers to learn and make judgments about education policies, practices, programmes and initiatives in order to modify, change, improve or, in extremis, abandon them. Of course, this places to one side for the moment (but see below) the critically important issue of who interprets the outcomes of research and/or has the power or not to act upon research findings in order to effect action or inaction in relation to improvement.

Definitions of evaluation abound. Readers might wish to consider the extent to which some of those proffered by Clarke and Dawson (1999: 2), for example, place an overriding emphasis upon evaluation as applied research which is concerned less to produce new knowledge but more 'to study the effectiveness with which *existing* knowledge can be used to inform and guide effective action' (our emphasis). Meanwhile, the common factors associated with a broad spectrum of definitions (Clarke and Dawson, 1999; House, 1993; Pawson and Tilley, 1997; Robson, 2000; Rossi and Freeman, 1993; Scriven, 1991) appear to encompass the following aspects, that the:

- evaluation is about a determination of the value and worth of something;
- 'something' is most usually education and social programmes;
- focus is upon programme activities, characteristics and outcomes;
- methodology is policy orientated, in encouraging recipients of the evaluation to make decisions about what such programmes actually achieve and how they might be improved;
- methods are systematic, accepted by parties to the evaluation, and judged in accordance to criteria which are fully explained and justified;
- evaluation strives for impartiality and fairness, and to represent the range of perspectives among those engaged in such pro- grammes.

There appears to be less overarching agreement about:

- the extent to which the above, in combination, represents evaluation as a distinctive type of research from other research;
- the extent to which evaluation is dependent upon existing social science research;
- whether distinctiveness matters and why, although there are

discernible and important trends towards 'scientific' and/or outcome- and impact-driven 'measurements' from evaluation;

- the role of evaluation in paradoxical times that combine the certain, the manageable and the predictable with postmodern tendencies towards the opposite, which might, in turn, lead to scepticism about evaluation findings, and their worth and applicability.

In the 1980s and 1990s, writers like Bulmer (1982: 159) were tending to position evaluation 'at the "hard" end of applied social science' or as 'a loose or "almost" discipline' (House, 1993: 77). More recently, Pawson and Tilley (1997: xii–xiii, their emphases), stress three determinants of evaluation that they entitle 'realistic evaluation':

1. That evaluation deals with the *real*
   All social programs involve the interplay of individual and institution, and of structure and agency. All ... involve disagreement and power-play ... All social interaction creates interdependencies and these ... develop into real world customs and practices, which are often quite independent of how people would wish them to be. These are the emergent realities which social programs seek to change ... which always begins with a sociological understanding of the balance of resources and choices available to all participants involved in a program.

2. That evaluation should deal with a *realist* methodology
   We do not shrink from the goals of 'detachment' and 'objectivity' ... The most powerful advocates of the privileged, progressive nature of society are the *scientific realists*. We suggest that it is high time to reassert the need for scientific evaluation and do so under the banner of realism.

3. That evaluation needs to be *realistic*
   The goal of being realistic should be regarded as a decree forbidding evaluators from hiding behind ... secret, scientific languages ... To be realistic is to acknowledge that there is no universal 'logic of evaluation', no absolute 'science of valuing', no 'general warranty for decision making' applicable to all judgments ... The 'evaluation community' is an overblown fiction and ... we can no longer corral together the 'action researcher' and the 'auditor', the 'experimentalist' and the 'ethnographer', the 'product' and the 'program' evaluator, the 'management consultant' and the 'mathematical modeller'.

In some respects, the emphatic words of such authors reposition or return evaluation to its earlier role in education research, namely an activity which, by design and method, examines the effectiveness of a specific educational activity that is targeted at a specific educational problem(s), as 'a way of engaging rigorously with piecemeal social [or educational] reform' (Pawson and Tilley, 1997: xiii).

Evaluation might now be regarded as a pluralistic enterprise in which most, if not all the methods, both qualitative and quantitative, described elsewhere in this text might be utilized, depending upon the specificity and the purposes of the activity(ies) being evaluated. For readers intending to engage in evaluation research, it will, of course, be necessary to foreclose definitional debates in order to concentrate on the nature and the scope of the educational evaluation they are intending to undertake. Usefully, Clarke and Dawson (1999) compare the activities denoted as evaluation with those which might be described as auditing, monitoring and inspection, and readers may find this helpful in thinking through the ideas underpinning evaluation.

Auditing

An audit concentrates on checking what actually happens against prescribed normative 'standards'. Here the evaluative element may be auditor comments when the activity falls below or exceeds those standards. According to Chelimsky (1985), cited by Clarke and Dawson (1999), it is evaluation rather than audit that addresses three sets of questions: descriptive – how many people are involved in this educational activity?; normative – is this initiative operating as it was originally intended?; and cause-and-effect – what has resulted from the initiative and in terms of which observed interventions?

Monitoring

Monitoring focuses upon the systematic surveillance of a series of events and includes the collection of information at regular intervals, often to provide feedback. Again, monitoring is part of evaluation but its more usual applicability is for accountability purposes especially 'fiscal, process and programme accountability' (Clarke and Dawson, 1999: 6). Though monitoring devices are far from neutral, both in terms of the choice of collection data, the manner of collection and the uses to which collected data are put, evaluation is distinctive in the sense that it most often takes the form of an in-depth study of a specific programme or activity at a certain point in time.

Inspection

'Like monitoring, [inspection] can be described as a top-down approach to check that codes of practice are adhered to and that minimum standards are achieved' (Clarke and Dawson, 1999: 7). For education researchers, an inspection report, for example that provided by Ofsted, is most usually used as an external data source, along with monitoring data, for evaluating a programme or activity and judging the underlying rationale and logic for its strategic planning and operations.

The most enduring distinction in evaluation discourse is between *formative* and *summative* evaluation. Credited to Scriven (1967), formative evaluation provides feedback to people engaged in a programme during the period of evaluation in order to support the processes of improvement. In particular, it addresses the perceptions and motivations of participants, and offers interim assessment to effect improvement. Summative evaluation focuses upon the overall outcomes and impact of the programme, and evaluators are enjoined to make recommendations about whether specific programmes or activities should continue to run, and in which forms. Most often, educational evaluation includes both forms, in which the formative elements are usually contained as interim reporting and for within-institution participants. Summative evaluation is a formalized end-point, usually geared towards a wider target audience, with an emphasis on outcomes and impact, and is, in current climates, increasingly geared to the measurement of outcomes and impact. More recently, the dichotomy between formative and summative has been considered of increasingly limited value. Instead, Chen (1996) draws upon four types of evaluation: process-improvement evaluation, process-assessment evaluation; outcome-improvement evaluation; and outcome-assessment evaluation. The key point is that implementation and effectiveness are not the only two dimensions that educational evaluators need to take into account; process-implementation evaluation, for example, described elsewhere as 'front-end analysis' (Patton, 1982) and 'pre-evaluation' (Rossi and Freeman, 1993), might also be used instrumentally and conceptually to develop the evaluation.

From the above, it can be asserted that evaluation has been, and is likely to remain, a highly political and contested activity. The constituents of that politicization are linked to the nature, scope and size of the educational evaluation, macro and micro policy climates, the type of evaluator and motivations of sponsors. Colin Robson (2000) offers advice that is geared more towards the first-time or small-scale researcher, often researching practices or programmes in his/her own institution. Here the parameters are likely to be local or localized, and involve a single evaluator who needs to draw on a limited range of resources, including shorter timescales. Evaluators in this situation are likely to carry multiple roles in an institution or in relation to the subject matter of the evaluation, and conduct studies that are commonly referred to as 'insider evaluations'. Specific challenges might be highlighted, such as those arising:

- Where the evaluator is an advocate *for* the programme, and where that advocacy affects both the collection and analysis of the data. In this case, a reflexive attitude may reduce the contamination of the data or increase evaluator awareness about what Pole (1993: 111–12) describes as 'positive contamination'.
- When there is a danger of being over-influenced by a familiarity with the history and understanding of the key issues.
- When the evaluator is likely to be over-influenced by the views of managers or superiors – the corollary may be a lack of influence in persuading other stakeholders in an institution to participate in the evaluation.
- From multiple roles in the institution and related ethical sensitivities (see also below).

On the other hand, the lone internal evaluator is likely to be:

- strongly focused and goal-directed;
- familiar with the detailed history of the institution, intervention or programme;
- focused on its key attributes or concerns;
- have the 'trust' of participants who may be more willing to contribute to the evaluation as active stakeholders.

The challenges for 'external' evaluators are similarly discernible. External evaluators may have:

- a greater range of resources at their disposal;
- wider background knowledge, understanding and/or insight, including an overview of other programmes, interventions and initiatives in other institutional settings;
- wider and deeper experience in the use of evaluation methods;
- the power to resist intimidation or refusals to cooperate by senior stakeholders.

On the other hand, for external evaluators with primary responsibility to an external body or sponsor:

- wider knowledge is not necessarily coupled with a depth of interest in the subject matter of the evaluation;
- issues of insensitivity to the norms of the institution and internal relationships may hinder the evaluation;
- limited knowledge and understanding of internal matters and/or of key educational actors may separately, or in combination, lead

to inaccurate portrayals of complex realities and of the potential to be misled by participants.

In the wake of such complexities, various roles for internal and external evaluators have been advocated. They include collaborative roles between evaluator and participants and empowerment for all stakeholders. Such processes have been championed by Fetterman (1994a; 1994b) and Guba and Lincoln (1989), for example, under the headings of 'empowerment' and 'fourth generation evaluation' respectively. Underpinning both approaches are two central ideas: the *first* is to encourage all staff to engage with the evaluation so that it becomes an integral part of the programme or initiative; the *second* is through empowering stakeholders by working with evaluation models that stress participant self-determination and self-evaluation, thereby undercutting the evaluator as *the* power holder. More recently, commentators like Clarke and Dawson (1999) have pointed to the danger of 'pseudo-empowerment', given the significance of the external evaluator's role, and limited prospects for stakeholder participants, particularly those located at micro-institutional levels, to influence the subsequent direction of programmes. In addition, as Clarke and Dawson also point out, the reality is likely to be more complex and includes programmes in which external evaluators take on a range of roles at different points in the evaluation, and in different combinations (Clarke and Dawson, 1999: 30).

In common with all forms of educational research, educational evaluation has important ethical and political implications. With regard to the former, program evaluation standards were published by the Joint Committee on Standards (1994), and these are summarized as an appendix item by Robson (2000). Key issues pertain to consent, privacy and confidentiality and risks related to benefits, viewed in terms of the feasibility, utility, propriety and accuracy of the evaluation. Finally, no matter how carefully an evaluation is conducted, its utility always remains uncertain. At publication, evaluations are frequently subject to accusations of outdatedness, and the vagaries of *limited* use by funders or sponsors, particularly when outcomes do not support the agendas of sponsors, and *partial* use by the same when selective evaluative outcomes are considered more appealing than the composite whole.

See also:
Action Research (3); Critical Realism (21); Dissemination (32); Empowerment (37); Ethics (39); Method (64); Methodology (65); Mixed Methods (66); Power (77); Qualitative Research (80); Quantitative Research (81); Values (115).

43 Evidence-based Practice

Within the field of education, recent consideration of 'evidence' has focused largely on the use of evidence to inform practice. Following criticisms of the nature and use of educational research made by a number of key players in the field, government initiatives to promote evidence-based practice were quickly replaced by an emphasis on evidence-*informed* practice, recognizing the interplay between evidence and other imperatives in education decision-making. Developments that followed have included the funding and setting up of The Evidence for Policy and Practice Information and Co-ordinating Centre (EPPI-Centre), and a widespread debate on the nature and uses of research evidence, conducted largely by academics and government-related personnel in the UK. However, the debate focuses on academic research evidence and generally has not engaged with wider questions about how players at all levels, including practitioners, understand evidence.

'Evidence-based practice' is a term borrowed from the field of health to identify a particular type of work-based practice. It fits with a view of practice espoused by governments, and is a belief that practitioners should put to one side their own values, preconceptions and experiences, and replace them with knowledge that is objective, value-free and authoritative; or at least, they should adopt practices that are based on evidence. This proposition leads to two positions. Usher *et al.* (1997: 132) describe this first model in the following way:

> ... the solving of technical problems through rational decision-making based on predictive knowledge. It is the means to achieve ends where the assumption is that ends to which practice is directed can always be predefined and are always knowable. The condition of practice is the learning of a body of theoretical knowledge, and practice therefore becomes the application of this body of knowledge in repeated and predictable ways to achieve predefined ends.

This technical-rationality model assumes that a body of evidence-based knowledge can be accrued about educational processes that practitioners should then use to improve their practice.

This can be contrasted with action research and more deliberative models of improving practice where an assumption is made in both cases that practitioners are concerned with the solving of practical problems *in situ*, which involves more than just deliberating about the most efficient means to achieve certain predefined ends. Practice-based knowledge in the deliberative mode is therefore particularistic, nonpropositional, non-replicable and cannot be generalized to other situations and settings in any straightforward way. However, this model does not exclude an assumption being made that practice and deliberative activity that informs practice is always improved by the collection of evidence about that practice. The teacher therefore understands their practice and the setting in which they work in a fuller and more rounded way, and this enables them to make more finely tuned decisions about what they should do.

An assumption is frequently made that transferring this notion of evidence-based practice from the field of health to schools, colleges and universities is unproblematic, or at least, that the two settings have enough in common to make it feasible. Evidence-based practice in health studies has tended to rely on randomized control trials, which allow protocols to be developed about how practitioners should behave. In the field of education, however, the use of these methods for collecting and analysing data is replete with difficulties. This is because it is more difficult to place teaching and learning within the scientific model, where the development of propositional, replicable and generalizable knowledge is the norm. In educational settings, context, experience, personal values and instinct play a more important role in the workplace and in workplace learning.

See also:
Action Research (3); Empiricism (36); Experiment (44); Generalization (50); Objectivity (70); Positivism (75); Prediction (78); Values (115).

44 Experiment

Though successful experiments in the field of education are rare, quasi-experiments, which do not meet the rigorous requirements of the experimental method, are commonplace. At its simplest, the experimental method requires the researcher to intervene in the natural setting and control a number of variables to determine a causal relationship between two or more properties of an individual or unit. A *one-off case study design* consists of the identification of an experimental group, which is then exposed to a planned intervention that would not naturally have occurred. The effects of this intervention are then observed and measured. Because this design lacks any forms of control, the results are likely to be unreliable.

A *single-group experimental design* builds into the process pre- and post-testing, so now the changes that have been caused by the intervention can be measured at two different time points (before and after the intervention) and then compared. If the results are better at the second time point, then the researcher can claim that the intervention has been successful.

A third type of experimental design, a *static group comparison*, introduces the idea of a comparison group. Here, two groups are identified. One of them is exposed to the intervention whereas the other is not. Both groups are post-tested, and their results compared. If the control group (the one that was not exposed to the intervention) shows weaker results in comparison with those obtained by the experimental group, then it is possible to conclude that the intervention has had the desired effect.

All of these designs have considerable weaknesses, common to most forms of quasi-experimentation. These weaknesses refer to the lack of control exerted over other factors that could have caused the increases in the test scores. The researcher, as a result, cannot be certain that it was the intervention that caused these increases and not other factors, such as the experiences of the experimental subjects during the process of the intervention, maturation effects, the possibility of pre-test sensitization, the reliability of the testing devices and selection problems that they may have encountered. For all these reasons, true experimentalists seek further controls over the process so that they can be sure that the effects they observe relate to the intervention and not to other factors.

Thus, a true experiment builds in both pre- and post-tests *and* experimental and control groups. Further to this, a process of randomization is applied to the selection of the control and experimental groups to ensure that members of the two groups are alike in their skills and capacities before the intervention takes place. This is known as a *pre-test post-test control group design*. Though this strategy allows a measure of reliability, there are still some weaknesses in the design, and one of these relates to the problem that effects may not show at the post-testing stage. With *time-series designs*, both the control and experimental groups are tested at a number of points in time, especially at the post-testing stage, to allow the researcher to examine the effects of the intervention over time.

More complicated designs are also possible where two or more interventions are made to a variety of different groups (*factorial design*); or where a series of interventions are contrasted (over time) with a series of non-interventions (*time sample experimental design*); or where a number of experimental treatments are compared using an appropriate number of groups over a number of different time periods (*counter-balanced experimental design*). All of these designs involve variable analysis, and controlling for different influences that might or might not contribute to the way an intervention is received.

And yet, these methods have not proved popular with educational researchers. Some of the reasons for this are practical and ethical. It is sometimes difficult to obtain the necessary permissions from interested parties to set up artificial learning situations, especially if the design is intended to be rigorous, and experimentalists still have to confront the problem of providing different interventions to two or more sets of individuals when they do not know before they start the experiment which of the two will be more beneficial.

The problems, however, are more serious than these. *First*, the process involves variable analysis and mathematical modelling, and these reductive operations may reduce the validity of the findings. *Second*, the experimental design lacks ecological validity, since treatments are made in non-naturally occurring settings. Generalizability is therefore difficult. Mathematical modellers, conscious of these weaknesses but still wanting to retain a variable analysis design, argue that it is now possible to control for different factors after the naturally occurring event has taken place. So, for example, longitudinal designs overcome the problems associated with cross-sectional studies, and multilevel modelling of naturally occurring data allows statistical control of factors that the researcher deems are not relevant to the issue being examined.

See also:
Correlational Research (18); Ethics (39); Generalization (50); Longitudinal Observation Studies (61); Mathematical Modelling (62); Reductionism (84); Reliability (91); Statistics (100); Tests (109); Validity (113); Variable Analysis (116).

45   Fallacies

Scott (2000) has identified nine fallacies in educational research.

1. *The Epistemic Fallacy*. This is where matters to do with the nature of reality (the ontological dimension) are conflated with matters to do with how researchers can know that reality (the epistemological dimension).

2. *The Causal Fallacy*. Correlations or associations are frequently conflated with causal relations. Educational researchers make causal claims from observations of regularities.

3. *The Homogeneous Fallacy*. Characteristics that the researcher gives to a group are then applied to individual members of that group.
4. *The Essentialist Fallacy*. Attributes or properties of individuals are dehistorized and assumed to be trans-social, whereas in fact they are specific to particular time–space loci.
5. *The Value-free Fallacy*. The assumption that is frequently made is that knowledge of the social world can be value-free, and this ignores the pervasiveness of procedural, observational and epistemic values in the conduct of educational research.
6. *The Prospective Fallacy*. Retrospective explanations are frequently conflated with prospective explanations.
7. *The Reductive Fallacy*. The assumption is made that human behaviour can be reduced to a set of properties that adequately describe that individual or their activities. These properties act as quasi-descriptions of the real characteristics they have and the real relations that constitute society.
8. *The Deterministic Fallacy*. Frequently, educational researchers neglect or marginalize human intention and creativity, so that structural descriptions reduce the actor to a pale shadow of their real self.
9. *The Pragmatic Fallacy*. Frequently, educational researchers understand research as a practical activity, which can be performed without reference to philosophical concerns, such as the place and role of values in research.

See also:
Causation (11); Correlational Research (18); Determinism (29); Epistemology/Ontology (38); Prediction (78); Realism (83); Reductionism (84); Values (115).

46   Fallibility

The idea that knowledge is fallible should not be confused with the idea that individuals may be wrong about the world, though this last may be construed as a type of fallibilism. In the first case, because the observer is positioned as a member of a society and in a time and place, then it is impossible for that person ever to acquire absolute and perfect knowledge of the social world; the relationship between contingent human beings and reality is such that absolute knowledge is not possible. In the second case, the claim is made that absolute knowledge is possible, but only so long as the correct methods are deployed. This position in turn makes a further claim that these correct methods can be successfully identified.

However, it is more complicated than this. What is considered to be perfect or correct knowledge depends on the ontological and episte-mological positions that are adopted, that is, the position taken about what reality is determines how it can be known and how much certainty one can have about it. If the researcher or observer adopts a social constructivist perspective, for example, where it is believed that different and incommensurable perspectives are equally credible and that these perspectives or discourses are real, then knowledge of this reality has to take account of this multi-perspectival view.

Error is a constant possibility in social and educational research, and this is illustrated by the frequent disagreements between researchers conducting parallel research studies. Error can occur for a number of reasons:

- the researcher mistakes appearances for reality;
- the researcher uses inappropriate methods;
- correlations or associations are conflated with causal relations;
- resources at the disposal of the researcher do not allow him or her either to explore the subject matter of the research in any great depth or to triangulate using different methods which strengthen the validity and reliability of the findings;
- respondents in interview studies and surveys may not give truthful answers.

However, all these forms of error are at least in theory correctable. The identification of such errors, indeed the notion of error itself, implies that a better or more correct way of proceeding is possible. Fallibility, on the other hand, goes beyond simple error, and implies that social actors are contingently positioned and therefore always observe the world from a fixed position. There is no outsider perspective that allows the individual access to complete knowledge.

Fallibility, therefore, may refer to three different positions in educational research:

1. The researcher or observer may make procedural mistakes in their research projects, but these can be identified and in theory corrected.
2. The researcher or observer always operates from a particular perspective, and therefore cannot step outside this perspective even for a moment. Thus fallibilism here refers to the impossi-bility of acquiring true and complete knowledge of the world.
3. The researcher is always one step behind the evolving and

emergent nature of the social world, and the looping nature of the relationship between discourse and reality means that descriptions of the world, because they have the capacity to influence and change that world, rapidly become redundant.

See also:
Causation (11); Critical Realism (21); Discourse (31); Epistemology/ Ontology (38); Interview (57); Reliability (91); Replication (92); Social Constructionism (99); Survey (105); Triangulation (112); Validity (113).

47 Feminist Research

Feminist perspectives on research have made many impacts on education research, primarily from what is commonly known as 'the second wave' of feminist research beginning in the late 1960s through to the 'third wave' that constitutes the early twenty-first century. Such impacts have proliferated internationally, although, in common with other forms of education research, feminist research has been shaped and continues to be shaped by changes in policy and practice at local and national levels, and increasingly by globalization. Important intersections and developments have occurred at the level of theorizing, and these, in turn, have impacted upon the way that research that is described as feminist is being conducted. For feminists, research is fundamentally political. More than an issue of using appropriate methods to address research problems or questions, it is 'a way of *being* and *doing* research in which there is a shared assumption to place the diverse experiences of women at the centre ... of social investigation' (Webb, 2000: 35, her emphasis) and this position holds despite a 'diversity of feminist thought and actions' (ibid.). Importantly, distinct feminist epistemologies for creating and understanding knowledge and 'who the knowers are' (Stanley and Wise, 1990) is compounded by diversity in women's experiences. One outcome has been multiple assessments and considerations about the nature of reality and knowledge *within* feminist research as well as *between* feminist research and other forms of research.

Drawing upon the writings of Foucault and the theoretical framework of 'prevalent discourse', Weiner *et al.* (1997) have examined the ways in which gender-focused developments in education, and specifically in the UK, have been linked with concurrent developments in feminist theory and research. In the 1960s and 1970s, key interests related to the relative absence of women from public life coupled critically with the extent to which knowledge, policies and practices were seen from a male perspective. Applied to education, the knowledge-worth-learning as constituted in school curricula and academic disciplines was also seen as male in subject matter and interpretation. The task of feminist researchers in education was, therefore, to reveal and replace such distortions by seeing through a female rather than male perspective or lens, and to incorporate women who had been silenced. Such agendas would replace the equality of opportunities agenda more prevalent in the 1950s and precipitate research in the 1970s and 1980s around anti-sexist policies and practices, about which feminist writers like Weiner *et al.* (1997) write positively yet, in hindsight, guardedly. By the 1980s and 1990s, and linked to the breakdown of earlier approaches to state welfarism, the attention of policy-makers turned to matters of individual achievement. For feminist researchers, the complexities of gendered performance in schools and a 'gender fair culture' in relation to education, training, careers and employment (accompanied by a growing casualization of employment and a feminization of poverty), interest began to centre upon the ways in which the masculinities promoted in schools delimited and defined education for boys (Mac an Ghaill, 1994).

Leonard (2001: 185–6, her emphasis) has also described late-twentieth-century developments in feminist research as 'a painful process' and a backlash against earlier feminist research dominated by feminist lesbians, black, working class and disabled women, which then led to a culture of reflexivity, self-criticism and self-awareness about 'what we [girls and women] do *not* share, and indeed how some women oppress and exploit others'. For Leonard, this has meant a growing research emphasis upon the complexity of structured social inequalities and about the ways in which gendered and other identities are being negotiated and renegotiated.

In education, a number of research trends are discernible in the field. In combination, they reinforce the political nature of feminist research. Adapted from Weiler *et al.* (1999) and Leonard (2001), feminist research attends to the following:

- examinations of schools, colleges and universities as sites for the enactment of gender;
- explorations of state-supported provision, and how policy and provision is shaped by gender;
- investigations of the resistances subordinated groups have developed and are developing around ideas of knowledge, power and learning;
- the need for further developments in understanding the relation-

ship between gendered conceptions of citizenship, the family and the economy.

Most recently it addresses:

- the relationship between poststructural, postmodern and post-colonial theories and feminism;
- the impact of globalization, global technologies, and neo-liberal policies upon education policy and practice;
- the need for research to continue to mount challenges to accelerating hegemonic discourses which encourage gendered *as well as* other forms of discriminatory practice;
- an accelerating focus upon 'what about the boys?' (Yates, 1999) as well as 'what about the girls?' (as in Lingard and Douglas, 1999);
- research into the interconnections between gendered and other identities from a range of perspectives, including those that are cross-cultural (Weiler *et al.*, 1999: ix–x; Leonard, 2001).

Feminist research and feminist methodology

Concerns about the distinctiveness or not of the methods used in feminist research have been part of a long-standing debate within and beyond feminism about the relation between theory, research and practice. (See Ramazanoglu (1992) and Hammersley (1992a) for example.) Some feminists have argued strongly in favour of a distinctive reframing of methodology and method based on feminist ways of knowing, for example, Stanley (1994). Others have noted a preference among feminist researchers for qualitative research (Maynard, 1994) or deny that their methodological frameworks are necessarily distinctive from others (Gelsthorpe, 1992). For others still, distinctiveness remains the key feature of feminist research, and particularly with regard to ethnographic research (for example, Williams, 1993).

Elsewhere, Leonard (2001: 191, our emphasis) argues that feminist researchers:

> need the discipline of disciplines, whatever their sexist short-comings. Feminist work isn't distinct because of having specific methods or methodologies, or even epistemologies ... Feminists can be found working within positivist, structuralist and inter-pretativist paradigms, using random control experimentation, ethnography, or semiotics. Rather, feminist research is character-ized *by asking questions in a specific topic area and with a specific emancipatory agenda* ... Actual feminist research practice ... can be competitive, for personal aggrandizement, and written in an elitist genre.

Therefore, as Leonard (2001) suggests, feminist researchers engaging in educational research in 2005 do so from rather different starting points from those of the 1970s, 1980s and 1990s. Yet parallels remain. *First*, central to the formulation of research problems are notions of empowerment for participants, and that research should be for women. *Second*, the context for the research is that it should be politically engaged and engaging, and an arena for 'passionate scholarship' (Leonard, 2001: 192). *Third*, the roles of the researcher and the research participants should be mutually implicating and participatory, with a keen interest in giving voice to the silenced. Here, there is continued concern to reduce the power differentials between research participants and the researcher, and much emphasis upon the reflexive and autobiographical stance of the researcher, and acknowledgement of her presence in the research. *Fourth*, the methodology retains its emphasis upon a standpoint approach. Leonard (2001) and others have challenged the dichotomy between reason and emotion, fantasy and reality, objectivity and subjectivity, science and politics, and between mind and body, in the construction and conduct of research. Among the feminist contributions to methods has been an emphasis placed upon specific approaches to interviewing, for example, and the construction of texts from the same. *Fifth*, there is a concern to make the findings of feminist research accessible to wider audiences and in a language that is widely understood (Leonard, 2001: 192) (an aim not always achieved, and sometimes restricted in outlet).

Most recent concerns in feminist research have centred upon men's pro-feminist theory and politics, in particular, an increased number of texts on boys, men and masculinity (for example, Lingard and Douglas, 1999). Some feminists have argued for a clear distinction between feminism and feminist perspectives; others argue for a ' "politics of alliance" between men and feminism, and for the acceptance of both "strategic essentialism" and "strategic pluralism" in its repertoire of action' (Yates, 1999: xiii).

Increase in concern about boys' underachievement has been viewed by some feminists as the latest among a long line of diversionary tactics or 'moral panics' to regain or reinforce patriarchal forms that are considered to have been central to education thus far (Weiner *et al.*, 1997). Meanwhile, while within and beyond the academy there is an amalgam of policy-makers, academics and practitioners who continue to choose to ignore or marginalize feminism, feminist researchers have made sufficient impact to continue to challenge the conventions, policies and practices of education and research. The ongoing imperative for such a stimulus has global ramifications.

See also:
Empowerment (37); Epistemology/Ontology (38); Gender (49); Method (64); Power (77); Qualitative Research (80); Quantitative Research (81); Subjectivity (104).

48   Focus Groups

Despite recent political interest, focus groups have a provenance in social research that predates their use in the distillation of government policy intentions. Used by social scientists, and subsequently by market researchers, focus groups have become increasingly widespread in education research, especially since they have the potential to 'reach' the research 'parts' that individualized responses from questionnaire surveys or one-to-one interviews cannot 'reach', and, indeed, such responses may not be required for research purposes that preclude individualized attention to the minutia of deeply personal moments. Focus groups may also have particular relevance when there is an increased emphasis upon researching communities of practice and learning. However, this does not exclude their use in 'sensitive' research where challenging or controversial issues might be raised more appropriately in group settings that minimize ethical challenges for participants, whether researchers or researched.

There has been some confusion about what distinguishes focus groups from other kinds of group interactions known variously as 'group interviews' or 'group discussions' (see also Oates, 2000). Perhaps the clearest enunciation comes from Kitzinger (1994: 103 and 116, our emphasis) in her focus upon 'the *explicit* use of the group *interaction as research data*' and in examining 'how knowledge, and more importantly, ideas, both develop, and operate within a given cultural context'. Two features, in particular, can be used to distinguish focus groups from other kinds of interaction that involve face-to-face interaction with more than one informant simultaneously. *First*, focus groups are focused in the sense that they usually involve collective activity(ies) to provide the framework for the interaction. In educational settings, for example, this might be a video or audio recording, photographs, charts, diagrams, short readings or word prompts for teacher, pupil or parent groups. *Second*, the core purpose of focus groups is to collect and analyse data that are primarily concerned with the *interaction* among members of the group (ibid.). This is not to argue that focus groups might, and frequently do provide qualitatively insightful data about individual group members, but rather that its primary purpose is linked to furthering researchers' understandings about group processes and norms, and how these develop in specific cultural contexts.

Moreover, as Morgan has suggested (1988; 1993), focus groups are especially useful in helping to investigate why people hold the views they do, precisely because a key aspect of group participation is the need for members to explain opinions and attitudes, especially when challenged by others, when asked to respond to a question or to provide further justification for what they have done or said during the group encounter.

Kitzinger (1994) highlights nine advantages of focus groups as a means to:

- highlight informants' attitudes, priorities, language and frames of reference;
- facilitate a wide range of communication;
- identify group norms;
- gain insight into social processes;
- encourage conversation about 'embarrassing' or sensitive subjects;

and to allow researchers to:

- explore differences in the group;
- use conflict to clarify why people do what they do;
- explore arguments to see how participants change their minds;
- investigate the ways in which some forms of speech affect group participation.

The use of an example reported in Pole and Morrison (2003) highlights some of the challenges in using focus groups for social research. Unlike their use with school pupils in class time where members are, in a specific sense, a 'captive audience', Roach and Morrison (1998) used focus groups as part of a research study designed to investigate young people's use of public libraries. The first challenge was in accessing informants and deciding upon location, size and number. (In other contexts, Oates (2000) reports on similar challenges.) Repeated advertising and promises of free refreshments and library advice did result in three groups of eight participants. A comfortable location in the centre of a municipal library that provided a safe, rather than isolated space for discussion proved helpful. The focus group leaders applied vignettes of library experience, real and imagined, and books, as props to promote discussion. The task was complex and the researchers took a twin-pronged approach, one researcher acting as discussion 'moderator' and the other as 'reticent discussant', taking careful note of group dynamics, movement and body language. Both roles were demanding and required skills of moderation and listening as well as targeted observation. The focus groups presented different challenges that were linked to the varying dynamics of the groups. The use of a tape recorder with a conference microphone attached was not without problems; some voices were hardly audible, and transcription was a lengthy, sometimes frustrating process of discerning between voices, people and language.

But the advantages outweighed the disadvantages. Used in conjunction with document analysis and interview data, they provided data from twenty-four participants that would otherwise have been impractical on a one-to-one basis. The groups allowed the researchers to interact directly with participants who had hitherto been unknown to them, and, in several cases, to one another. Participation evolved as informants were gradually able to build upon one another's comments through pro-active and re-active verbal and non-verbal interaction. Young people appeared to like this form of engagement. While the focus group data were challenging in terms of analysis and interpretation, they gave the researchers access to a wide range of issues concerning young people's understandings and views about what library use meant for them, and gave the researchers new insights into young people's perceptions of what constituted 'safe' or 'risky' environments in which to work, learn, rest and socialize. In the triangulation of different methods, it was, therefore, possible to compare and contrast the different kinds of data collection that took place in the relatively 'private' and 'public' arenas of individual interview and focus group encounters.

Caution might be appropriate in using focus groups as a first-stage strategy. For example, when Janesick (1998) studied deaf culture in Washington, USA, and addressed the question 'How do some deaf adults manage to succeed academically and in the work place given the stigma of deafness in this society?', she used individual interviews and observations first. This was followed by focus groups once she had come to learn more about perspectives on deafness among the 12 participants in her study.

Elsewhere, there is support for the use of focus groups as an appropriate method for conducting research with children and young people as well as with adults. O'Kane's (2000) recent account of using participatory techniques, like focus groups, in facilitating views about decisions which affect children, as expressed by 'looked after' children in local authorities in England and Wales, are especially insightful. Focus groups provided a method 'to break down the power imbalance between adults and children, and ... create[d] space which enable[d] children to speak up and be heard' (O'Kane, 2000: 136–7).

Despite the advantages cited, the above examples also point to limitations. In common with other interpretive approaches, focus groups are open to the criticism that findings may be limited to group members rather than wider populations. How serious a limitation this is depends upon the purposes of the research and the questions being addressed. At a practical level, focus groups are especially demanding of interviewing and moderation skills among researchers, and their management of both. For this reason, focus groups generally require the participation of more than one researcher. Adequate time also needs to be allowed for researcher feedback and joint analysis. Careful consideration needs to be given to analysis. Focus groups can be used to collect quantitative data coded via content analysis (for example, Stewart and Shamdasani, 1990) but are most often used to obtain qualitative data (Roach and Morrison, 1998). Finally, focus groups may be especially prone to sabotage by reluctant or over-dominant participants and perhaps for this reason should be considered the basis for rich and deep data collections that require special foresight and planning.

See also:
Conversation Analysis (17); Culture (23); Discourse (31); Documentary Research (34); Ethics (39); Interpretivism (56); Interview (57); Research Community (95); Survey (105); Triangulation (112).

49   Gender

Most research with and upon human beings has a gender dimension. It would be surprising if it did not, given the centrality of gender to the identities and directions of lives experienced in the private as well as public domains of family, work and careers that, in turn, interact variously with education. However, where gender takes centre stage in educational research, it does so in relation to the structured inequalities in society which are exemplified as gendered identities and educational experiences, notwithstanding diverse manifestations globally, and interconnections with other forms of inequality like disability, class or ethnicity. In education, the focus has been upon 'the gender regime within educational systems' (Lingard and Douglas, 1999: 4), and in research, especially of the past 50 years, this has been accompanied by new orientations, as well as reorientations to gender. This has brought epistemological, ontological and methodological challenges, at the core of which, for feminists, is the notion of research which, in its production as knowledge, and as process and activity, is masculinist (discussed elsewhere in this volume under Feminist Research, see Chapter 47). There are also important overlaps between the centrality of gender to education and educational research, and the theoretical frameworks of hermeneutics and interpretivism, especially in relation to knowledge created as partial and perspective-dependent. Similarly, postmodernism is implicated, especially concerns among its proponents to expose research partiality and boundedness and concepts that guide and constrain it (Lyotard, 1984).

Theoretical as well as practical debates about gender are, for the most part, reflected in developments which emanate from within feminist research where the term gender was linked by feminists to notions of patriarchy and sexism. Discussion of the term was also prioritized by women rather than men (though there has been a recent emergence of pro-feminist writing by men, and an alternative and simultaneous backlash of anti-feminist writing by men and women). Leonard (2001: 178), following Barry (1993), pursues this in relation to perspectives on gender that might be aligned to equal opportunities or to feminist perspectives. Exemplars of the former would be to locate gender perspectives in terms of the differences in opportunities and rights of women and men as requiring legislative change because they are disadvantageous for both, but especially for women; that seek to tackle gender discrimination as a separate issue from other forms; identify politics only in its public sphere; and remain 'ambivalent' towards feminism. Exemplars of the latter would be to locate structured forms of gender inequality throughout public and private spheres and in mutual relations. Both recognize that the power which operates in personal relations is fundamentally political; and configures relations between the sexes in terms of a dominant masculinity and male-defined structures, in which class and race are also implicated. This implies an explicit political commitment to women as a group and 'to women's action', in education as elsewhere (ibid.: 178).

In reality, there is fluidity between these two positions which also under-emphasizes the fragmentation of the feminist movement in the 1980s, specifically as it relates to contested notions about holistic gendered experiences as women and men, evidenced in the rise of black feminism in the 1980s and, more recently, as pro-feminist writing by men about gender. Early approaches to gender, especially to problems of inequality in access to life chances (notably first to education) were underpinned by theoretical debates about 'difference' in terms of distinctions between sex and gender that tracked 'the dualist conceptions of mind/culture and culture/nature' (Lingard and Douglas, 1999: 21). In early forms, it could be argued, some feminist stances on the nature/nurture debate denied 'meaningful significance to sexual difference' and posited 'gender as a social construction that overlays the mute body (as identified with sex)' and 'the body ... as "a blank slate" upon which are imprinted cultural mores' (ibid.: 21). More recently, deconstruction has taken different forms, to the extent that gendered subjectivities are less likely to be seen as kinds of generic blueprints upon which gendered socialization is overlaid, but one in which, following Gatens (1996), gender and its relation to the body (female or male) is not ' "taken up" by culture but *lived in culture*' (Lingard and Douglas, 1999: 21 our emphasis). Such reconfigurations of gender might, in part, be construed as an attempt to prise definitions away from earlier essentialist positions about gender in male-dominated societies, to which women must always struggle to gain access, given the patriarchal privileging of being male over female.

Constructions and deconstructions of gender have also been influenced by poststructuralist theory which seeks to disentangle reflexively understandings about gender, body and power by interrogations of language and the power of language-in-use to define such relationships. One outcome has been the burgeoning of research about gendered lives using texts that can be interpreted in a range of ways. In education, Walkerdine (1990) provides a notable example. Deconstruction has raised some concerns, especially among those who consider that a growing emphasis upon discourse, and the language being used to define gendered identities, may have led to an over-emphasis upon language rather than 'the material facticity of [women's] material subordination' (Leonard, 2001: 193) and its basis for action towards empowerment. As Leonard declares:

> Sometimes the fact (some would query if it is a 'fact') of 'sub-ordination' is missing: and women's agency is seen to override any contexts and constraints (if indeed, any 'real' 'constraints' are recognized).

As a counterpoint, there is current and renewed emphasis upon the relationship between gender and recent educational reforms, including those that relate to educational 'managerialism' (Acker, 1994) and its specific aspects as they impinge upon gendered politics (for example, Gewirtz *et al.*'s (1995) study of the marketization of schooling and the influence of parents upon young people's choices).

Finally, commentators (like Dillabough and Arnot, 2001: 47) point to political theory as a new direction for gendered theorizing and research in which gender is seen as a political as well as social and educational identity. Indeed, research into citizenship *as* education as well as the links *between* citizenship *and* education will need, if it is to fulfil its promise, to make links between the political, social and educational dimensions of gender as it is experienced in schools, in further and higher education and as lifelong education in the UK and internationally.

See also:
Deconstruction (26); Discourse (31); Empowerment (37); Feminist Research (47); Hermeneutics (52); Interpretivism (56); Narrative (67); Social Constructionism (99); Structure (103); Subjectivity (104); Textuality (110).

50   Generalization

Educational researchers, and indeed educationalists, frequently make generalizations. Sometimes it is asserted that the purpose of social science and educational research is the making of these generalizations. And yet there are few enduring generalizations about educational activities and relations that are not either trivial or mistaken. A traditional view of generalization is that it allows statements about a property of an individual or educational unit, which also belong to a class or population of that individual or unit. Again, these usually refer to the quantitative dimensions of these objects, i.e. size, breadth and frequency. Generalizations that involve quantitative modelling of this relationship may be deterministic or probabilistic. When the object's qualitative attributes are being considered, then generalizations may be made, but the relation between the sample and the population is bound to be approximate. As a result, a notion of transferability has been suggested by qualitative researchers (cf. Guba and Lincoln, 1985) as a replacement or alternative to generalizability. Here, the burden of proof is left in the hands of readers and users of research.

Traditional, and thus quantitative, notions of generalizability have been criticized on a number of grounds (cf. Sayer, 1992):

- The object is dehistoricized: the generalization that is being made is given law-like dimensions, whereas it cannot and does not transcend the boundaries of time and place.
- Generalizations ignore the emergent nature of relations between people and institutions.
- Generalizations imply a causal relation between two objects or properties, when in reality, what is being claimed is an associational or correlational effect.

- Generalizations are prone to the reductive effect of mathematical modelling, where characteristics of a group are frequently applied to an individual who has been placed by the researcher within that group, and the property given substance by the generalization is assumed to apply in a deterministic way to that individual; so, if a racial property is given to an individual, it is assumed that the individual will always behave in conformity with that property.
- Generalizations may be ambiguous. Sayer (1992: 132) argues that 'tests might show that in a sample of people 80 per cent do x and the remainder y. This can be interpreted either as an effect of the presence of two types of people, one of which always does x and the other y, or else as a generalisation about a homogeneous population in which each member has the same propensity to do x or y.'

Quantitative generalization seeks to determine the relationship between a sample from which the educational researcher collects data and a population from which the sample is derived. Though this relationship is frequently expressed as a mathematical one, this cannot solve the problem of whether in reality the subset of individuals that make up the sample belong to the population that they are being placed within. For example, a sample of mathematics teachers would seem to have a relation to a population of mathematics teachers, and yet frequently the property being examined cannot be derived from the loose categorization of being a mathematics teacher.

See also:
Causation (11); Critical Realism (21); Determinism (29); Fallacies (45); Mathematical Modelling (62); Nomothetic Statements (69); Prediction (78); Qualitative Research (80); Quantitative Research (81); Reductionism (84); Sampling (98); Statistics (100); Transferability (111).

51 Grounded Theory

A theory is a system of ideas which conceptualizes experience. In the analysis of qualitative data, the key concern of researchers is to ensure that research findings are grounded in the information that is collected in the field and becomes the key data of the study. What qualitative researchers do with the information that becomes data is to categorize it and make connections between categories. Such data is mainly, but not exclusively, concerned with meaning rather than numbers. This is the key task for qualitative analysts, which has its foundations in analytical induction and is based on Glaser and Strauss's (1967) *The Discovery of Grounded Theory*.

It may be helpful to begin by distinguishing between analytical induction (defined elsewhere in this volume in Chapter 51) and grounded theory, since the latter has important elements of the former contained within it. Analytical induction proceeds by a series of steps or stages. For example, the researcher identifies a problem or an issue, for example, Bullying in Secondary School. A series of case studies might then be conducted and a possible explanation of the phenomenon formulated. Further cases are examined in order to establish the 'fit' between the initial explanation or hypothesis and the further data collected. If that 'fit' is missing then the researcher or research team will need to reformulate the explanation and conduct more research. What then follows is an iterative interplay between data and explanation to the extent that the first explanation may need redefinition. Data collection case-by-case continues until a lack of fit between revised explanations/theorizing and case does not appear. The process is time consuming and resource heavy, and as Bryman and Burgess (1994) point out, its demands are such that it is used relatively infrequently.

Grounded theory resembles analytical induction in two particular ways: *first*, there is continued emphasis upon the interplay between data collection and theorizing; *second*, the generation of categories from data collection continues until the researcher feels confident that the meaning and the importance of the data is established and that categories are 'saturated'. Next steps are to formulate more general or abstract expressions of these concepts, from which more theoretical reflection flows. As data collection and theoretical collection continue, hypotheses about the links between them are 'tested' further in the field. Silverman (2001: 71) defines a 'simplified model' of this as follows:

- an initial attempt to develop categories which illuminate the data;
- an attempt to saturate these categories with as many appropriate cases in order to demonstrate their relevance;
- developing these categories into more general analytic frameworks with relevance outside the setting.

Drawing on Glaser and Strauss's (1967) account of death and dying, Silverman (2001: 71) distinguishes between grounded substantive theory and grounded formal theory:

They [Glaser and Strauss] show how they developed the category 'awareness contexts' to refer to the kinds of situations in which people were informed of their likely fate [grounded substantive theory] ... The category was then saturated and was finally related to non-medical settings where people learn about how others define them (e.g. schools) [grounded formal theory].

Elsewhere, Denscombe (1998) and Pole and Morrison (2003, in relation to ethnography) have explained the building blocks of grounded theory that have become integral to general approaches towards qualitative data analysis. Five key themes emerge: *first*, the advocacy of pragmatic guidelines for research, rather than inflexible rules; *second*, that qualitative research should be concerned with analysis even more than description, thus emphasizing the central role of the researcher, and that the meanings of data as interpreted by participants are always reinterpreted by the researcher in the course of his/her engagement with the same; *third*, that theories should emerge from the empirical research and not be added on; *fourth*, that the researcher embarks upon research with an open mind, and not with pre-established theories to 'test' in the field; *fifth*, that the selection of research participants cannot be fully known at the outset of the research. The last point precludes early or definitive sampling.

Grounded theory has been subject to a number of criticisms or, as it might be more accurate to state, a number of criticisms levelled mainly at those for whom grounded theory may have been applied as a kind of whitewash in order to disguise poorly conducted and analysed qualitative research, or research that is empiricist and mostly or entirely devoid of theoretical import or content. Elsewhere, grounded theory has been criticized for its failure to acknowledge the theoretical and conceptual frameworks that guide researchers in the initial stages of their work, including decisions about the research topic.

The spectre of relativism also haunts grounded theory although, we would argue, key aspects can be countered. Criticism is usually two-fold. The first relates to the explanations advanced in the name of grounded theory. The second relates to 'knowing' *when* saturation has occurred. In process and outcome, qualitative research is dependent upon the relationship between the researcher and the data. As Pole and Lampard (2002: 206) comment, it is the 'intimate relationship' between the researcher and the data upon which the analysis depends: 'The discovery of theory within the data is a construction of the researcher, brought about by his/her knowledge of the data and the capacity to identify codes and concepts within it.' In which case, how do we know that analysis of this kind is little more than 'the creative ability of the researcher'? (ibid.). Dey (1993) offers a helpful counterpoint in his interpretation of reliability and validity as they apply to the analysis of qualitative data and the emergence of grounded theory. A key under-pinning for qualitative research, he argues, is openness and transpar-ency at all stages of data collection and analysis. More than an audit trail is implicated. There are concerns to examine the fitness for purpose of the methods used to investigate the research 'problem' and to ensure that outcomes and conclusions are appropriately nested as part of the epistemological and methodological rationales for action. Context is crucial, as is the richness of the data and the need for the researcher to attribute the significance of what is seen, heard, reported and interpreted. In brief, Pole and Lampard's (2002: 209) summary of key issues is pertinent to the analysis of qualitative data that draws upon grounded theory. These are: 'knowing the data; thorough coding; the identification of concepts; grounding the concepts in the data; [and] opening the findings for scrutiny' by others.

Proponents and exponents of computer-aided analysis (for example, Tesch, 1990; Miles and Huberman, 1994; Richards and Richards, 1994) are growing in number. As Pole and Morrison (2003: 98) comment, advocacy rests upon three main advantages: *first*, 'its ability to manage data'; *second*, 'its capacity to assist the actual process of analysis, and *third*, 'its approximation to (or emulation of) quantitative or positivist approaches to research'. But the issue of whether the logic of the computer is the most appropriate basis for the analysis of qualitative data is not without controversy. Coffey and Atkinson (2000: 35), for example, contend that grounded theory has been received in two ways: *first*, as a 'general strategy of social inquiry' and *second*, 'as a method that can be reduced to prescriptive recipe-knowledge'. In this sense it is argued that 'computerized' analysis has the potential to lose some of the connections to humanist ethnography and commitments to 'thick' understandings of the subjective world of educational actors. Moreover, it also loses some of the connections to postmodern insistence on multiple voices and perspectives. Their critique rests not upon a view that necessarily proscribes the use of computers, but rather that it reduces analysis to matters of 'search and retrieval' of coded segments. 'Grounded theory is more than coding ... the danger lies in the glib association between the two' (ibid.: 36–7). Taking this point further, it can be argued that a sub-culture of specific and converging ways of thinking about the relationship between grounded theorizing and analysis is developing, and this is reinforced by a burgeoning number of software programs (Pole and Morrison, 2003: 101).

Writing more than ten years ago, Bryman and Burgess (1994) were of the view that the major influences of grounded theory upon social and educational research had been two-fold. *First*, it had 'alerted qualitative researchers as to the desirability of extracting concepts and theory out of data' (ibid.: 220). *Second*, it had 'informed aspects of ... analysis ... including coding and the use of different types of codes and their role in concept creation' (ibid.: 220). How much the application of grounded theorizing has moved beyond this position is still discussed. Silverman (2001: 71–2, his emphasis) is blunt:

> At best, grounded theory offers an approximation to the creative activity of theory building found in good observational work, compared to the dire abstracted empiricism in the most wooden statistical studies. One way to save grounded theory from being a trite and mistaken technique is to treat it as a way of building theories from a particular *model* of social reality ... a social constructionist will use grounded theory in a very different way to ethnographers who believe that their categories simply reproduce nature.

Readers may want to judge for themselves the extent to which grounded theory requires rescue, from whom and for which purposes.

See also:
Categorization (10); Coding (14); Empiricism (36); Epistemology/Ontology (38); Ethnography (40); Induction (55); Method (64); Methodology (65); Postmodernism (76); Qualitative Research (80); Reflexivity (87); Social Constructionism (99); Subjectivity (104).

52 Hermeneutics

The hermeneutic method comprises the study and interpretation of texts. In the twentieth century it developed into a method for understanding human actions, and the activities of researchers themselves. In particular, it sought to address the issue of how a member of one culture could understand the experiences of someone from another culture, or from another historical period. Various solutions were suggested, ranging from the phenomenological reduction, where a pure form of consciousness could be developed liberated from social and historical influences, to a belief that history could be viewed only from the inside, and this involved piecing together the fragments of meaning from the present, and contextualizing them in terms of the whole picture.

Gadamer (1975) in turn argued that this process had a circular nature. What he meant by this was that all sense-making has to be located within cultural and historical perspectives. Thus any knowledge developed about human beings is perspective-bound and partial. There can be no outside reference point to evaluate or judge that knowledge. It is locked into a circle of interpretations made in the present in the context of a myriad interpretations made in the past. If this is accepted, then knowledge always has a provisional character, and has to be understood differently from a positivist conception of knowledge.

A further variant on this theme is the double hermeneutic suggested by Giddens (1984: 31). This is where theories, concepts and ideas developed by researchers not only describe the social world, but also have the potential to change it, because lay actors incorporate into their belief systems this new knowledge, thus changing the original knowledge and the way they behave. The implication of this is that knowledge about educational activities and institutions may remain stable but also has built into it the potentiality for instability. It is important to be careful here not to over-emphasize the inevitability of such change as new knowledge about society may also have little effect and indeed be discarded or marginalized. The double hermeneutic therefore does not work in any mechanistic fashion; however, new knowledge has the potential to change the world thus making that original knowledge redundant. Giddens (1984: 31) describes it in the following way:

> The Social Sciences operate with a double hermeneutic involving two-way ties with the actions and institutions of those they study. Sociological observers depend upon lay concepts to generate accurate descriptions of social processes; and agents regularly appropriate themes and concepts of social science within their behaviour, thus potentially changing its character. This ... inevitably takes it some distance from the 'cumulative and uncontested' model that naturalistically inclined sociologists have in mind.

A further meaning can be given to the idea of the double hermeneutic, and this relates to the idea of interpretation, and it again complicates the act of doing research. For interpretivists, the most significant facet of human behaviour is that individuals make interpretations about the world, or at least they are always striving to give meaning to it. Educational researchers in turn are engaged in the same type of activity, that is, they also are interpreting the world, albeit it in a more systematic way than most lay actors. Research is therefore understood as an activity that involves interpretations by researchers of interpretations made by individuals in society, and this can be described as a double interpretation or double hermeneutic.

See also:
Interpretivism (56); Objectivity (70); Phenomenology (73); Positivism (75); Subjectivity (104).

53 Historical Research

The locus of interest for the historical researcher is the past. Historical research is the systematic collection and evaluation of data to describe, explain and understand actions and events that occurred in the past. Doing historical research involves a number of interrelated research tasks which may be summarized as follows:

- the identification and limitation of a problem or area of study;
- the formulation of a hypothesis or set of questions;
- the collection, organization, verification, validation, analysis and selection of data;
- testing or answering the questions where appropriate;
- writing a research report involving a new understanding of the past and its relevance to the present and the future. (Adapted from Cohen and Manion, 1984: 48 and Fraenkel and Wallen, 2003.)

The purposes and values of historical research have been understood in a number of ways, but are summarized as follows:

- to make people aware of what happened in the past and what might be learnt from past successes and failures;
- to investigate what happened in the past to see whether findings can contribute to the resolution of existing problems;
- to assist in predicting the future;
- to allow for a revaluation of data, including the testing of hypotheses to explore trends and/or relationships;
- to understand present education policies and practices in relation to the past. (Fraenkel and Wallen, 2003: 548-9)

The main focus of attention for the historical researcher may be an individual, a group, an institution or an idea (Cohen and Manion, 1984: 49). However, this is not to argue that any of these are studied in isolation but rather that a specific focus is foregrounded. Historical research proceeds through a number of stages. Several are common to all research; others present unique challenges that relate to studies of the past.

So, the initial stage is to identify a topic which is feasible and justifiable, and where appropriate, to include a hypothesis about relations between variables. Fraenkel and Wallen (2003) warn would-be researchers about selecting topics about which scant historical evidence is available or accessible. Locating historical sources is a key feature of such research, since the researcher has no recourse to 'direct observation', instead relying on the records, relics and 'traces' (Hockett 1955 cited in Cohen and Manion 1984: 54–5) that previous individuals or observers have left behind. In this sense, the primary sources which are central to historical research are also secondary observations by other individuals who were neither necessarily trained observers nor individuals who could have predicted the uses to which their testimonies (in a variety of forms) would be used.

Historical sources include a variety of documents presented in a range of formats, some for private and others for public consumption; numerical records; statements made through songs and stories told orally that become part of oral history (and where living raconteurs can be interviewed by researchers for oral accounts for specific events and situations); and relics, namely the physical and visual objects that can provide the researcher with evidence from the past. Sources are divided into two categories: primary and secondary. The core feature of primary data lies in its direct relationship to the events being studied. These might again include relics but also direct eye-witness accounts from individuals, alive and deceased, who were first-hand witnesses to the topic of study. Secondary sources are 'one-step removed' (Fraenkel and Wallen, 2003: 551) and include second-hand accounts from individuals who did not witness events, magazine, newspaper and journal reports of the time. Wherever possible, historical researchers prefer to use primary sources, given the likelihood that secondary sources might be less accurate or more 'sketchy'. Nonetheless, most researchers will need to use both sources during the course of the research.

A second stage involves the evaluation of sources, and follows many of the processes engaged in by all researchers who conduct documentary research, discussed elsewhere in this volume and much earlier by Platt (1981). In historical research the two processes of evaluating sources are known as external and internal criticism. Following Cohen and Manion (1984: 57–8), key aspects may be summarized. External criticism is aimed at establishing the authenticity of the source, rather than the truthfulness or accuracy of what it contains. Researchers search for clues in terms of the circumstances and times in which, for example, written sources were produced, in terms of authorship, and whether alternative versions of the same source or document exist. Internal criticism involves an evaluation of the accuracy or worth of the data contained in the source. In this sense, researchers try to establish the credibility of the witness, but, in doing so, also need to take into account their own potential biases and relationships to the sources of evidence. Researchers investigate whether the author of a document, for example, was present at the event being described, in which capacity, whether the author had a specific or vested interest in what he/she wrote, in terms of its sense-making and language, and whether other versions of the same event exist.

A key task for historical researchers, as for all researchers, is the analysis and synthesis of the data collected, although in historical research this has a particular nuance. Mouly (1978) cited in Cohen and Manion (1984: 61) pose a number of questions for historical researchers to address. Of specific importance is the need to confirm whether there has been an over-dependence on secondary sources, whether the dependability of the data has been established, whether adequate historical perspective is displayed, whether bias on the part of the researcher distorts evidence, whether the hypothesis is plausible and the relationship between the data and 'other' historical facts is sufficiently established.

The processes used by researchers to arrive at synthesis vary, and inspiration is drawn from both quantitative and qualitative approaches to data analysis. Predominantly, qualitative data analysis is preferred. More recently, some researchers have deployed quantitative analysis drawn mainly from official statistics to further validate their findings, and statistical forms of content analysis have been applied to selected elements of historical and educational research.

While the extent of the challenge might be exaggerated, it has been suggested that historical researchers have particular problems with generalizability to the extent that their subject matter is totally dependent on what remains, and is available to them as evidence. Much depends on the purpose of the research and its key research questions. In summary, the main advantage of historical research lies in its uniqueness in terms of its sole focus on the 'past' (in contrast to contemporaneous retrospection). According to Fraenkel and Wallen (2003) its main disadvantage lies in the historian's inability to control for threats to internal validity. Such disadvantages are apparent in other forms of documentary research, but are further exaggerated in historical research in relation to its dependence upon specific kinds of primary and secondary sources.

See also:
Coding (14); Diaries (30); Documentary Research (34); Life History (58); Writing (118).

54 Ideal Speech Situation

Jurgen Habermas, the German philosopher, developed the idea of the ideal speech situation as an alternative to correspondence theories of the relationship between discourse, or speech acts, and their referents. The importance of this idea for educational research is that it provides an alternative to both positivist/empiricist approaches to validity and radical relativist approaches that sever the relationship between discourse and reality. However, there is a more important reason for paying attention to this concept, and this is that it provides an underpinning for critical epistemologies and ultimately critical approaches to the curriculum.

Educational research aims to determine the truth of statements that are made about educational activities and procedures. Habermas (1972; 1974; 1989) suggests that it is not possible to establish a one-to-one relationship between description and reality. Educational researchers cannot establish facts about the world, an aspiration of positivist/empiricist methodologists. All they can do is describe procedures by which truth claims are evaluated. This means that certain conditions have to be fulfilled before they can determine the truth of the matter. Habermas argues that in an ideal speech situation, all impediments to understanding have been removed, so participants fully understand all the technical issues involved in the discussion, have competence in, and understanding of, the procedural issues and dynamics of the discussion, and have participative competence, in that they are able to participate fully in the discussion. Implicit in this is the elimination of power differentials between participants. The communicative act is sealed off from the real world in which powerful people are able to distort the process of communication. Relations of power therefore have been equalized.

What this implies is that the language game must be played so that rhetorical devices such as concealment of position, irony, assertiveness, over-emphasis and the like are removed from the equation. Participants in the ideal speech situation, without the impedimenta of differentiated positioning, may now debate and reach agreement that is truly rational. Rationality is therefore understood as properly conducted discourse or communication. Habermas is making a number of validity claims here. In any undistorted communication, participants must accept that:

- what is being argued for is intelligible or meaningful;
- the propositional content of what they say is true;

- they are justified in what they are saying;
- they are sincere when they speak.

Thus, truth refers to the reaching of agreement through critical discussion when all the barriers that distort communication have been removed.

The ideal speech situation has been criticized on a number of grounds. First, it is regarded as an ideal, something to which participants can aspire, but ultimately not reach. It is therefore in this sense a regulative idea. Second, it has been criticized by positivists/empiricists because it builds into the research act an implicit ideological element; it is opposed to the idea that a simple relationship exists between reality and language. Scott and Usher (1999) suggest further problems, albeit from a different ideological perspective than positivism. The ideal speech situation requires language to be undistorted, a pure and transparent medium of communication, which even if it could be realized, would end all communication rather than undistort it. No argument, even purged of ideological elements, would be possible, as language would simply reflect the truth of the matter. For postmodernists, the ideal of rationality is inherently unsound, as they would understand the promotion of rationality itself, even if constructed through undistorted communicative processes, as an ideological matter.

See also:
Critical Theory (22); Discourse (31); Empiricism (36); Positivism (75); Postmodernism (76); Power (77); Realism (83); Validity (113).

55   Induction

Induction is a principle that is much used in educational research, and is frequently contrasted with deduction. Whereas a deductive approach starts off with a hypothesis about the relationship between two educational variables and then proceeds to prove or disprove it, an inductive approach is concerned with collecting facts about educational activities, and then combining, compressing and synthesizing those facts into a coherent theory which takes account of all of them. Induction, deduction, retroduction and abduction are modes of thinking that underpin particular methodological strategies. Indeed, these various modes of thinking are related to particular strategies. For example, grounded theory is essentially an inductive strategy, whereas experimentation is essentially deductive.

Harré (1972) represents the inductive principle in three stages:

1. Scientific knowledge in this mode is characterized by the process of accumulation. Scientific knowledge consists of a series of facts about the world, and it grows by the addition of new facts, which do not affect the integrity of the old facts.
2. 'There is a form of inference of laws from the accumulated simple facts, so that for true statements describing observations and the results of experiments, true laws may be inferred' (Harré, 1972: 42).
3. There is a process of instance confirmation, where a greater number of instances of an event being observed allow a greater degree of belief in the law.

Blaikie (1993) subsumes these three principles into a four-stage model:

1. All facts are observed and recorded without selection or guesses as to their relative importance.
2. These facts are analysed, compared and clustered, without using hypotheses.
3. From this analysis, generalizations are inductively drawn as to the relations between them.
4. These generalizations are subject to further testing.

As we suggested above, a typical inductive strategy is grounded theory, but even here, there are elements of deductive theorizing. In its purest form (Glaser and Strauss, 1967) the researcher is enjoined to avoid presuppositions, other hypotheses and previous research studies, and enter the research field with an uncluttered mind. Grounded theory procedures entail ten steps: data collection; transcription of the data; category development; category saturation; definitional abstraction; theoretical sampling; axial coding; theoretical integration; theory grounding; and gap filling. Glaser and Strauss later modified their original *tabula rasa* approach and accepted that researchers are theoretically sensitized before they enter the research field. However, this points to two main criticisms of inductive theorizing (cf. Popper, 1976). The first is that because a number of similar events have occurred, educational researchers should not then conclude that a causal relationship has been established; they cannot extrapolate from past experiences to future occurrences. The second criticism is more serious, and this is that all observations are theory-dependent. It is literally not possible to observe anything without some pre-conceived schema to understand it, even if subsequently that schema undergoes modification.

Most inductive strategies have elements of deduction built in, so that it is possible to talk about dominant–less dominant designs, where the dominant component is inductive and the less dominant component is deductive. This is because, though theory is developed from the data, that theory is subsequently tested against new data, and because the researcher generally accepts that they should be theoretically sensitized before data collection starts. Inductive strategies, or even the use of an inductive device as a part of a strategy, are commonplace in educational and social science research, and usually take a grounded theory form. The key to using an inductive approach in educational research is that the theory that is subsequently developed both emerges from and is grounded in data collected in real-life situations.

See also:
Abduction (1); Causation (11); Data Reduction (25); Deduction (27); Experiment (44); Generalization (50); Grounded Theory (51); Observation (71); Positivism (75); Retroduction (97); Variable Analysis (116).

56 Interpretivism

The interpretivist tradition has exerted a strong influence on educational research over the last 30 years, and is best exemplified by symbolic interactionist approaches. The basic tenets of interpretivism can be easily expressed. Social actors negotiate meanings about their activity in the world. Social reality therefore consists of their attempts to interpret the world, and many other such attempts by those still living and those long since dead. These are real and constitute the world as it. Thus interpretivists subscribe to a realist ontology. Educational researchers insert themselves into this continual process of meaning construction in order to understand it.

Interpretivism, therefore, in its purest form separates itself from social constructionism, adherents of which argue that social reality can be described in a number of different ways, all of which are equally valid. For interpretivists, it is those interpretative processes that constitute reality. The researcher is therefore engaged in a process of re-describing or reconstructing these processes, and turning lay accounts into social scientific explanations of social phenomena. The key questions for educational researchers are whether it is possible to represent adequately these lay accounts in a different language, and whether this different language immediately distorts what it is trying to re-describe. Interpretivists, therefore, rely on the self-reported accounts of lay actors as they engage in the various meaning-making activities that constitute their lives.

There are a number of problems with this research perspective. The first criticism has been alluded to already, and this is that in its purist form it does not take account of the multi-perspectival nature of descriptions of social reality. Second, rarely do social actors engage in deliberative activity about their actions. As Giddens (1984) suggests, routine is the most common form of behaviour, and as a result continuous reflection or reinterpretation occurs infrequently and then perhaps only at the behest of the researcher. Third, unadulterated re-description of someone else's reasons for their actions is not possible. This is because that re-description always involves a re-evaluation of the account and re-setting of it in a different context. Social scientific accounts are therefore always significantly different from lay accounts.

Fourth, purist forms of interpretivism are unable to account for institutional and discursive structures that position the individual in various ways. This is in part because social actors are unaware of them, and therefore cannot take account of them in the self-reflexive and self-reporting interpretations that they make. The fifth criticism that has been made is more fundamental. This suggests that it is illegitimate to conflate these interpretive activities with a full and complete understanding of the world. Educational researchers may want to argue that self-reports of their interpretations and deliberations by social actors are central to understanding social life, but this cannot exhaust knowledge of social reality. Further to this, the individual is unlikely to be in a position to understand fully the conditions for their actions. For all these reasons, interpretivism in its purest form is not usually considered to comprise a full and adequate account of social reality and how it can be known.

Within the field of educational research however, the notion of interpretation as distinct from the interpretive paradigm has considerable currency. This is best expressed in interview studies that focus on how lay actors construct meanings about their activities and actions; or biographical/autobiographical research perspectives that focus on past and present constructions of meanings by individuals; or in depth research studies that use self-reported accounts as the first phase in understanding educational processes and activities. In this latter case, educational researchers offer critical accounts of lay actors' understandings of these processes and always go beyond what they are told by respondents. The justification for this is both in terms of the adequacy of the accounts that they themselves eventually produce, and in terms of a depth ontology to which they subscribe. Though interpretivists have some commonalities with empiricists/positivists in the sense that their ontology is realist and they reject a multi-perspectival epistemology, they are different because they prioritize the construction and negotiation of meaningful activity in their research projects.

See also:
Biography/Autobiography (8); Critical Realism (21); Critical Theory (22); Discourse (31); Epistemology/Ontology (38); Interview (57); Realism (83); Reflexivity (87); Social Constructionism (99); Structure (103); Symbolic Interactionism (106).

57 Interview

Much has been written and published already about *how* to conduct interviews in educational settings. (See Powney and Watts, 1987; Hitchcock and Hughes 1995; Pole and Morrison, 2003, for examples.) Here we focus on the key ideas which underpin them. Interviewing seems a deceptively simple way to find out what interviewees think, say and do, and how researchers interpret the telling. The most common of all methods used in education research, interviews yield different kinds of data depending on the purposes for which they are being used and the kinds of interview most amenable to those purposes. As a starting point, all interviews focus upon a verbal stimulus to elicit a verbal response (Silverman, 2001) but purposes will determine different approaches to the collection, management and analysis of such 'responses' as data that involves different approaches to explication and justification.

At a general level, interviews sit in various positions upon a continuum of qualitative–quantitative approaches to research. At one 'standardized' end are highly structured interview surveys that pay close attention to the task of collecting large amounts of data, in as focused a way as possible, through use of proforma like ringing codes, the use of numerical values, tick boxes, and so on. Here, as May (1993: 93) puts it, the interviewer attempts to control and 'teach' interviewees to 'reply in accordance with interview schedules'. At the other end, there are semi- and unstructured interviews that encourage interviewees to respond open-endedly and 'to answer a question in his or her own terms' (ibid.). Interviews vary, then, in relation to the degree of structure, interview purposes and length, depth and range, relationships between interviewer and interviewee and the locations in which interviews take place. More importantly, however, interviews vary in accordance with the philosophical starting points that underpin them. This means that a reading of the epistemological and methodological bases of interviews and interviewing is a necessary prerequisite in research designs that involve them, and include the inferences that might be most appropriately drawn from the analysis of such data.

Structured interviews are usually survey-based and are designed to explore certain predetermined areas using questions that are designed in advance, and are prepared in accordance with one or more specifically stated research hypotheses or questions considered in a descending 'ladder' of abstraction from broad hypotheses to specific questions. They are standardized to the extent that the question, its wording and sequence in the interview are fixed and identical for every interviewee who is usually referred to as the respondent. Using a relatively large sample of the total population and drawing upon statistical techniques in order to draw inferences that might be applied to the whole population, the use of the term 'respondent' is not, therefore, accidental since a core issue is to effect a design that transfers large amounts of data for analysis with minimum 'contamination' of the data by the interviewer and involves a more 'passive' role for the interviewee, thus ensuring the application of reliability and validity instruments most closely aligned to the 'scientific' method. This makes probing and clarification more problematic though not impossible, usually in terms of a pre-designed code or value that can be assigned to the probed-for responses. Philosophically, the core underpinning is positivist, and the endpoints of such approaches are to 'supply' facts about the educational world that are, in combination, reliable, valid and independent of the settings in which the interviewer(s) collected the data.

Towards the other end of the interview continuum, while qualitative researchers might differ about the extent to which they apply 'standardized' interview techniques, the core issue for researchers who use interviews in qualitative research is to seek in-depth understandings about the experiences of individuals and groups, commonly drawing from a small sample of people, frequently selected purposively, and with a de-emphasis rather than a necessarily whole-scale rejection of generalizability. The terms usually applied to such interview forms are 'unstructured' and 'semi-structured', although, as Pole and Morrison (2003: 30) argue, such terms are something of a misnomer, in the sense that 'unstructured' interviews *are* structured in accordance with a systematic research design, and ' "semi-structured" has become a kind of "catch-all" half-way house between structured and unstructured interviewing that commonly allows the interviewer greater flexibility to introduce "probes" for expanding, developing and clarifying infor- mants' responses'. The key issue and purposes for such interviews are requirements for the interviewer to define the interviewee as a person who is actively constructing his/her own world, and to draw upon the interview text to develop insights into such worlds. Again, the use of the term 'informant' rather than 'respondent' is not accidental, since it signals a specific kind of relationship between the interviewer and the interviewee, in which there is awareness by the interviewer of the ways his/her orientations and experiences will affect the collection and interpretation of data, and that the relatively 'open' framework for information gathering will result in new themes and issues emerging in the course of data collection. The sense here is of emerging themes that are grounded in the data collected from interviewees, rather than pre-determined prior to data collection.

The use of a continuum to refer to kinds of interview almost inevitably disguises subtle differences in understandings about different kinds of interviewing, including those which relate to its key purposes. For example, qualitative approaches to interviewing may draw on a range of perspectives. Following Silverman (2001: 87), we might draw on two perspectives, namely those of emotionalism and construction-ism, to identify subtleties in purpose and scope. Hence, from the perspective of emotionalism, informants are:

experiencing subjects who actively construct their social worlds. The primary purpose is to generate data which can give an authentic insight into other people's experiences. The main ways to achieve this are unstrucutured open-ended interviews usually based upon prior, in-depth participant observation. (ibid.)

This telling-it-as-it-is mode contrasts with the perspectives derived from constructionism in which

interviewers and interviewees are always engaged in constructing meaning. Rather than treat this as standing in the way of accuarate descriptions of 'facts' or experiences, how meaning is constructed becomes part of the researcher's topic ... A particular focus is upon how interviewees construct narratives of events ... and people and turn-by-turn construction of meaning (ibid.).

That many adjectives have been used to describe different kinds of interview reflect their multiple and diverse purposes. 'Structured' and 'formal' are usually applied to survey interviews. 'Ethnographic' is frequently applied to qualitative versions of semi- and unstructured interviews, notwithstanding debates about the need and/or the interviewer's capacity to capture the informant's 'voice', and in a range of formats in which, for example, 'conversations' can sometimes overlap with interviews (Hitchcock and Hughes, 1995: 163). 'Directive' and 'non-directive' are also used to denote maximum or minimum interviewer control over the interview, its direction and its content. 'Life history' interviews provide opportunities for in-depth understandings about individuals, usually achieved through sequenced interviews, and the development of constructed narratives of events, episodes and lives within and beyond education. 'Diary' interviews are increasingly used to supplement the 'mute' evidence provided by diaries, either in the form of pre- or post-diary interviews in order to reinforce purpose and access and retrospective analysis respectively (Morrison, 2002a). 'Group' interviews are often used interchangeably with focus groups. The distinctive nature of the latter, however, lies in the sense in which its key rather than supplementary purpose lies in the importance and nature of the interaction between group members, rather than the cumulative effect of a range of individual perspectives that might be encouraged either through the presence of others or to enable sensitive issues to be aired in a group rather than on an individual basis. The term 'enriched' is sometimes applied to individual or group interviews when interviewees are presented with specific material as a spur to reflection and engagement with the key purposes of the interview.

Whichever prefix is applied, the analysis of interview data will also reflect the epistemological and methodological purposes of the research, in order to arrive at conceptual and theoretical coherence. For large-scale survey interview analysts, the emphasis will be upon an initial exploration of the data to check for data or sampling errors, followed by detailed statistical analysis to inform the inferences that might be drawn from the data to a wider population. For small-scale unstructured interview analysts, the emphasis will be upon an iterative and reflexive engagement with the data through all phases that are also subject to systematic audit. Watling (2002: 272) describes this as 'formative analysis' to 'reflect the epistemological and ontological aspects of qualitative research projects which seek to provide understandings and actively shape the types of data collection that will go on'. In qualitative interviewing, initial analysis begins when detailed data is summarized by the use of a descriptor, most often described as a code. Codes develop from being descriptive and/or literal data to interpretative and then explanatory and abstract data, moving towards a conceptual analysis which owes much to a discovery or grounded approach to research. From a quantitative perspective, survey interview analysis similarly reflects its epistemological purposes, in which, in order to arrive at a satisfactory predetermined question, piloting is crucial. Surveyists frequently prepare coding books in advance of an interview survey, code data twice to increase reliability, and prepare coding frames that are transposed onto the interview schedule, commonly known also as the interview questionnaire. There is an emphasis upon the application of measurement, and a number of tests are applied in order to establish relationships between independent and dependent variables (that are addressed by responses to interview questions), measure the strength of such relationships, compare means, establish a correlation between variables, measure that relationship through regression analysis, and so on (Pell and Fogelman, 2002).

Increasingly, the contrasts provided by a continuum between quantitative and qualitative interviewing are not as clear-cut as might be inferred from above. However, in Chapter 66 we highlight the epistemological as well as methodological challenges, as well as strengths, in mixing methods (see Mixed Methods (66)). Interviews will continue to play an important part in the education researcher's toolkit, as long as their strengths and limitations are appreciated:

> Interviews focus on what people *say* they say, write, and do *rather* than what they [necessarily] do say, write and do ... meanwhile, interviews demand much of the researcher in terms of sensitivity and ethical awareness. (Pole and Morrison, 2003: 35, their emphasis)

Different kinds of interview make a range of demands and over varied timescales. It is, therefore, essential that, in combination, all of the above are considered carefully before selecting interviewing rather than other kinds of research activity.

See also:
Coding (14); Conversation Analysis (17); Diaries (30); Discourse (31); Ethnography (40); Focus Groups (48); Generalization (50); Grounded Theory (51); Life History (58); Mixed Methods (66); Narrative (67); Qualitative Research (80); Quantitative Research (81); Questionnaire (82); Reliability (91); Sampling (98); Social Constructionism (99); Survey (105); Telephone Interviews (108); Validity (113).

58   Life History

Life histories are stories or narratives recalling events in people's lives. Their form varies as has their use by a variety of disciplines. In education and social research their popularity has waxed and waned but more recently life history research has been revitalized. Earlier disfavour linked to disjuncture from positivist paradigms. More recently, their use in education research has increased, initially with respect to teacher and pupil trajectories, but also in relation to the interrelations between educational policy and practice, and to the multiple effects of gender, class, ethnicity and, most recently, disability, upon the experiences of individuals in education institutions and beyond.

Hitchcock and Hughes (1995) make the distinction between 'retrospective' and 'contemporaneous' life histories. In the former, the emphasis is upon the reconstruction of a life from memory; in the latter, life histories focus upon individuals' daily lives 'in progress'. The distinction might be seen as exaggerated in the sense that all life history accounts are retrospective in that they involve reflection and 'looking back'. It is the conjunction between the education researcher's curiosity to understand contemporary culture by seeking out the voices of educational actors in order 'to make the familiar strange' and 'the oral historian's interest in understanding the past' that is of key interest (ibid.).

It is not difficult to understand why life history accounts appeal specifically to qualitative researchers. As Coffey (1999: 128) points out, research informants portray, and researchers interpret, 'lives' as 'sequences, consequences, time, causality, structure and agency'. Life histories, therefore, provide opportunities for detailed understandings usually in the context of a constructed narrative of events and episodes.

As Pole and Morrison (2003: 35-9) explain, the disciplinary heartland of life history is anthropology. Educational researchers' interest lies in how the 'folks' encountered in educational settings 'cope with' the educational experiences encountered by them, rather than upon the way that educational systems and structures 'cope with' the stream of individuals who pass through them (Mandelbaum, 1982). In such ways:

> Life history interviews allow researchers to consider what informants *think* is happening in education, what they *expect/ have expected* to happen, what they *make happen* and what *has happened* to them as a consequence of schooling and/or educational experiences. (Pole and Morrison, 2003: 35, their emphases)

Life histories have biological, cultural and social dimensions. Often the emphasis is upon what Mandelbaum (1982: 148) described as 'principal turnings' or changing points in individuals' lives, and how individuals adapt to such experiences, in order to make sense and give meaning to lives and careers.

In educational research, life histories have been used in a variety of ways, sometimes to link pupils' and teachers' histories with school histories and patterns of curriculum development and educational innovation (Goodson, 1983; Goodson and Sikes, 2001; Hitchcock and Hughes, 1995).

In addition, as Pole and Morrison (2003: 36) record:

With increasing emphasis upon reflexive and reflective practitioner practice among teachers and teacher researchers (discussed, for example, by Skilbeck, 1983; Elliott, 1991), there has been a resurgence of the genre that foregrounds autobiographical and, on occasion, intensely personal, sensitive, and provocative aspects of teacher, pupil, and researcher experience.

In this connection, Pole (2001) recalls the use of life histories with teachers of black and minority ethnic origins in which he was able to locate their teaching careers within wider life experiences, in multiple, consecutive interviews that lasted between one and two hours.

Conducting life histories requires much of both the informant and the researcher. Patience, inquisitiveness and empathy on the part of the researcher are key. For informants, the approach demands a willingness to be open and analytical, often confronting issues in their lives not confronted previously. As Goodson and Sikes (2001) suggest, the use of life histories is not for the faint-hearted. Moreover, as Pole and Morrison (2003: 36, their emphases) note:

Considerable skills are required by researchers who probe the lives of participants who are seen as 'active doers and seekers' rather than 'passive research participants' in educational activity (Mandelbaum, 1982: 50). It should also be apparent that life history interviews are usually multiple and time-consuming and demand prolonged commitment to people and situations. Life histories bring into sharp focus research skills in *getting in, getting on*, and *getting out* of research situations and relationships.

The rationale for life history is that it provides unique insights into people's lives. The approach is not without methodological concerns. In part, these relate to the specificity of the data that is based on single instances. The tools of 'storying' also vary. Individuals may write experiences down, in the presence of the researcher or not, or speak into a tape recorder. Or, accounts may be written down by the researcher either in note form or tape-recorded in interviews with the researcher. The researcher then analyses the data and presents the final account. The 'writing up' also varies – from transcripts left relatively unchanged by the researcher, to more heavily amended extracts of the life history, again edited by the researcher. The extent of editing may vary, as might the level and depth of analytical insights incorporated by the researcher into the life history report.

All this suggests that the reconstruction of life history texts varies in form, with recent emphasis upon minimal rather than maximum reconstruction, that has been influenced, for the most part, by ethnomethodological, feminist and postmodern tendencies. For Stronach and MacLure (1997), for example, the telling-it-as-it-is aspect of life history becomes part of the process of 'subduing' and ordering the data in order to produce coherence in the final account. Such coherence is viewed by them as problematic in the sense that 'narratives that promote coherence, singularity, and closure, and aim to set up a close camaraderie with the reader are ultimately conservative' (ibid.: 57).

All interviews demand much of the interviewer in terms of sensitivity and ethical awareness. Life history interviews make specific demands. These require particular vigilance in the 'storying' of individual experiences that remains at the heart of educational research, especially in its ethnographic and qualitative forms that focus upon interviews and journal or diary keeping.

See also:

Agency (4); Anti-racism (6); Biography/Autobiography (8); Culture (23); Diaries (30); Ethnomethodology (41); Feminist Research (47); Gender (49); Interview (57); Narrative (67); Positivism (75); Postmodernism (76); Qualitative Research (80); Structure (103); Writing (118).

59 Linguistic Discourse Analysis

What people say and do is of key interest to researchers in education. Linguistic discourse analysis focuses upon the minutiae of talk and texts, written and spoken, and can be located historically in classroom research, and, in particular, the analysis of classroom talk. Linguistic discourse analysis has been defined as 'the study of language in use' (Cameron, 2001: 10 cited in MacLure 2003: 182). The term 'in use' suggests that language is a system which is then applied and interpreted in a 'real world' context, such as that of the classroom or school management team meeting. Linguistic discourse analysts have studied language use in a wide range of formal and informal education settings. Early studies on classroom talk (for example, by Sinclair and Coulthard, 1975) focused upon a three-part structure in a classroom exchange, described by them in terms of 'initiating' moves by teachers, 'responses' by pupils, and 'feedback' by pupils. Such research would later capture the imagination of sociologists of education who were particularly interested first in relations of power, authority and subordination in classrooms, later in the effects of class, gender and ethnicity, and the comparative studies of 'home' and 'school' language (see Brice Heath, 1983), which later coincided with curricular concerns to provide pupils with the linguistic and student-centred skills they would need for life and careers (MacLure, 1994).

Linguistic discourse analysis constitutes a *bricolage* of approaches, borrowing insights from linguistics, sociology, education and psychology. As such, it remains centred in the discourses of the classroom and/ or the small-scale and specific, rather than upon the macro-discourses which might inform, yet extend beyond, what is spoken and written about in the contexts of bounded micro-structures like the classroom or staffroom. For critics, this tends to exclude 'other' readings of what might be going on in classrooms and staffrooms. For example, Stronach's (1998) early work pointed out that the so-called emancipatory discourse of student-centred learning, typically heralded under the banner of vocationalism, might otherwise be 'read' in terms of changes in the regulation of young people from externally imposed disciplines, invoked by teachers as 'external' disciplinarians, to 'internal' forms of self-regulation (or, in Stronach's terms, subtle forms of 'witchcraft').

Critics of linguistic discourse analysis accuse its proponents of crude empiricism and of a rather opportunistic scavenging of social theory; proponents defend their approach in terms of their skilled and insightful linguistic understandings about talk and texts. As MacLure (2003: 186) has recently noted, in all forms of discourse research, 'each "side" ... finds something lacking in the other'.

See also:
Conversation Analysis (17); Critical Discourse Analysis (19); Documentary Research (34); Empiricism (36); Textuality (110).

60 Literature Review

The literature review is a guiding light for the whole research process. It can be a guide to readers and writers of research in finding an appropriate path through the research, or it can be like a warning flash light marking out potential obstacles and problems. Our starting point is to encourage readers to consider literature review as a method in its own right. A review is a detailed interrogation of the literature underpinning a research topic. The term interrogation has a specific meaning and involves a critical examination of sources not only from a range of theoretical perspectives but also in terms of the definitions and methodologies underpinning those sources, linked to their importance for the research study. A literature review is *not* a literature search, although the latter is a technical process essential to the former. A search is the process of producing a summary list of published literature in the researcher's area of interest and requires distinctive skills. These are crucially important in the exercise of research, but are not equivalent to, or a substitute for, critical review.

Critical readings of published literature are integral to academic inquiry, although the form taken shows cultural variations. With increased globalization and the growing internationalization of student experience, some but not all variations are diminishing. The interplay between critical reading and critical review writing can understandably generate anxiety, especially among those new to research in education. This is more than a competency issue; there is a complex intermeshing of factors, like deference to experienced and/or published authors or a reluctance to engage in readings that stand in direct or 'threatening' opposition to one's own perspectives or experiences in education. However, although some academics in education may not always provide the most appropriate role models to follow, especially in relation to such challenges, it is the critical literature review that lies at the heart of academic inquiry and is rooted in critical engagement with the published discourse of significant 'others' in education and education research.

The term 'critical' is therefore central to interpretation of literature review. A range of authors have offered useful pointers to its meaning (Wallace and Poulson, 2003; Haywood and Wragg, 1994; Lofthouse and Whiteside, 1994). So, what makes a review critical?

- It shows insight and a subtle blend of perception and understanding. This requires 'an attitude of scepticism' (Wallace and Poulson, 2003: 6) towards researchers' own as well as others' knowledge, and the processes deployed to produce such knowledge.
- It provides the researcher and the reader with a 'picture' (historical, methodological and/or theoretical) and an understanding about the issues that the 'picture' raises and, as importantly, omits. This requires a questioning and scrutinizing approach in checking and cross-checking published claims to 'truth'.
- It requires an open-minded and constructive approach in covering the thinking of writers who do not support the ideas of the researcher as well as those who do, and, as importantly, 'a willingness to be convinced if scrutiny removes your doubts, or unconvinced if they do not' (ibid.).

Finally:

- It excludes destructive criticism including that which challenges 'other people's worth as people' (ibid.).

For all research writers, reviewing the literature is a continuous process. It begins before a research problem is fully formulated and it continues until the research is finished. There is something of a paradox here (see also Kumar, 1999: Chapter 3). An effective review cannot be undertaken fully until the researcher has formulated his/her research problem/focus yet the initial literature review also enables the researcher to formulate the problem. However, it is also the case that while most reports of academic inquiry locate the literature review near the front of the report, its uses in defining a hypothesis (or not), in predefining concepts (or not), will depend on whether the research is primarily quantitative or qualitative in orientation and the latter will also, in part, be determined by methodological orientations to exploring 'new' literature that arise from, or are grounded in, emerging data, and are more commonly associated with qualitative approaches.

Because a literature review provides the reader and the writer of research with the state of knowledge in the area of study, it is important to identify the types of knowledge that will be variously identifiable in published texts (although not as clear-cut as the distinctions below might suggest).

Such knowledge may be:

- Data-focused, that is, clearly concerned with the collection, analysis and outcomes from the empirical research previously conducted by the author(s).
- Theoretically focused in relation to the identification of themes, concepts and theories. In education, these may be expressed at the micro-, meso-, or macro-levels. Commonly in education, there are a number of theories described as 'middle range'. In each case, reviewers will need to interrogate the paradigmatic, epistemological and methodological concerns, perspectives and contexts (whether temporal, cultural, or geographical) that underpin the words of the author(s) and their reported actions. Often these are made explicit but sometimes they are not.
- Practitioner-focused, in which the primary interest is upon the perspectives, actions and experiences that, in combination, comprise the practice-knowledge that drives the writing.
- Policy-focused, that is, often visionary and/or prescriptive in defining 'what is' or 'what ought to be' in the researcher's area of interest, and with, as well as without, the support of related

published research or consultation with practitioners. (Adapted from Haywood and Wragg, 1994; and Lofthouse and Whiteside, 1994.)

There are a number of challenges in the production of a critical literature review. The most common is to misrepresent the review as a summary of a literature search that may also be unfocused. A 'leaving-no-stone-unturned-and-summarizing-any-literature-that-is-remotely-connected-to-a-research-topic' approach is not unusual among first-time researchers in education, and is especially problematic when a primary purpose of research is to tell a coherent research 'story'. In this respect, the advice of Wallace and Poulson (2003: 27–8) is especially helpful in identifying eight features of a potentially 'high-quality' review. It is:

1. focused on an explicit substantive, conceptual or methodological question or sub-questions.
2. structured to address that question or sub-questions.
3. critical, in the manner described above.
4. accurately referenced.
5. clearly expressed.
6. reader-friendly.
7. informative, with analysis and synthesis in response to the question and/or sub-questions clearly articulated and delimited.
8. balanced, in the sense of a careful weighing of argument and counter-argument, in which judgments are based on the relative strengths and weaknesses of the literature.

In 2005, there are three additional challenges facing the reviewer and reader of published education literature and research. These are briefly summarized below.

Literature sources

Even before the acceleration of search and retrieval strategies and the widespread availability of literature (by multiple and electronic means) brought about by advances in ICT, the potential for literature overload existed. This has now accelerated even further and has both practical ramifications both in terms of search and retrieval up-skilling and also the complexity of the researcher's task in selecting out from a wider literature base that which will form the basis of his/her review, some elements of which may be more credible than others. This demands even more of the researcher in terms of monitoring current and emerging trends in the researcher's topic area, but is also an accelerating indicator of the need to resist seeing a literature review as a finite activity that occurs at the start-point of research. All researchers will 'stop reading' towards the end-point of their project, if only to ensure that the project report writing is completed! The key point is advocacy of integrative and critical reading through the lifespan of the research topic, which also takes into account finite resources and realistic expectations of what a review can and might achieve.

ICT, Meta-analyses and plagiarism

The second point is a corollary of the first in the sense that accelerating technological advance is also giving rise to a growing 'industry', frequently web-based, of off-the-peg literature reviews that are available in almost all disciplinary areas. This is, of course, not to undermine the legitimacy of meta-analyses, statistically based, which have been conducted to provide summaries of individual studies, and are discussed, for example, by Fraenkel and Wallen (2003: 89). However, even putting aside the question of whether such meta-reviews are, in reading, summaries of available studies, rather than critical reviews (and in which sense), the temptation for first-time researchers may be to import them as 'data' into their own research. Two issues arise: the first relates to the nature of the importation and whether the reviewer can do, or does, a 'review of the review'; the second relates to acknowledgement of use and reported increases in incidences of plagiarism, especially of the web-based variety, in other words, taking the work of (an)other writer(s) and using it as if it was one's own in order to mislead the reader. Such plagiarism can extend to accompanying illustrations, tables, maps and diagrams, and is an important reminder of the need for accurate referencing in a literature review.

Literature types

The third point is that while the breadth of literature may be increasing at an accelerating rate, the issue of its depth and range may be more challenging. This is increasingly the case where the funders of education research, for example, restrict funding to the most applied forms of research and/or place limitations on dissemination by published writing. In the UK, for example, it has been located as part of 'the larger framing debate about what research on education policy is, or should be, in whose interests it is undertaken, who does it and how problems in education policy research and resources for addressing them are defined' (Ozga, 2000: 3), written up and published (or not). Such issues reinforce the importance of scrutinizing both the presence *as well as the absence* in the types of knowledge being reviewed or, indeed, made available for review. This may be especially the case when a reviewer is attempting to evaluate the methodological approach that underpins a specific inquiry, and discovers that these are either excluded or summarized briefly, as an appendixed item, for example.

Finally, it is important to note the importance of distinguishing between published documents as integral to the critical review of sources that underpins all research, and the use of documents as a means of surveying education policy and practice in ways that provide an alternative to observation, interviews or questionnaires, for example, which are discussed elsewhere in this volume.

See also:

Dissemination (32); Documentary Research (34); Epistemology/Ontology (38); Evaluation (42); Historical Research (53); Methodology (65); Paradigm (72); Qualitative Research (80); Quantitative Research (81); Referencing Systems (86); Writing (118).

61 Longitudinal Observation Studies

An example of a longitudinal observation study is Blatchford (2003), which focused on classroom size effects. Though this study included a qualitative dimension, longitudinal studies, and this one was no exception, are in the main quantitative, as the purpose is to make comparisons over a period of time. Blatchford's study sought to compare student achievement (expressed as performance on a range of literacy and numeracy tests) over three years of full-time study. The rationale for the study was to examine how class sizes with different students and with the same students at different points in their education impacted on their performance in these tests. This was an observational study conducted in real-life time and not an experimental study in which the research team deliberately manipulate the social setting by randomly allocating students to differently sized groups for the purposes of making comparisons between their achievements over a period of time.

Two cohorts of children were observed. The first of these numbered 7,142 spread out over 330 classes in 199 schools; the second numbered 4,244 spread out over 212 classes in 134 schools. Each cohort was followed for three years of schooling in English schools beginning at Reception (4–5 years), continuing through Year 1 (5–6 years), and finishing in Year 2 (6–7 years). Information was collected for each child about: term of entry, free school meal eligibility, age, ethnic background, pre-school attendance, English as an additional language, special needs status and gender. Information was further collected about class size at a given time point, and numbers and presence of other adults. Teachers completed questionnaires in relation to age, experience, non-contact time, professional training and job satisfaction.

Data about pupil performance was collected by means of the Avon Reception Entry Assessment at pre-Reception. Tests on reading progress and mathematics were administered at the end of the Reception year; Young's Group Reading and Mathematics tests at the end of Year 1, and National Curriculum Assessments at the end of Year 2 were used to ensure that scores could be recorded on a number of attributes at a series of time points during the first three years of compulsory education. In addition, a classroom mapping process to plot group composition and involvement was used. An instrument was devised and used to determine teacher estimates of time allocation, in particular as this related to teaching activities and classroom management and other non-teaching activities. Systematic observations were conducted with Reception-year children, involving pre-set category identifications at 5-second intervals to determine how children behaved in interactions with their teachers, with other children and on their own. Question-naires were also sent out to teachers to record their experiences of class size and how it affected teaching and learning over the year, and the contribution from other adults in their classrooms. Case studies, involving the collection of qualitative data, were made to provide a more in-depth picture of how individual classes functioned, focusing in particular on different class sizes. Finally, a pupil behaviour rating scale was used to measure hyperactivity/distractability, aggressiveness, anxiety/fearfulness, sociality and exclusion.

This long list of data-collection activities indicates the extent to which the research team sought to take account of all the various factors that they thought might impact on how class sizes affect pupil learning. Using multilevel modelling techniques to control for different variables at different points in the analysis allowed the research team to make a number of claims. These related to the relationships between class size and attainment, class size and within-class groupings, class size and teaching, class size and teachers' and pupils' behaviour and class size and pupil attentiveness. The use of mixed methods allowed a measure of triangulation and deepened understanding of the processes under scrutiny.

There are a number of distinctive features of this type of research. First, data categories are pre-set to allow for mathematical modelling of the relationships between the variables. Though qualitative data in this particular project were collected in the form of case studies, they were not used in the primary analysis but as a confirming and validating measure. Second, the primary focus of longitudinal observation studies is on statistical relationships and associational or correlational con-structs from which causal relationships are inferred. Critical realists would argue that this underplays the workings of mechanisms and depth structures. Third, research subjects are reduced to sets of observable and measurable categories and therefore essentialized.

The longitudinal nature of this study, the attention to detail, and the collection of large amounts of information about the effects of class sizes allowed the research team to have greater confidence in their conclusions. This was clearly an advantage of this method. Further to this, the design used was non-experimental and thus the team of researchers felt better able to make claims about the transferability of relationships between the variables to other settings in place and time, and this strengthened the external validity of their study (cf. Blatchford, Goldstein, *et al.*, 2002; Blatchford, Moriarty, *et al.*, 2002; Blatchford, 2003; Blatchford, Edmonds, *et al.*, 2003).

See also:
Assessment (7); Case Study (9); Causation (11); Correlational Research (18); Critical Realism (21); Experiment (44); Gender (49); Generalization (50); Mathematical Modelling (62); Mixed Methods (66); Observation (71); Qualitative Research (80); Quantitative Research (81); Question-naire (82); Reductionism (84); Regression Analysis (88); Statistics (100); Tests (109); Triangulation (112); Validity (113); Variable Analysis (116).

62 Mathematical Modelling

Researchers who mathematically model educational systems and processes generally use non-experimental designs which attempt to make associations and draw correlations between data that refer to naturally occurring events. In other words, mathematical modellers work on data that is collected after the event, and in some cases would have been collected anyway without any direct intervention from the research team. In contrast to experimental designs, mathematical modelling has strong ecological validity and proponents therefore feel entitled to make strong generalizability claims. The knowledge that is produced is intended to be propositional, predictive, quantifiable and reliable. Policy-makers are particularly attracted to this type of educational research, as it provides information that can be used to develop policies to allow control over the various parts of the education system.

Mathematical modellers have been criticized in a number of ways.

- The effect of their work is to trivialize and distort knowledge of educational systems and activities, and they make deterministic assumptions even if they are of a probabilistic kind.
- They examine regularities in nature and not underlying causal mechanisms, though they frequently conflate the two. This is because qualitative dimensions can only be inspected by instruments that are sensitive to this type of dimension.
- They misunderstand the nature of the systems they are examining, so they assume that they are referring to closed systems, whereas most educational activities take place in open systems.
- Though they are successful at describing the relations between quantitative properties of objects, they assume that the same types of treatment can be applied to qualitative dimensions of objects.
- They adopt a form of analysis in which the individual is reduced to a set of properties that work in a deterministic fashion, although the data that has been collected for inputting into the model is time- and place-bound.
- The property, the way it works and relations between properties can never be directly inspected, so mathematical modellers work with indicators, which are approximations of the property to which they refer.
- The quality of the modelling is determined by the quality of the data from which it has been derived, so value-added modelling of schools and colleges is only valid if the original data that is collected also properly relates to the setting it is seeking to describe.
- They make certain parametric assumptions about the behaviour of objects that do not allow them to examine the emergent nature of objects and relations between them.

Models of educational and social systems are only successful if they can predict how those systems and individuals within the system will operate in the future. It is highly significant that few nomothetic statements about educational systems have been made.

See also:
Causation (11); Closed and Open Systems (13); Critical Realism (21); Determinism (29); Empiricism (36); Prediction (78); Qualitative Research (80); Quantitative Research (81); Reductionism (84); Reliability (91); Statistics (100); Value-added (114); Variable Analysis (116).

63 Media

The media play an important part in the way educational agendas are framed. Newspapers and the spoken media select some items for inclusion in their outputs and exclude others. Furthermore, each item is constructed in a certain way to have a specific effect. Galtung and Ruge (1973) identified two sets of conditions which partially explain why some events are reported and others not. They are: 'general news values' and those that 'specifically relate to the Western news media'. The list of conditions is as follows:

- *Immediacy*. A newspaper or broadcasting outlet has certain deadlines to keep and a news item is included if it fits better with these deadlines.
- *Competition for space*. Whether an item is included, and where it is placed in the newspaper or news programme, is dependent on the amount of space available on the particular day, which in turn is determined by the amount of newsworthy items available to hand.
- *Continuity and coherence*. Whether an item is included, and how much space it is given, is to some extent determined by whether it fits with the ideological slant of the newspaper.
- *Scope*. The 'size' of an event determines its newsworthiness.
- *Cultural proximity*. In a similar way to the idea of geography, cultural boundaries are drawn daily as a result of decisions made by editors of newspapers and news programmes. Events that make better sense in terms of the cultural values of the editor are more likely to be reported on than events that do not accord with them.
- *Unambiguity*. Journalists and broadcasters generally seek to reduce the complexity of events so that their meaning is relatively unambiguous and focused. This works in three ways. First, choice of event or item is made in terms of whether the argument that the reporter makes is relatively straightforward and does not refer to too many other events or items. Second, the event is chosen on the grounds that its reporting is able to give a coherent message to its readership or audience. Third, and more importantly, the event is chosen if it is able to support a coherent ideological message that is favoured by the newspaper or broadcasting station.
- *Ability to excite*. Educational events and activities are more likely to be reported if it is thought they might excite or provoke a reaction in their readers.

- *Ideological agenda.* This refers to the way items of news are selected because they conform to the agenda of the news outlet.
- *Reference to elite persons and nations.* Reporters and editors map the world in certain ways. There is an established hierarchy of values, i.e. some people and some events are more important than other people and other events.

The second issue concerns the way the item of news is constructed. This is achieved in a number of possible ways.

- *The creation of consensus.* Newspaper reporters and broadcasters seek to create a consensus that is often expressed as 'our'. For example, they may refer to 'our nation', 'our schools', 'our people'.
- *Stereotyping.* Language works by creating taxonomies of meaning and attaching evaluative connotations to particular words. It does this by creating ideal types and the media uses these ideal types to frame particular educational events or, the actions of particular people, or to characterize certain individuals.
- *Personalization.* The highlighting by the media of persons is an important part of the way reporters construct stories. The media have to sort and process a mass of information and present a coherent and compelling picture of it to its readers and viewers. This inevitably involves the simplification of a complex picture. This simplification is achieved by personalizing individuals, but only as examples of types, those types having been established in the minds of regular readers and viewers by other stories and by other discursive devices.
- *Positive and negative legitimizing values.* Journalists construct a moral as well as an ideological agenda. This is partly a function of their desire to influence the political agenda, and partly a function of the process of simplification referred to above. Simple negative and positive values are attached to certain types of people and certain kinds of activities.
- *Selection.* Reference has already been made to the way items of news are selected and understood as newsworthy. These criteria comprise: immediacy, competition for space, continuity, coherence, scope, cultural proximity, unambiguity, ability to excite, ideology and reference to elite persons and nations.
- *Audience.* Finally, journalists always have a particular audience in mind and thus treat the issue being reported in terms of how they understand that audience. This means that a tabloid journalist works in a different way from a broadsheet journalist and tailors their reporting accordingly. This refers to complexity of meaning, complexity of argument, length of words used, length of

sentences used, length of article, relationship between illustrative material and written text, amount of illustrative material used and seriousness of content.

See also:
Reductionism (84); Values (115); Writing (118).

64 Method

This term refers to the tools or techniques used to collect, analyse and interpret data in education research. Commonly, methods are described in terms of quantitative techniques that apply statistical calculations as well as the many other techniques described elsewhere in this volume under headings like interview, naturalistic and systematic observation, and focus groups, for example.

Methods also constitute the procedures and, as importantly, the procedural rules that enable education researchers to confirm that the knowledge they have created has reliability and validity. Methods can be further categorized in terms of three types of rule-focused procedures. The first pertains to the rules for establishing the key elements of the study, like hypotheses, theories and concepts. The second pertains to the rules for collecting the data, and the third to the rules for analysing and interpreting the same.

Method is, therefore, clearly distinguishable from methodology that describes the philosophical and epistemological frameworks within which the rules and techniques are applied. It is the relationship between methodology and method which gives the research study its intellectual credibility and legitimacy.

Readers of research might understandably be confused by the diverse and overlapping ways in which terms like research 'approach', 'strategy', 'method' and 'methodology' are used (and abused). Moreover, there are debates about whether some 'techniques' like survey or case study, as two examples, constitute 'methods' or 'approaches' or 'strategies'. Denscombe (1998: 7), for example, defines survey as a 'strategy that encompasses a broad range of methods such as questionnaires, interviews, documents, and observations'. What makes the strategy distinctive is 'commitment to a breadth of study, a focus upon the snapshot at a particular point in time and a dependence upon empirical data' (ibid). Elsewhere, 'case study' can be viewed as a 'method' that contrasts with a survey or experiment in its detailed and bounded focus upon one or a small number of units for analysis, but also as a 'distinct research paradigm' (discussed by Gomm *et al.*, 2000: 5–7) that entails specific assumptions about 'how the social world can and should be studied' (ibid.: 5) and involves 'a contrast between [survey and] positivism, on the one hand, and naturalism, interpretivism, and constructionism on the other' (ibid.).

Finally, there are overarching concerns (by Scott, 1996, for example) to view method in terms of the mutually implicating relationships between method, theory and what comes to be defined as data or authoritative evidence in educational research, that is then judged by researchers and others as legitimate knowledge. Some researchers have preferred to focus upon the appropriateness or otherwise of particular methods for addressing specific kinds of research problems, while other researchers look at the fit or lack of fit between some research methods and 'standpoint' or 'empowerment' research, for example, or between research methods best suited to study the macro-, meso- or micro-aspects of education. In combination, such debates continue to draw researchers' attention to the epistemological as well as practical and technical issues that confront researchers who apply specific methods in their investigations.

See also:
Case Study (9); Empowerment (37); Epistemology/Ontology (38); Experiment (44); Methodology (65); Strategy (101); Survey (105).

65   Methodology

Methodology is the theory (or set of ideas about the relationship between phenomena) of how researchers gain knowledge in research contexts, and why. The 'why' question is critical since it is through methodological understanding that researchers and readers of research are provided with a rationale to explain the reasons for using specific strategies and methods in order to construct, collect and develop particular kinds of knowledge about educational phenomena. Methodological interest in the design, process and outcomes of educational research requires that readers do more than draw conclusions on the basis of data that is provided as evidence, since it is the researcher's interpretation of what is worth knowing, how to collect the knowable, and then to interpret it, that is a core aspect of what becomes known as 'truth' (notwithstanding that such readings will be interpreted differently in relation to truth(s)). As Scott (2000: 25, our emphasis) points out, the interpretation of data has to be set in a variety of contexts that may be 'epistemic, cultural, historical, personal, *and even more importantly, methodological'*. This lifts disputes about which research method or strategy has most veracity to issues that relate methodology with epistemology (or knowledge) and ontology (the reality we seek to know) (ibid.: 11).

In education, it is argued, methodology has specific significance since its core concerns are human beings. As Griffiths (1998: 36–7) comments, 'unlike the physical sciences, educational research is always on/for/with other people – and getting knowledge is a complex matter'. Complexity is signaled for three key reasons: 'human agency; social relations, especially the effects of power; and ethics' (ibid.). In terms of human agency, 'human beings construct meanings for the events in which they participate' which impacts on what is knowable about human beings and how researchers 'could come to know it (methodology)' (ibid.). Griffiths points further to the issue of unequal power relations between the researcher and research participants, particularly when there is a tendency for researchers to come from a particular sector of society. Such issues have been of key concern to anti-racist and feminist researchers. This leads Griffiths to the third, perhaps most fundamental aspects of methodological interest, namely, those which relate to ethical issues. She argues:

> Research can be on/for/with human beings, and the categories 'on' 'for' and 'with' are ethical categories ... Thus in the human sciences there are ethical issues which have methodological implications. This is something of no concern in the physical sciences. In drawing this distinction I am drawing attention to only one set of ethical concerns. There are others which are shared by all researchers, including those in the physical sciences. An ... example ... is the ethical concern surrounding the uses to which knowledge can be put. This is as much a matter for nuclear physics ... as it is in studies of race in education. However, such concerns have no methodological implications. (ibid.: 38–9)

Not all educational researchers are as convinced about the relationship between epistemology and methodology as the writers cited above. Elsewhere, research methods texts have given primacy to the level of a fitness between methods used and their purposes in enabling researchers to address specific research problems. In part, this might be considered to represent a reaction against 'the somewhat doctrinaire posturing' characterized by debates across the qualitative–quantitative research divide (Bryman, 1988: 173). Another relevant development has been the blurring of what might be thought to constitute 'professional development' activities and those viewed as 'academic' research activity. While the popularization of practitioner and action research has largely been welcomed in relation to a Stenhousian emphasis upon reflexive professional research inquiry to effect improvements in educational practice, warning notes have been sounded about the 'all-singing/all-dancing practitioner-researcher' and the 'fetishing' (Brown and Dowling, 1998: 165) of research methods in the absence of a dialogic engagement with methodological and epistemological concerns.

See also:
Action Research (3); Anti-racism (6); Epistemology/Ontology (38); Ethics (39); Feminist Research (47); Method (64); Power (77); Qualitative Research (80); Quantitative Research (81); Writing for Academic Purposes (119).

66 Mixed Methods

Traditionally, methodological strategies and methods have been designated as mainly or entirely quantitative or qualitative. Indeed, in important respects, the two Qs have been thought to represent more than different ways of researching the world; instead they have been considered as competing perspectives or as largely uncontaminated (by the other) 'bundles' of epistemological assumptions, sufficiently divergent to constitute different ways of knowing and finding out about the social world.

More recently, attempts have been made to question the assumption that 'quantitative' and 'qualitative' methods represent opposing ways of researching educational phenomena. Arguments in favour of mixed methods are both technical and epistemological. Let us introduce the technical position first. Here, key concerns are about practicality and appropriateness; the idea is that mixed methods can and should be applied if, in combination, they provide the best opportunity to address the research problem set. The problem then becomes a technical one, namely, how best to deploy hybrid approaches to address the research problem (Bryman, 1988). This view has been variously expressed. For example:

> Can qualitative and quantitative research be used together? Of course. And often they should be ... The important thing is to know what questions can best be answered by which method or combination of methods. (Fraenkel and Wallen, 2003: 443)

The second position is epistemological. Here, it is asserted that qualitative and quantitative approaches do not necessarily belong within different paradigms (while not denying that different paradigms exist). In which case, it may be sensible, on epistemological as well as technical grounds, to deploy mixed methods within the same study (Hammersley, 1992b). Discussed in Scott (1996), Hammersley identifies seven ways by which qualitative methods have been distinguished from quantitative methods, in order to demonstrate that such distinctions are of limited value and can lead to misleading conclusions.

1. Both qualitative and quantitative researchers use numbers and, in either case, numbers may not be the best way of reflecting precision or accuracy.
2. Claims made by qualitative researchers about the ecological invalidity of quantitative research are misleading, first because valid and representative data can be collected in artificial settings, and second, because artificiality is also a feature of participant observation, in which the researcher always affects, albeit to varying degrees, the 'naturalness' of the research setting.
3. The distinctions between the focus on meanings in qualitative methods and behaviour in quantitative methods are thought to be exaggerated since investigations of both meanings and behaviour have applied both methods.
4. The concentration upon the natural/social science divide is also considered to be exaggerated. Here, Hammersley argues that many educational researchers would not be unhappy to position themselves in both camps.
5. Furthermore, the deductive/inductive divide is similarly false. He cites the example of ethnographers who would argue that their studies are not merely descriptive but also draw upon the testing of previously formulated hypotheses.
6. The distinction that is made between qualitative and quantitative examinations of culture is also viewed as exaggerated.
7. Finally, the distinctions drawn between the two Qs in terms of idealism and realism are similarly misleading. Here, Hammersley argues that researchers from both 'camps' usually accept that their accounts are constructed but that as researchers they do not invent reality.

In response to Hammersley, Scott (1996) reminds us of the key distinction to be made between different methodological positions and issues in using different research techniques or methods. He reminds us that overarching methodological frameworks provide distinctive ways of approaching research that, following Guba and Lincoln (1994), bring specific understandings about purpose, foci, data, analysis and, indeed, which information collected actually counts as 'data' and why and how. It follows that, at each level of Hammersley's argument, readers may need to distinguish between methods and methodological frameworks, and what appear to be fairly 'surface', and, therefore, minor distinctions (or quibbles) at the level of method are understood as more fundamental at the 'deep' level of overarching research framework.

Moreover, Scott (1996: 63) poses two further questions:

First, do these distinctions refer to what is or what ought to be? Second, is there one correct approach or are different approaches and strategies appropriate for different [research] tasks?

Arguing from an a-paradigmatic position, writers like Bryman (1988) appear to accept as non-problematic that not all researchers make overt the epistemological underpinnings of their work. Scott (1996: 63) questions this: 'what researchers have done in the past, cannot be a guide as to what they will do or should do in the future'. The second point refers to the debate about whether research can accommodate different but complementary approaches. In contrast to Hammersley (1992b), who appears to favour a multi-paradigmatic approach, Scott (1996) places a strong onus upon researchers to select the paradigm in which it is most appropriate to locate and address the research question(s) posed, arguing that this selection will then affect every aspect of research design and outcomes. This includes the nature and method of data collection and the ethical dilemmas to be confronted.

So, is it possible to combine qualitative and quantitative methods? The short answer is yes, but there is strong disagreement about where 'mixing' should begin and end. It is a truism that more researchers *are* mixing methods. Indeed, increasingly, funders and sponsors of educational research openly advocate and require such mixing, in their terms, to enhance the validity of research findings, and, it might be said, to provide a range of findings that maximize value-for-money. Creswell (1998: 564–78) describes at least three kinds of mixed methods designs.

In a *design triangulation*, the researcher simultaneously collects qualitative and quantitative data. S/he then compares results and uses the findings to see if they validate each other. In the *explanatory design*, the researcher collects and analyses quantitative data and then obtains qualitative data to follow up and refine the quantitative findings. In an *exploratory design*, the researcher collects qualitative data and then uses the findings to give direction to quantitative data collection. This data is then used to validate or extend the qualitative findings. (Cited in Fraenkel and Wallen, 2003: 443–4, our emphasis.)

In summary, advocates of mixed methods argue that:

- combination enhances triangulation;
- qualitative research can be used to facilitate quantitative research;
- quantitative research can be used to facilitate qualitative research;
- combination gives a fuller overall research 'picture';
- combination facilitates both 'outsider' and 'insider' perspectives and the research is thus improved by this;
- combination helps to overcome the 'generalizability problem' for qualitative research (this will, of course, depend upon whether generalizability is key to the aims and purposes of the research study);
- combination may facilitate a better understanding of the relationship between variables;
- combination can encourage better links between micro and macro levels of analysis;
- combination allows appropriate emphases at different stages of the research process.

But there are important challenges:

- To what extent is combination 'really' possible when/if both approaches start from different epistemological positions?
- Do researchers have the resources for combined approaches?
- Do published research accounts suggest that even when so-called combination occurs, it is, in reality, more a case of separate work proceeding in tandem rather than combination? (One consequence has been conflict over which findings 'count' most, especially when one set of findings appear to contradict another.)
- Do researchers have sufficient expertise and training to operate in this way?

Two summary comments may be apposite. *First*, much of the debate about mixing methods appears to hinge on whether, in design, process and outcomes, researchers are attempting to mix methodologies or mix methods. Thus in an interpretive case study about the role of teaching assistants in one large secondary school, and where most emphasis is placed upon qualitative approaches, a closed-ended questionnaire survey of teachers, governors and pupils might inform the longitudinal design and processes involved in understanding what teaching assistants do and (others) think they do in that school. Indeed, it is not inconceivable for the researcher to consider teacher assistant practice beyond the boundedness of the case in order to inform his/her understandings of the meaning, experiences and activities that constitute the work and culture of teacher assistantship in the said case.

Second, researchers need to be aware that when mixing qualitative and quantitative methods they may be asking distinctively different, rather than similar, questions. Quantitative researchers generally show a predilection for establishing causes, for testing established theories and for identifying and isolating variables. Qualitative methods appeal to researchers who wish to ground research studies in social actors' specific understandings of educational reality. Even the most enthusiastic advocates of mixed methods sound cautious:

> Nevertheless, it must be admitted that carrying out a sophisticated quantitative study *and* an in-depth qualitative investigation at the same time is difficult to pull off successfully. Indeed, it is *very* difficult. Oftentimes what is produced is a study that is neither a good qualitative nor a good quantitative piece of work. (Fraenkel and Wallen, 2003: 443, their emphasis.)

Perhaps the best that researchers can do, notwithstanding a rigorous and systematic approach to research activity that needs to be understood and valued as distinctive, is to recognize that:

> there is ... always a gap between different [research] accounts, regardless of the sophistication of the representational devices we use. It is in this sense that our claims to knowledge about education must always be approximate. (Scott, 1996: 71)

See also:
Deduction (27); Design (28); Epistemology/Ontology (38); Induction (55); Interpretivism (56); Method (64); Methodology (65); Positivism (75); Qualitative Research (80); Quantitative Research (81).

67 Narrative

A narrative is an account or story. The account is structured in various ways (Labov, 1972; Cortazzi, 1993). Commonly, narratives include an introduction or preamble, a tale or 'string' of critical incidents and an ending, sometimes framed as a conclusion or an evaluation. In education research, narratives are used in several forms where first, the research participant is narrator and second, the researcher is narrator.

Research participant as narrator
Here, the main distinction is between *first*, a narrative by the participant that has been recorded with the interception and intervention of an

interviewer, and subsequently becomes transcribed text, and *second*, written texts that have not. In the *first* category, there are important distinctions to be made with regard to the type and purpose of the interview – from general conversation to highly structured – and about the status of the interview data. The type, purpose and status of the interview and data are linked to the researcher's methodological standpoint.

We can further subdivide the *second* category of participant narrative into solicited and unsolicited accounts. Some written narratives are requested by researchers who invite research participants to write or tell (often into a tape recorder) a story or account that is subsequently analysed by the researcher (with and without the further intervention of the story teller.) Another form of written account is that which has *not* been requested by researchers but is accessed by them as documentary evidence for the purpose of informing the research topic. In education research, the latter has often been used as background or secondary data to inform the research, although the genre of content analysis provides a helpful counterpoint to relative neglect, and can and does elevate such accounts from background status to centre stage. Moreover, as Silverman (2001: 120–2) points out, the rhetorical devices used in such narratives often provide important insights into how writers work to achieve particular effects or descriptions of themselves and the settings in which they operate(d).

Narratives that occur as 'natural' conversations are often viewed as more reflective but less coherent than accounts which are solicited. Natural conversation is not necessarily seen as a disadvantage but as an opportunity for the story teller to think and choose their words, often a key element in action and practitioner research where the potential is to reflect upon and then improve the professional practice of self and those with whom the researcher is working. In education research, teachers' stories have been important elements of this approach (Cortazzi, 1993; Woods, 1985, 1993a and b), especially linked to life history (Pole and Morrison, 2003; Goodson and Sikes, 2001).

Where interview is used as the main narrative tool then it is important to ascertain how the status of the data is understood, and by whom. Silverman (2001: 86–7) identifies three ways in which researchers from three epistemological positions might interpret an interview narrative. First, from a *positivist* perspective, interview data give readers access to 'facts' which can be readily summarized in tabularized forms. Second, from an *emotionalist* perspective, 'interviewees are viewed as experiencing subjects who are actively constructing their own worlds. The primary issue is to generate data that gives an authentic insight into people's experiences' (ibid.: 87). The mode of interview is open-ended or unstructured and the researcher draws upon analyses that approximate, in varying degrees, to the participant telling-it-as-it-is. Third, from a *constructionist* perspective, the interview narrative becomes a topic for investigation in itself. The focus is upon how interviewees construct meanings of events and people, and how this, in turn, is affected by the turns-taking aspects of the interview, as conversation analysis. Each understanding has its strengths and weaknesses but what they all reveal is the key role played by researchers in interpreting and reinterpreting the narratives that will finally become part of the researcher's meta-narrative and research report/outcomes.

Researcher as narrator

In qualitative approaches to research, qualitative description is important, especially in ethnography. Here, the term narrative is used to describe a mode to portray events, in which researchers translate field notes into text using 'a narrative construction of everyday life' (Hammersley and Atkinson, 1995: 250) that following Richardson (1990) is 'valued as a basic tool in the ethnographer's craft' (Hammersley and Atkinson, 1995: 250). What is often described is not a single event, but written analysis as synecdoche, in which the narrative account by the researcher is used to describe and exemplify experiences and action (Pole and Morrison, 2003: 89–90). Qualitative description often treads a careful path between providing vignettes of the 'familiar' and the 'strange' to evoke understandings about 'what is going on here?' and the field worker's notes are often included, which gives readers a sense of the researcher 'being there' (ibid.) and where the search for patterns in the data provides building blocks that are assembled and reassembled to produce 'an intelligent, coherent, and valid account (Dey, 1993, cited in Pole and Morrison, 2003: 92).

In summary, the appeal of the narrative as a research tool is multiple and a number of features are discernible. Crucially, narratives:

- are important as sense-making strategies used by individuals, and years of experience can be 'compressed' into one account;
- are often highly personal and share with all qualitative data the complexities of 'truthfulness' (Gabriel, 1991);
- supply important insights into the story teller (including the researcher) as well as the story;

- are incomplete, and what remains unsaid or unwritten may be as important as what is said and written;
- often 'lead' the listener and reader in specific directions, often linearly with a central thread, an ending, sometimes a moral (Labov, 1972) or an evaluation of the account.

Narratives, then, provide important insights and understandings into the subjective experiences and understandings of individuals and groups. By their nature, findings may be difficult to triangulate, and it might be argued that this makes claims about 'what really happens', in a life or at work or through a career, challenging. Methods applied from mainstream qualitative research, from literary theory, socio-linguistics, discourse analysis and historical research each have a place in narrative research. Elsewhere, postmodernists call for much closer attention to the 'tyranny of the text' (Stronach and MacLure, 1997: 56) and argue the need for continuing attention to the relation between methodology(ies) and the text. Thus researcher

> narratives that promote coherence, singularity, and closure and which continue to set up a close camaraderie with the reader, are ultimately conservative and uncritical of prevailing ideological and representational arrangements. If we refuse to interrogate these forms, we run the risk of promoting an uncritical research practice which, in seeming to present teachers as they 'really are' simply serves to perpetuate whatever iconographies of teacherhood happen to be circulating in the various professional cultures (research, practitioner, academic) at any given time. (ibid.: 57)

It appears that narrative research continues to generate its own, sometimes contested narrative.

See also:
Action Research (3); Biography/Autobiography (8); Conversation Analysis (17); Critical Discourse Analysis (19); Discourse (31); Documentary Research (34); Historical Research (53); Life History (58); Linguistic Discourse Analysis (59); Textuality (110); Writing (118).

68 Naturalistic Observation

For qualitative and ethnographic researchers, observation is centrally implicated. Observation is a key feature of qualitative research. In *naturalistic* or *participant observation*, participation in the activities being observed is essential in attempts to get to the 'inside' of rich and vicarious educational experience. As Pole and Morrison (2003: 20) point out, this has important implications:

> The observer-cum-ethnographer's account includes autobiographical elements, in which researchers are the main research instruments. Among the 'folks' of interest are, therefore, ourselves. And while the degree of participation may vary, all ethnographies involve participant observation in the sense that it constitutes 'a mode of being-in-the-world characteristic of researchers'. (Hammersley and Atkinson, 1983: 249)

As participant researchers write themselves 'in' to the text, they also bring a specific kind of theoretical focus to educational phenomena, described variously by Silverman (2001: 70) as a critical interweaving between research, data collection and emergent theory building; and by Hammersley and Atkinson (1983: 175) as the progressive 'funneling' of observations. Researchers work in educational settings in which they have different degrees of understanding and this may require different levels of participation. A range of observational typologies for naturalistic observations have been described elsewhere (Gold, 1958; Denscombe, 1998). These range from 'total participation' through 'participation in the normal setting' to 'participant as observer' (Gold, 1958: 218). As Pole and Morrison (2003: 23) illustrate in their work, 'most ethnographies in educational settings adhere to versions of the second and third category'.

While all observers face access and maintenance of role issues, 'insider' observers do so in a particular form that extends beyond the issue of making a familiar setting strange:

> While much participant observation will be *overt*, there will be times when it will be less obvious to the research informants that the educator-as-[participant observer] has stepped outside ... his or her role as 'educator' in the setting being explored. In this sense, ... observation can take on more *covert* characteristics, and this delicate interpenetration of roles remains a key aspect of the balancing act between observation that precludes 'interference' in the action being observed, and the maintenance of relations that require both ethically informed consent and the need to maintain distance from informants. (Pole and Morrison, 2003: 25, their emphases)

Fieldnotes are key elements of participant observation and 'while it is rare to record *too much*, the importance of storing and organizing the writing as you proceed can never be underestimated' (Pole and Morrison, 2003: 26, their emphasis). What fieldnotes should contain depends on the research topic but Wolcott's (1981) advocacy of four staged approaches remains pertinent – 'observation by broad sweep; observation of nothing in particular (especially in the early stages); searching for paradoxes and searching for problems facing the group being observed' (Pole and Morrison, 2003: 28). The systematic auditing, management and analysis of qualitative observational data are crucial to judgments about its plausibility, credibility, authenticity and meaning.

Participant observers, especially lone researchers, are especially vulnerable to issues of personal perspectives drawn from one set of senses rather than from multiple observers and/or the tendency to observe the exciting or dramatic. Reflexivity is critical and the approach demanding. For these and other reasons, participant observation is most often used in conjunction with other methods.

See also:
Action Research (3); Correlational Research (18); Ethics (39); Epistemology/Ontology (38); Ethnography (40); Interpretivism (56); Longitudinal Observation Studies (61); Mixed Methods (66); Observation (71); Positivism (75); Qualitative Research (80); Quantitative Research (81); Reflexivity (87); Systematic Observation (107); Variable Analysis (116).

69 Nomothetic Statements

One of the distinctions made between the natural and the social sciences is that the natural sciences allow law-like, or nomothetic, statements to be made about their subject matter, the natural world, whereas the social sciences, including education, only allow ideographic statements because they are concerned with individual cases. This is too stark a distinction, and yet there are few enduring statements about educational institutions and activities. A number of reasons have been suggested as to why educational and social researchers have generally been unsuccessful in developing theories that last over time.

- Social life has an emergent quality to it, in that institutional and discursive structures change over time, and thus descriptions about them are always giving way to new ones.
- The constructs used to describe social life are an implicit part of the life itself. With natural phenomena, the descriptions that are made of them do not and cannot affect the way they operate. Observations of these natural phenomena may in some circum-

stances be affected by the act of observation, but what this refers to is the relationship between the instrument and the phenomena. The constructs developed about these phenomena cannot affect them, though they may have an influence on how researchers investigate them.

- The looping nature (Hacking, 1999) of the relationship between the constructs developed about social life and future occurances means that the original constructs may become redundant and thus have to be reformulated. Hacking is here referring to the way lay actors amend these constructs, so that new ones are needed to explain new social phenomena.
- Human beings reflexively monitor their actions and the conditions under which they perform them. This allows new knowledge to be developed and this new knowledge may affect future processes of reflection and action. Natural phenomena do not have this reflexive capacity.

What this means is that nomothetic statements about social phenomena have this element of instability, and may be replaced at any time by statements that take account of emergent phenomena, including new discursive and institutional structures. The distinction between nomothetic and ideographic statements however, is a false one, in the sense that educational researchers and social scientists, though interested in individual cases, are also concerned with the social and collective dimension to life, trends in behaviours and persistent patterns of human interaction, abstractions and deeper-lying structures or mechanisms that cause observed behaviours. The real distinction is between statements that reflect enduring behaviours in the natural world and fallible statements that reflect emergent structures of both a discursive and institutional nature that are temporary, but at the same time are a part of those emergent structures.

See also:
Critical Realism (21); Discourse (31); Fallibility (46); Hermeneutics (52); Observation (71); Reflexivity (87); Structure (103).

70 Objectivity

Objectivity is an important concept in the field of educational research methodology. It is a contested concept and is therefore used in a variety of ways. It also has a long lineage and has been discussed by philosophers over the last two millennia. The different ways it is used by educational researchers are as follows.

- It is synonymous with the idea of truth, so a conclusion or finding from an empirical research study is said to be true if it is objective. In this sense it carries very little weight as a concept, and only has meaning in so far as it has attached to it those attributes that are associated with truth. Its function is polemical as it seeks to persuade the reader or listener that the finding or conclusion has greater status than one that is said to be untruthful or not objective.

- It is attached to a particular type of research method, strategy or analytical frame, so, for example, a questionnaire is said to be objective because the values of the researcher have been eliminated from the data which is subsequently collected; whereas a semi-structured interview is said to lack objectivity because it is impossible to eliminate the researcher's values from this type of data collection. However, this use of the notion of objectivity is disputed, because the general claim is made that the construction of any research instrument involves the incorporation of values, and the specific claim is made that a questionnaire is so constructed that it incorporates values in the way the questions are framed. Values in this last case are therefore present prior to the collection of data, whereas with other methods of data collection, they are present either during the data collection process or at the analysis stage.

- A third way in which objectivity is used by educational researchers is when it refers to the elimination of bias. A finding or conclusion from an empirical research study is said to be objective if various professional, personal and conceptual biases have been eliminated. A first type of bias may therefore be described as interest-bound. The educational researcher is rewarded by their sponsor, the educational research community or their stakeholder group if they fulfil their part of a bargain, i.e. they are offered remuneration, status or advancement. These drivers may lead the researcher to bias their findings to meet the requirements and expectations of the sponsor, research community or stakeholder. If the researcher is able to identify and then subsequently resist such pressures, their work is said to be objective. A second and more important form of bias is where the belief systems of the researcher contaminate the data and the way it is analysed, so that religious, ethical, political or social biases constitute a distortion of the reality that is being described. These forms of bias may also extend to the intellectual and conceptual frames of the researcher, and for some types of research, i.e. those located within positivist/empiricist perspectives, the overriding concern is to eliminate them from the research activity.

Gadamer (1975) suggests that the elimination of bias is a misconceived enterprise. For him all knowledge-construction is inevitably biased as knowing has to be contextualized in terms of those pre-existing states within which the researcher is located. The process of understanding reality comprises the incorporation of the strange into the familiar so that in any future knowledge-creation activities the researcher is positioned differently from what they were before. He describes this as a hermeneutic circle, and he argues that researchers cannot operate outside it.

For educational researchers, objectivity is a difficult idea to make sense of, and is frequently used as a polemical device. As we have suggested, the elimination of bias, or the achievement of objectivity, is not as straightforward as it seems. This is because educational researchers operate from different epistemological perspectives and therefore construe notions of bias and objectivity in different ways. Further to this, there is the problem of identifying whether one is biased or not, as bias, however it is defined, may be concealed or unconscious. This should not detract from its importance as a concept in educational research, and its continuing use by educational researchers testifies to the need to address the many issues that adhere to the idea.

See also:
Empiricism (36); Epistemology/Ontology (38); Ethics (39); Hermeneutics (52); Interview (57); Method (64); Positivism (75); Questionnaire (82); Research Community (95); Strategy (101); Values (115).

71 Observation

Most people have a sense of what observation is. What distinguishes the everyday observations of 'watchers' from those of educational researchers and social scientists is the 'something extra' done with their data when they 'engage in social scientific writing about "folks" ' (Silverman, 2001: 45). A recurrent activity, all education researchers apply observation in some form as it is their opportunity to listen, watch and record (and often share subsequently with informants) what informants say and do in specific educational settings and time frames.

Herein lies its particular appeal. Moreover, observation provides the opportunity for researchers to record the extent to which research participants actually 'do' what they might say they do when asked in interview or diary, for example. And, in observation, the emphasis is upon what the observer sees people doing and the researcher's application of meaning to the actions observed. This brings attendant challenges; these are initially as follows.

Opportunities

Observation highlights detailed and specific information about educational activities and practice that would be difficult to ascertain in other circumstances. It also enables researchers to sample educational experience first-hand rather than depend on what participants say they do. For a range of reasons, what participants say they say and do in specific situations may be inaccurate. Inaccuracy may be a factor of distorted or limited memory, a determination to present especially favourable (or for other reasons, unfavourable) accounts of 'what goes on here'.

Depending on the circumstance, observation may also be preferred by informants precisely because research might then be regarded by them as a more valuable and valid experience as researchers record that which is rooted in informants' actions rather than distilled from 'remote' theoretical literature reviews, a point made by Foster (1996: 13) in relation to research with student teachers, for example.

Observation also gives another perspective or interpretation of what is being observed, again described by Foster as 'being able to "see" what participants cannot' (ibid.: 13); such forms of 'seeing' benefit from the observer's own experience and expertise, or what Delamont and many others have described as 'making the familiar strange' (Delamont, 1981).

For some groups of research informants, observations provide a means to research which may not be feasible or possible to conduct in other ways with specific groups, like very young children, for example (though it would be important not to exaggerate the distinctive limitations of working with such groups).

Challenges

Intrinsic to such opportunities lie the key challenges. Fundamentally, what the observer sees and then records depends both on the observer's values and the purposes of his/her observations. In such ways, observers may see what they want to see, see what they are used to seeing and understand their observations in ways that they are accustomed or predisposed towards. Observations are thus affected by the values and judgements brought to the observation by the observer, though it is a matter of debate whether such value predispositions are more or less problematic for observation than for other research methods.

Observation is time consuming, potentially both physically and mentally demanding of the observer, and, therefore, resource heavy. Practically, observers are restricted in what they may be able to observe and this raises issues about representativeness. Above all, concern is expressed about whether informants consciously change their behaviour when they are being observed though it might be argued that this tendency might decline in the longer rather than the shorter term (although this may bring to the fore other, equally important ethical issues).

In observation, a variety of methods are used. These depend upon the purposes of the research and its methodological and epistemological bases. There are two principal types: naturalistic or participant *and* systematic or structured.

See also:
Action Research (3); Correlational Research (18); Epistemology/Ontology (38); Ethics (39); Ethnography (40); Interpretivism (56); Longitudinal Observation Studies (61); Mixed Methods (66); Naturalistic Observation (68); Positivism (75); Qualitative Research (80); Quantitative Research (81); Reflexivity (87); Systematic Observation (107); Variable Analysis (116).

72 Paradigm

The word paradigm has become commonplace in educational research and in social theory since its use by Thomas Kuhn in his seminal *The Structure of Scientific Revolutions* (1971). Kuhn argued that science is characterized by a sequence of activities. Normal, conventional and accepted science undergoes a crisis, where current theories and perspectives cannot explain new facts. This in turn leads to new theories and perspectives being developed, which account for both the new and old facts; and which in a revolutionary fashion replace the accepted way of understanding. In turn, these new perspectives become the norm. This way of understanding science is paradigmatic, in that one paradigm and one set of epistemological assumptions have replaced another. In the social sciences and in educational research, paradigms are sometimes also referred to as epistemes (Foucault, 1972) or traditions (MacIntyre, 1988).

Kuhn was heavily criticized for building in a relativist element to his theory of the development of science. However, he himself later suggested that he never intended this, but merely wished to argue for a cumulative theory where science is characterized as the development of better and more comprehensive theories which better explain the world. Revolutions occur when the old and new science seem to be so different that it is possible to describe them as competing. It is still possible, however, to make judgements about either from the perspective of the other.

A more radical reading of Kuhn's work would suggest otherwise, and social constructionists have embraced the relativist dimension of his work. What this means is that any judgements which are made about material or social matters can only be made from within the boundaries of the particular paradigm, episteme or tradition from which they originate. Science and indeed social science loses its cumulative orientation because paradigms are not considered to be inferior or superior to each other (if they were, they would not be paradigms as such, since they could then be arranged in a hierarchical fashion). What exists, if this perspective is adopted, is a series of competing ways of understanding the world, none of which are superior to each other. What this also means is that when a revolution occurs, everything is seen from a different perspective. Since the paradigm is an epistemological construction, it affects everything that individuals do in the world.

In the field of educational research, different paradigms have been developed which are, because of their constituent components, incommensurable. One such grouping is as follows.

- *Positivism/empiricism*, where it is accepted that facts can be collected about the world; language allows us to represent those facts unproblematically; and it is possible to develop correct methods for understanding educational processes, relations and institutions.
- *Phenomenology*, where the emphasis is placed on the way human beings give meaning to their lives; reasons are accepted as legitimate causes of human behaviour; and agential perspectives are prioritized.
- *Critical theory*, where it is accepted that values are central to all research activities; describing and changing the world are elided; and the researcher does not adopt a neutral stance in relation to understanding the world.
- *Postmodernism*, which rejects universalizing modes of thought and global narratives; understands knowledge as localized; and seeks

above all else to undermine the universal legitimacy of notions such as truth and objectivity.

In recent times, the notion of a paradigm has been used to indicate a change in perspective, but this does not imply a radical and epistemologically orientated re-visioning. So, Gipps (1994) refers to different and, in her view, incommensurable ways of understanding educational assessment, where traditional psychometric perspectives are replaced by more holistic and pedagogically orientated perspectives. In its older sense, the notion of a new paradigm refers to a radical epistemological break with what went before.

See also:
Agency (4); Assessment (7); Critical Theory (22); Epistemology/Ontology (38); Interpretivism (56); Phenomenology (73); Positivism (75); Postmodernism (76); Relativism (89); Social Constructionism (99).

73 Phenomenology

This concept has its origins in the work of Edmund Husserl, and was extended and refined by Alfred Schutz and Maurice Merleau-Ponty. Its central idea is the phenomenological reduction, and phenomenologists usually locate themselves in interpretivist or post-empiricist philosophies. This is because they reject the idea that knowledge can only be gained from the senses, but would also want to add that knowledge can be developed from the imagination and through self-reflective activity. The reduction involves a process where the individual puts to one side everything that they know about an object, and traces back how they came to know it. This comprises a suspension of everyday commonsense beliefs in order to know better how those commonsense beliefs were acquired, and the application of a pure form of consciousness.

If this reduction is successfully achieved, then the individual is left with a melange of perceptions, colours, sounds and sensations, which do not literally make sense. This is because those categorizations and relations between phenomena that order the particular world of the individual are no longer relevant to consciousness. The phenomenologist then attempts to build up those pure sense-impressions into meaningful structures. It is a process of self-conscious reduction and construction. Schutz (1972) argued that this involves typification, which is a process of categorizing, synthesizing and differentiating phenomena. This process of construction is particularly applicable to the social world, which involves typifying people and actions, and thereby accessing commonsense, taken-for-granted knowledge about people and relations between people. The process of reduction and construction has the effect of changing the way reality is understood, not least because of the self-reflexive element of the procedure. Furthermore, it allows the social actor access to the way knowledge is socially constructed, and could indeed take a different form in a different setting. It also adds a historical dimension to knowledge.

Educational and social researchers borrowed much from the idea, and many of them operating in the present day would refer to themselves as phenomenologists. However, the phenomenological reduction has in most instances been discarded, as researchers argued that the method, i.e. the stripping away of everything known about the object under investigation, should itself be subject to the reduction, and this could not be achieved without making the whole process impossible to carry out. What has survived from the early writings on phenomenology is the emphasis on the way social actors build up understandings of the world by continually interpreting sense data and re-working previous understandings of the same phenomena, set within the context of other people going through the same processes. Reality is therefore a social construction, and though this has been heavily critiqued for its relativist implications, versions of it are still influential among certain types of educational researchers. These researchers are more likely to place themselves within interpretivist, critical and postmodernist schools of thought, rather than positivist or empiricist ones.

See also:
Agency (4); Critical Theory (22); Empiricism (36); Historical Research (53); Interpretivism (56); Positivism (75); Postmodernism (76); Realism (83); Reflexivity (87); Social Constructionism (99).

74   Plagiarism

Plagiarism is a form of intellectual dishonesty and is the practice of taking the work of another person and using it as if it was one's own in such a way as to mislead the reader. The University of Manchester's guidelines (1991 cited in Bell, 1999: 209) regard plagiarism as 'the theft or expropriation of someone else's work without proper acknowledgement, presenting the material as if it was their own'. Cryer (2000: 137) refers to the Australian Vice-Chancellor's Committee's definition of plagiarism as a form of 'misconduct in research' in which there is 'the direct copying of textual material, the use of other people's data without acknowledgement, and the use of ideas from other people without adequate attribution'.

Some forms of plagiarism are witting thefts of the intellectual copyright or intellectual property rights of authors' works. More often, and specifically in the case of small-scale or first-time researchers, plagiarism may be the result of poor work and study practices, and unwitting falsehood. Understanding how to use and properly acknowledge the work of others usually begins with good learning habits that are derived from accurate note-taking from the early stages of research, and includes careful attention to the technical aspects of referencing and bibliographies as well as careful records of direct quotations and page numbers (see also sections on Writing and Writing for Academic Purposes described elsewhere in this book).

What Denscombe (2002: 59–60) calls 'the temptation to plagiarise' has increased mainly because of the vast increase in sources from which the work of others can be obtained, predominantly through Internet searches, but also because it is now much easier technically to download large amounts of information (or the texts of others) from the same. Forms of plagiarism vary. Maps, tables and illustrations, in common with text, need appropriate acknowledgement. In oral presentations, due acknowledgement to quotes from authors, whether displayed on PowerPoint or overhead transparencies, and/or paper-copied from both, is also necessary.

See also:
Literature Review (60); Referencing Systems (86); Writing (118); Writing for Academic Purposes (119).

75 Positivism

Positivism is a social theory, which views the natural sciences as the paradigm for social enquiry, a major tenet of naturalism. Both positivists and non-positivists disagree about its precise definition. There are three reasons for this. First, it consists of a number of beliefs about the natural and social worlds and ways of investigating them, only some of which are shared by researchers who may still want to describe themselves as positivist. Second, its theoretical base has not remained stable, as a number of distinct variants have emerged in the light of criticism and development. Third, for some researchers, it has become a term of abuse, and this has resulted in a reluctance on their behalf to call themselves positivist, and equally an essentializing of the term by their opponents who reject the general belief without proper consideration being given to some of its parts. It is also related to an empiricist view of the world, which rejects metaphysical and transcendental philosophies and focuses on sense data.

In its traditional form, the following beliefs can be said to characterize positivism (cf. Blaikie, 1993):

- *Phenomenalism*. The only true knowledge is that which can be gained from the senses. Experience therefore is prioritized over metaphysical speculation or rational contemplation. Furthermore, only a certain type of sensory experience is accepted, that is, sense data untainted by consciousness or subjective activity.
- *Nominalism*. Nominalists argue that abstract concepts have no meaning unless they can be derived from experience. Where observations are not possible, then knowledge gained through other means is illegitimate. Religious, aesthetic, metaphysical and ethical notions have this illegitimate status. Language in its purest and legitimate form has a correspondence to reality, and can be described as theoretically neutral. Descriptive terms which are unobservable (abstractions or metaphysical notions) are meaningless unless they can be translated into observable terms.
- *Atomism*. Objects in nature and experienced by human beings constitute the world. Generalizations refer to the constant conjunction of atomistic events, and not to real objects in the world, which have the potential to influence events and observations of those events. These generalizations refer not to causal relations but to empirical regularities.
- *General laws*. This involves a belief that the construction of general laws about social and physical relations are both possible and desirable. Furthermore, these general laws are universal and therefore apply across time and space.
- *Value judgements*. Factual statements can be separated from value statements, so that secure knowledge of the world can be obtained free from any types of values. Observations can be theory-free, and thus it is possible to construct a science of education, which consists of enduring law-like statements.
- *Single method*. There is a single appropriate method for constructing knowledge in the world, which applies equally to the natural and the social sciences.

Various critiques have been made of phenomenalism, nominalism, atomism, nomethetism, value-freedom and single-method. These focus on the difficulties with accessing untainted sense data, the problems with accepting correspondence views of the relationship between language and reality, the a-causal nature of empirical regularities, the non-universality of educational precepts or laws, the value-embedded nature of observations and the differences between the natural and social worlds where human beings, unlike material phenomena, are conscious and can provide reasons for their actions.

Outhwaite (1987) has suggested that there are three principal varieties of positivism. The first is the classical and historically prior variant, popularized by Auguste Comte, where causal laws can be derived from observations and these observations are value-free. However, he did not believe that the natural sciences and the social sciences were so similar that a common method could be developed. The second variant, known as logical positivism, emphasized the virtues of nominalism, but also suggested that in all essential respects the methods of the natural sciences could be applied to the social sciences. Finally, the third variant, variable analysis, led to the development of statistical explanations for social phenomena in the form of universal laws or generalizations, constructed from the constant conjunctions of events. This third variant has been critiqued extensively by, among others, critical realists who have developed a social theory based on a depth and stratified ontology.

See also:
Causation (11); Critical Realism (21); Empiricism (36); Generalization (50); Nomothetic Statements (69); Observation (71); Realism (83); Reductionism (84); Subjectivity (104); Values (115); Variable Analysis (116).

76 Postmodernism

Postmodernist research perspectives embrace a number of different approaches to the study of the social world. However, these different approaches share a number of beliefs. The first of these is a rejection of correspondence views of reality; so the relationship between discourse and reality is never straightforward. Indeed, many leading postmodernist thinkers would subscribe to a view that Bhaskar (1989) calls radical relativism. Here, the only meaningful phenomenon is the text; there is nothing beyond it. The second of these foundational principles is a distaste for universalizing modes of thought and global narratives. Knowledge is local and specific; has no trans-social dimension to it; and is constructed within communities that develop their own criteria for determining what is true and what is false. Judgements made about other social settings and systems across place and time can only be made from the viewpoint of the social setting to which the observer belongs. Knowledge is therefore relative to particular time/space loci. The third foundational principle involves a rejection of ethical and teleological ideas. Foucault (1983: 9) suggests, for example, that

(t)here is always something ludicrous in philosophical discourse when it tries, from the outside, to dictate for others, to tell them where their truth is and how to find it, or when it works up a case against them in the language of naïve positivity.

One of the consequences of this approach is that it then becomes impossible to identify progress in society, which may act as a driver for social change, but in reality merely replaces one social configuration with another. Given that postmodernists reject foundational principles, it is perhaps difficult to categorize a postmodern way of thinking, and this self-imposed lack of legitimacy is a serious problem. Frequently, postmodern ideas are criticized for claiming legitimacy and authority, as any set of ideas must do, and at the same time undermining that claim by denying credibility to these notions.

Postmodern approaches to research therefore reject the idea that it is possible to identify a set of procedures which if researchers follow will result in valid and reliable accounts of social reality. However, what cannot be inferred from this is that every configuration of research approach is equally legitimate; so it is sometimes suggested that the use of quantitative and qualitative approaches within the same research design constitutes a postmodern approach. The arguments for combining quantitative and qualitative approaches are firmly located in rational argument about how best to describe the setting being researched. Postmodernist thinkers would want to argue against the natural legitimacy of this combination of ideas; and locate such argument within the historical development of particular ideas and their combinations, and as relative to the society of which they form a part. In this sense, postmodernism is not a research strategy or approach as such, but a way of transgressive thinking which challenges modernist thinking about research methodology to recognize its own relativistic character.

Lather's (1991) postmodern approach to research seeks to displace orthodoxy and reconfigure research in new ways. It attempts to:

- provide a space for alternative voices and undermine the priority usually given to the agendas held by powerful people in society;

- surface the textual devices used in conventional research and as a result attempt to show how powerful discourses are constructed;
- question how authors construct texts and organize meanings, and again in the process show how language works to construct certain types of truths;
- challenge realist assumptions that there is a world 'out there' waiting to be discovered and reassert the idea that research acts to construct the world;
- explore the various possible ways of constructing alternative realities;
- be concerned with power and the politics of research; indeed, show how these impact on research projects and on the writing of research reports;
- reintroduce the researcher into the picture, and locate the researcher within those frameworks that act to construct them as researchers and as human beings.

In reality, postmodernist researchers generally adopt an ethical position of one type or another, and we can see the development of this in Lather's approach above. The virtue of such an approach is the way it concentrates the researcher's mind on power relations between subjects in the research setting and on the way knowledge is constructed both by respondents and researchers alike.

See also:
Design (28); Discourse (31); Ethics (39); Fallibility (46); Historical Research (53); Mixed Methods (66); Objectivity (70); Power (77); Realism (83); Relativism (89); Reliability (91); Textuality (110); Validity (113).

77 Power

Issues of power are central to an understanding of educational research methodology, though more so with post-positivist perspectives than with positivist/empiricist approaches. This is because some post-positivist perspectives are anti-realist. Reality, for them, is constructed by groups of people operating within communities of practice, and that construction takes place within language. How language is constructed is ultimately a matter of powerful people in society imposing a particular view of the world on that world. This is not to suggest that individual human beings can describe reality in any way they want (a solipsistic viewpoint). Reality is constructed as a result of decisions made by people in societies, many of them long-since dead. On the other hand, realists understand language as representative of a reality that is separate from the way it is described, and though it is possible to be deceived about that reality, social actors can still know that they have been deceived and therefore work out from this a better or more correct description of the world.

Foucault (1979) argued that power should not be understood as merely what someone in a powerful position in relation to someone else does to that other person, but that power is ever-present in all human activity. He describes this as a productive form of power, and sets this against oppressive forms of power. What this means is that knowledge-construction is always a result of the operation of power, and indeed, he elides power and knowledge, so that the one cannot be understood without reference to the other. Productive and oppressive forms of power have significant implications for educational research methodology. On the other hand, philosophers from analytical schools of thought make a distinction between power and authority, thereby legitimizing some forms of influence and delegitimizing others.

If it is acknowledged that the researcher brings to the research setting their own set of values, and more importantly, a particular, even if generally accepted, way of understanding the world, then the act of finding out is an act of imposition, or, as Bourdieu (1977) suggests, the researcher is always engaged in an act of symbolic violence when they interpret data collected from another person; that is, they are symbolically violating the way another person sees themselves. This sense of violation, even if the strength of the metaphor employed by Bourdieu is not accepted, applies equally well to all types of educational research, even if experimentalists and researchers operating with pre-formed sets of categories would want to deny that their instruments are value-laden. If it is accepted that values are central to the act of doing research, then power issues are an essential feature of research.

Two questions arise from this discussion. The first is: how is it possible to know and understand those power relations which structure knowledge-making activities; and the second is: what is the best way of expressing those power relations, since the demands for transparency would suggest that they should not be concealed. Educational researchers who acknowledge the presence of power in their delibera-tions would argue that research can and must be reflexive. Two approaches are possible. The first suggests that educational researchers should be self-consciously critical in their activities and surface those power relations between researcher and researched for the attention of the reader. The second is more pessimistic and this suggests that researchers are inevitably embedded in social structures and forms of discourse which means that they cannot ever fully grasp the specific ways in which power works through them as researchers. But even here, there is an acknowledgement that educational researchers should attempt at all times to surface these power constructs in the conduct of their research studies. In most educational research projects power issues are either ignored or marginalized.

See also:
Coding (14); Discourse (31); Empiricism (36); Experiment (44); Interpretivism (56); Methodology (65); Positivism (75); Realism (83); Reflexivity (87); Social Constructionism (99); Structure (103); Values (115).

78 Prediction

There are some compelling reasons for suggesting that the future is not predictable, that is, the observer can never accurately predict what will happen. MacIntyre (1981) argues that there are four sources of systematic unpredictability. The first of these is what he calls the possibility of radical conceptual innovation.

Any invention, any discovery, which consists essentially in the elaboration of a radically new concept cannot be predicted, for a necessary part of the prediction is the present elaboration of the very concept whose discovery or invention was to take place only in the future. (MacIntyre, 1981: 89)

Predicting a radical conceptual innovation is logically impossible. The second of his reasons for suggesting that prediction is not possible is that people make choices in terms of choices that other people make, and those choices would be meaningless unless they worked under the assumption that those choices had not yet been made. If the person were able to predict what choice they would make, they would not then actually be making a choice, because it would already have been determined. The third of his reasons is that human beings reflexively monitor their actions, and these reflexive moments have the potential to change the conditions in which they are acting and thus make future actions unpredictable. Finally, MacIntyre (1981) suggests that any explanation for what actually happened has to embrace the notion of contingency, and this should not be eliminated statistically from explanatory models because it is the most sensible explanation. And yet, some types of educational researchers are committed to a notion of prediction. For them, two types of prediction are possible. The first approach, a deterministic model, makes the assumption that antecedent conditions are understood as efficient causes of human behaviour. If it is possible to describe accurately the antecedent conditions, and equally to know how the causal mechanism works, then it is possible to predict what will happen when those antecedent conditions are in place. This has been referred to as the billiard ball scenario – the antecedent condition is the striking of the white ball by the cue; the cause and effect mechanism works through the laws of motion; the white ball, if it is accurately aimed, will strike the red ball in a certain way causing it to take a particular trajectory. This is a closed-system scenario. A variant on this incorporates the idea of probability, which allows for the possibility of counterfactual cases. By using various statistical tests, the researcher can determine the likelihood of the effect being observed in other similar settings across space and time. Probability, however, works under the assumption that complete knowledge of the system is neither possible nor forthcoming. Expressing the future in probabilistic terms does not solve the problem of the indeterminacy of social relations. It in effect identifies the number of counterfactual cases that are likely to occur, and their identification is in relation to the amount of knowledge held about the system and therefore the degree of development of the theory being espoused.

Probability however, does not only refer to the degree of ignorance the researcher has about objects and mechanisms, it also refers to the degree to which those processes work in a mechanistic fashion. Normal distribution curves, which underpin parametric probability calculations, are based on previous distributions of particular properties of individuals. Assumptions are made that these normal distributions will continue to operate; and that they correspond to laws in nature. An example of a fairly safe projection is a calculation from recorded birth rates at a set point in time that in five years the number of that age group will correspond given an accepted degree of mortality. Even then, this involves an assumption that the mortality statistics remain stable over the period of time and into the future. Future-orientated probability exercises therefore always make assumptions about the stability of trends over time. If these assumptions are not considered to be serious obstacles in the way of predicting events in the future, then it is possible to provide information that informs policy-making.

See also:
Agency (4); Causation (11); Closed and Open Systems (13); Determinism (29); Distribution (33); Generalization (50); Reflexivity (87); Statistics (100); Structure (103).

79   Publishing

Educational publishing takes a number of forms.

- *Books from independent publishers to which authors are contracted.* These publishers may have a national or an international base, though only two English-speaking countries in the world have a fully developed competitive system of educational publishers, the USA and the UK. Other English-speaking countries round the world have neophyte educational publishing industries or branches of major publishing houses located elsewhere. The industry in the UK consists of four or five major publishers and a number of others that publish shorter educational lists or specialize in other fields but are still interested in publishing educational books. Different educational publishing houses are held in different esteem by the educational research community and the potential readership, so some academic authors may choose one publisher over another to give greater status to their book than if they had chosen another.
- *Books and pamphlets produced by academic outlets.* Many educational departments in universities run seminar series or research series, which they publish themselves. Occasionally arrangements are made with independent publishers to publish jointly with them. This has the advantage of a wider dissemination, publicity and distribution base than can be afforded by the individual institution itself.
- *Academic journals from independent publishers.* These may cover a wide variety of topics within the field, are usually peer-reviewed and may be nationally based or international. Though some of these journals may advertise themselves as international, this has a number of different meanings attached to it: the readership is international; contributions are encouraged from an international field; either the editorial committee may be international or a separate international editorial board is appointed alongside a national board; or the focus of the journal is international or comparative. Academic journals have different statuses among the research community and among policy-makers, and these different statuses are sometimes driven by citation indexes and research assessment exercises. Thus, articles published in high-status journals will have greater credibility than those in low-status journals.
- *Professional journals either from independent publishers or from the*

professional outlets themselves. These may not be peer-reviewed, as the editor working either alone or with an editorial board decides on what is included and what is not included in each issue. The content of these professional journals is focused on practice, and therefore different judgemental criteria are used, and frequently different forms of writing are accepted.

• *The national and international press.* Again, this demands a certain type of writing, is usually of a shorter length, and has a shorter production timescale.

For academics, dissemination through publishing is considered to be a key part of their work. Other forms of dissemination are more orally based.

See also:
Dissemination (32); Power (77); Refereeing (85); Research Community (95); Writing (118).

80 Qualitative Research

Qualitative research has come to denote research approaches that are underpinned by a set of assumptions about the way the social world operates. It derives many of its basic tenets from the perspective that the science of the human world is fundamentally different from that of the natural world, and therefore needs to deploy distinctive (often interpretative) methods. Here, the focus is upon seeing the world through the eyes of those being studied and upon developing concepts and theories that are 'grounded' in multiple stages of data collection, in which the characteristics of design are constant comparisons of data with emerging categories and theoretical sampling of different groups to explore similarities and differences.

Drawing from Morrison (2002b: 19–21), qualitative research has a number of key features.

• Research centres upon the subjective realities of research participants (although qualitative researchers may disagree about the extent to which those realities are reconstructed and/or reinterpreted by themselves). This means that understanding those perspectives is critical, and that criticality pertains regardless of whether the subjects are children or adults. For example, Mayall (2000) emphasizes the importance of children's perspectives, as research 'with' and 'for' rather than 'on' children, and this reflects a powerful (re-)emergence not only of the need to empathize with research subjects but also to penetrate the meaning frames in which they (in this case, children) operate. This need to penetrate the subject's world strongly suggests a preference for lengthy immersion 'in the field' as a participant observer or by serial life history interviews. In 2005, the approach is replete with challenges, not least of which may be 'seeing through *whose* eyes' and the pressure to produce findings over the shorter timescales now characteristic of funded research. Nonetheless, the intention is to see 'from the inside' through empathetic understanding or *verstehen*.

- Qualitative researchers give detailed attention to observation, often described as naturalistic or participant observation. The essence is rich and deep description of individuals, events and settings, in which few details are excluded, in order to ask 'what is going on here?'

- In qualitative research, detailed attention is given to the holistic picture in which the research is embedded. This is more than attention to detail. The approach taken is that researchers can *only* make sense of the data if they are also able to understand the data in its broader educational, social and historic context.

- Because qualitative research is frequently concerned with processes of learning, adaptation, innovation or change, there is usually a longitudinal element to the research and no shrinking from the commonplace, or what Miles and Huberman (1994: 6) call the 'banal'.

- There may be a reluctance to impose prior structures on the research investigation so as not to foreclose issues unknown at the start, though this ought not to be misconstrued as a reluctance to be systematic. 'The researcher is the main "measurement device" of the study' (ibid.: 7) and a case can be made for 'pre-structured qualitative designs' as well as 'loose, emergent ones' (ibid.: 17). Linked to this point may be a reluctance to impose prior theoretical frameworks. Instead, notable writers in the field have written about the importance of 'sensitising concepts' (Blumer, 1954) and 'conceptual frameworks' (Miles and Huberman, 1994).

- The emphasis is upon words rather than numbers, although this should not be exaggerated. Nonetheless, textual analysis dominates with words, symbols and artifacts the main units of analysis. These 'can be organized to permit the researcher to contrast, compare, analyse and bestow patterns upon them' (ibid.: 7).

- Finally, above all, qualitative researchers recognize that they are part of, rather than separate from, the research topics they investigate. In such ways, researchers impact upon participants and participants impact upon researchers. Reflexivity is at the core of qualitative approaches.

It is clear that the links between qualitative and interpretative approaches are strong, but it is equally clear that the word interpretivism encompasses a range of philosophical traditions that include ethnography, phenomenology, ethnomethodology, symbolic interactionism and naturalism, and that these, individually as well as collectively, impact variously on the design, process and outcomes of qualitative research. What connects the philosophies is a set of distinctive principles about what it means to conduct research *with* people:

> Thus the world of the educational researcher is different from the world of the natural scientist, and all educational research needs to be grounded in people's experience. For interpretivists, reality is not 'out there' as an amalgam of external phenomena waiting to be uncovered as 'facts', but a construct in which people construe reality in different ways. (It may be that some human groups perceive reality similarly, but this does not diminish the potential for reality to be construed differently.) (Morrison, 2002b: 18)

In education, qualitative research has been used mainly to investigate the small-scale. While the appeal may be to the uniqueness of in-depth exploration, the extent to which it is possible to make empirical or theoretical generalizations from one or a small number of cases is widely debated (Gomm *et al.*, 2000). Some writers have argued that the kinds of inferences that can be drawn from the small-scale are different in type than those that might be drawn from the quantitative, or from large-scale scrutiny (Yin, 1994). Other writers refer to 'naturalistic generalizations' (Stake, 1978) or wider applications in terms of 'fitness for purpose' or 'transferability' (Guba and Lincoln, 1989). Bassey (1999) refers to the concept of 'fuzzy generalization' that carries an element of uncertainty. 'It reports something that has happened in one place and it may happen elsewhere. There is possibility but no surety' (ibid.: 52).

There are differences among qualitative researchers about the extent to which it is possible to 'write' other people's actions and perspectives as if unaffected by the researcher's presence. Hammersley and Atkinson (1995: 19) are unequivocal:

> Once we abandon the idea that the social character of research can be 'standardised out' or avoided by becoming 'a fly on the wall' or 'full participant', the role of the researcher as active participant in the research process becomes clear. He or she is the research instrument *par excellence*.

Finally, we may need to exercise some caution about the distinctiveness of qualitative in relation to quantitative research. As Morrison (2002: 23–5) points out, there may be a tendency to underestimate the degree of overlap between quantitative and qualitative research, noting in particular that qualitative research might also be used to test theories, and that both quantitative and qualitative approaches can and do use numerical data. The key point is to avoid the less than reflective cookbook approaches to combination that assume, rather naïvely, that the shortcomings of one approach can be balanced by the strengths of the other.

See also:
Epistemology/Ontology (38); Ethnography (40); Ethnomethodology (41); Generalization (50); Grounded Theory (51); Induction (55); Interpretivism (56); Mixed Methods (66); Observation (71); Phenomenology (73); Quantitative Research (81); Reflexivity (87); Subjectivity (104); Symbolic Interactionism (106); Transferability (111).

81   Quantitative Research

Quantitative research has come to denote research approaches that are underpinned by a set of assumptions that seeks to apply the natural science model of research to investigations of the educational world. Here, the focus is upon patterns, regularities, causes and consequences in which there is an application of the principles of positivism, that the patterns of the social world have their own 'real' existence.

Seen mainly in linear terms, Bryman (1988) provides an idealized model of quantitive research, although he reminds readers that the 'truth' is often messier than the ideal, with theory not always playing as large a part in quantitative research as might sometimes be assumed. He asserts:

> Quantitative research is often conceptualized by its practitioners as having a structure in which theories determine the problems, to which researchers address themselves in the form of hypotheses derived from general theories. These hypotheses are invariably assumed to take the form of expectations about the likely causal connections between the concepts which are the constituent elements of the hypotheses. Because concepts ... are frequently believed to be abstract, there is a need to provide operational definitions whereby their degrees of variation and co-variation can be measured. Data are collected by survey, experiment ...

Once the survey or experimental data have been collected, they are then analysed so that the causal connection specified by the hypothesis can be verified or rejected. (ibid.: 18)

From the above, it can be shown that quantitative research has a number of key features, also noted by Morrison (2002b: 16–17).

- The relation between concept formation, observations and measurements is crucial, so that how we objectify, observe and measure 'educational attainment', 'leadership styles' and 'intelligence', for example, are key concerns. With this comes the important notion of 'breaking down' the research problem into manageable 'bits' that can be observed and measured. Among commonly used measures in education research are structured observation and questionnaire surveys.

- Quantitative research is also interested in causality, making frequent use of variable measurement, associated variously with cross-sectional and longitudinal surveys, and more recent, mathematical modelling. How do we know a school has 'improved' and by 'how much'? How can we distinguish between an 'effective' and an 'ineffective' school? These are questions that would exemplify the approach.

- In cross-sectional surveys conditions have to be met in order to establish causal relations (Bryman, 1988: 30–4). Researchers need to draw upon statistical techniques to demonstrate that there *is* a statistical relationship between variables. They also need to show that the relationship is non-spurious, and that there is a temporal order to the data studied.

- Quantitative researchers have a key interest in demonstrating that their findings can be generalized beyond the location of their project. This reinforces concern about the representativeness of samples, or the extent to which experimental findings can be generalized beyond the circumstances of the original experiment.

- While quantitative researchers accept that research can never be entirely value-free, they are specifically interested in whether the research can be replicated.

- In quantitative research the emphasis is upon both the individual as the object of the research and the aggregation of individualized data to provide overall measures.

From the above, the affiliation between quantitative research, positivist approaches to educational research and the application of scientific method is clearly discernible. This has a number of distinctive aspects. People are objects of research, notwithstanding their uniqueness from one another and from other objects of the social world. Only phenomena that are observable through experience can validly be considered as knowledge. Internal 'states of mind' as an object for research are, therefore, ruled out unless they can be rendered observable or researchable, like 'attitudes', that can then be measured. Scientific knowledge involves the collection of 'facts' which can be observed 'out there' in the educational world and are distinct from the observer. 'Facts' may then be fed into theories. Many have law-like characteristics because they are based on empirically established regularities. So, for example, the notion that a theory of learning or of educational leadership can be built upon an edifice of empirically established facts is called inductivism. Theories provide an important backdrop to empirical research because hypotheses can be generated from them, usually in the form of postulated causal connections, and this implies that quantitative research is also deductive.

Positivists and quantitative researchers take a particular stance with regard to values. Again, as Bryman (1988) indicated, they do so in two senses. First, it is incumbent upon researchers to purge themselves of values that might impair their objectivity and undermine the validity of their research. Second, positivists draw a distinction between scientific statements and normative ones. Thus 'whilst positivists recognize that they can investigate the implications of a particular normative position, they cannot verify or falsify the position itself' (ibid.: 41). Such a stance has other implications. If positivists do not consider themselves as 'inside' the research milieux they investigate, then it ought not to matter who does the research, provided that others are equally 'expert' or well trained in applying the scientific method. In other words, one would expect that other researchers handling similar data would come to the same conclusions. This may also allow them to predict, in the sense that past observations may enable them to predict what will happen in the future, given similar circumstances and significant* associations between the data.

We have already noted the importance of variables and their measurement for quantitative research. For positivists, human characteristics and attributes can be considered as variables and discoveries about the relationship between them should enable positivists to explain the world they have uncovered.

A note of caution is needed here. The affiliation between positivism and quantitative research is not necessarily recognized by all researchers, and there may be a tendency by some researchers to rationalize their epistemological positions after the event. As Brown and Dowling (1998: 57) comment:

We have chosen not to present the choice of a particular way of collecting data as indicating a strong affiliation to a specific epistemological position. In our view, these associations are commonly post-hoc and are of limited help in either the design or interrogation of research. It is of greater importance in deciding how to collect your data, that the methods are consistent with the theoretical framework in which you are working.

As Morrison (2002b: 23–5) points out, there may also be a tendency to underestimate the degree of overlap between quantitative and qualitative research, noting in particular that qualitative research might also be used to test theories, and that both quantitative and qualitative approaches can and do use numerical data. The key point is to avoid the less than reflective cookbook approaches to combination that assume, rather naïvely, that the shortcomings of one approach can be balanced by the strengths of the other.

* Significance: this term has two meanings:

1. Researchers give reasons why and how the research is important or relevant. This might vary according to the aims and purposes of the research. Thus, importance might be seen in terms of: meeting the needs of specific audiences, adding to the scholarly literature, helping to improve practice, and/or in informing policy.
2. The term refers to measures or tests of confidence that are applied in order to ascertain whether an association between two or more variables is genuine or the product of chance. Statistical significance tests provide benchmarks for researchers to proceed on the assumption that the apparent association is real, or not.

The two terms should not be mixed and in this connection we refer to the second definition in which statistical significance does not necessarily imply social, legal, educational, artistic or political importance.

See also:
Causation (11); Correlational Research (18); Deduction (27); Empiricism (36); Epistemology/Ontology (38); Generalization (50); Induction (55); Mathematical Modelling (62); Mixed Methods (66); Objectivity (70); Positivism (75); Qualitative Research (80); Regression Analysis (88); Reliability (91); Replication (92); Representativeness (93); Statistics (100); Survey (105); Variable Analysis (116).

82   Questionnaire

There is an abundance of published texts about how to do questionnaires. This is hardly surprising given the popularity of survey research discussed elsewhere in this volume and the centrality, though not exclusivity, of questionnaire design to surveys. The emphases upon the linearity of the questionnaire process and the step-by-step delineation of what to do next among published writers might be thought to contribute, in part, to its popularity among first-time and small-scale researchers in education, a popularity that tends to be countered only by a resistance to, or fear of, the statistical analyses that accompany questionnaire surveys and/or a misunderstanding about the range of survey designs and questionnaires that might be used. Questionnaire surveys are often used in a combination of methods. While mixed methods are discussed elsewhere in this volume, it is hard to avoid the conclusion that questionnaires plus 'something else' are not infrequently advocated by both small-scale researchers in education and large-scale sponsors of education (who should know better?), as a safety net for objectivity, scale, breadth and generalizability. For the purposes of definition, the term 'questionnaire' is used here to signify the use of questions to elicit responses in self-completion (by electronic or postal means), face-to-face (survey interviews) and telephone formats in order to generate data that is quantified in a case-by-variable data matrix (Marsh, 1982). Our central focus lies in the ideas that underpin their design and use.

Questionnaires are rooted in the positivist paradigm and questionnaire surveys have been used as mantras for positive and negative critiques of quantitative research. Underpinning both, however, is the sense in which the questionnaire is an appropriate tool for conducting research in both the natural and social sciences, and that the researchable is only that which is amenable to our senses and capable of measurement. Interest in questionnaires falls into three main categories, philosophy, technique and politics. De Vaus (1996) and Burton (2000) discuss questionnaires in terms of these categories. Issues can be summarized as follows.

Philosophy
Philosophical concerns are that:

- questionnaires are empiricist and add little of theoretical value;
- questionnaires are based on a 'science' model of hypothesis and significance testing which lacks imagination or creative thinking;

- questionnaire surveys establish correlations between variables, not causes;
- the questions used in surveys are incapable of getting to the meaningful aspects of social action;
- questionnaires lack context and tend to produce atomistic outcomes;
- some educational 'things' are not measurable. (Adapted from Burton, 2000: 304.)

Amid arguments and counter arguments, we focus upon four aspects: theoretical value, causality, context and creative imagination.

Theoretical value
Questionnaires have been criticized as (simplistically) linear and a-theoretical. In response, Pole and Lampard (2002: 90), for example, consider that the researcher's substantive *and* theoretical agenda is centrally implicated and explicated in questionnaire design, since the choice of instrument ought to reflect a process of theorizing prior to and during data collection and analysis. Elsewhere, Burton (2000: 292) sees social science theory as the starting point for survey design in which the researcher constructs a hypothesis or set of ideas that can be tested: 'Concepts then need to be operationalised so that they can be measured by the use of indicators.' But, *the* key difference between questionnaire surveys and qualitative research, for example, is that conceptual and theoretical frameworks will, of necessity, be mainly predetermined by the researcher. Burton (2000: 293) does not underestimate the challenges involved, specifically in terms of defining concepts appropriately:

> Concepts are contested, in that they have no fixed meaning . . .
> One way of clarifying concepts is to obtain a range of definitions
> . . . an alternative way forward would be to collect together
> previous definitions and search for common elements that would
> form the basis of a definition . . . A much easier approach would be
> simply to use a definition that already exists.

Then indicators need to be developed that reflect the selected concepts. Again, this is more complex than a straightforward linear process of questionnaire design might suggest. For questionnaire designers, then, an important conclusion is that:

> Concepts and indicators are highly contested . . . [researchers and] research students need to be aware of concept and indicator ambiguity and provide a clear rationale for their choice [including the question(s) to be used as the basis for measurement]. (ibid.: 295)

Causality

While there is widespread agreement not to mistake correlation for causality, proponents of questionnaires query whether alternative approaches will necessarily have a firmer grip on causality. While the narratives of long-term qualitative research may sometimes (although not always) provide a clearer enunciation of causality, they often do so, as in case study, in relation to single instances or narrowly bounded systems. Similarly, experimentation might be rejected on ethical grounds. While Pole and Lampard (2002: 94) are clear about the need for researchers to reject 'spurious' relations between variables and the prerequisite to make pre-judgements about what constitutes 'cause' and 'effect', questionnaires are, nevertheless, considered to have advantages when they form part of 'longitudinal survey research, since causality can only work in one direction if it is temporally ordered'. Moreover, survey research, it is argued, can be effective in

> rejecting alternative causal explanations of observed phenomena, since multivariate statistical analysis can demonstrate whether a given third variable explains the relationship between two variables. (ibid.)

This still means that in questionnaires, causality is inferred rather than demonstrated, and the task of the researcher is then to ensure that the statistical analyses are also accompanied by a 'plausible narrative' that derives from 'theoretical reflection' and possibly 'additional data from quantitative or qualitative research' (ibid.: 95).

Context

A criticism of questionnaires is their tendency to divorce the response and the respondent from his/her social contexts, and from other respondents. A counter argument would be to assert that a dismissal of context is not an essential feature of questionnaires, since the research instrument could be designed to include questions about context. Another response would be to deny that contextual effects are central to questionnaire use in which case there may be an acceptance that supplementary methods are needed to investigate context.

Creative imagination

Questionnaire design and use, it is argued, are frequently misunderstood as rather sterile paper-and-pen or hand-to-computer exercises. An important counterpoint to this argument would be to see questionnaire design as a creative process rather than an event. Key aspects of that process would include:

• Theoretical reflection.
• Careful attention to the wording of each question as well as to the coherence of the questionnaire as a whole. The requirement is for careful piloting.
• Recognition that questionnaire administration is *also* a social process, in which the researcher needs to pay careful attention to the likely willingness of the respondent to answer the questions. Hence, attention is given to questionnaire appearance, length and layout.
• Attention to the meanings that would-be respondents will give to the questions, and, as importantly, to the commonality of meanings as understood by the same, and by the researcher. (Adapted from Pole and Lampard, 2002: 103.)

For Fowler (1993) and Oppenheim (1992), *the* key issue is that questionnaires are designed to provide measurement. Above all, this requires questions that must be judged in terms of the question's capacity to promote responses that link directly to that which the researcher sets out to measure, and an equivalence in each question and its asking. Hence, surveyists' preoccupation with question reliability (through test–retest, alternating item order, and so on), measurement consistency, respondents' understandings and propensity to respond willingly, are prime concerns. Not surprisingly, therefore, there is a preference for closed over open-ended questions, and careful attention given to sampling issues, coding and levels of response/non-response.

Technique

Concern about questionnaires is sometimes linked to the technical complexities of design and analysis. At one level, the critique centres on a superficiality that might derive from standardized techniques. At another, it is about the complexity that underpins the logic of statistical analysis and the meanings that can be derived from the same. Hammersley and Gomm (1997: 27) take the critique one stage further by attacking the validity of numerical data, in particular the extent to which numbers disguise 'their constructed character and sources of potential bias built into them'. Proponents of questionnaires accept such criticisms only where questionnaires are designed for inappropriate purposes or designed inappropriately. As importantly, there is an acceptance of the need for detailed qualitative explanation to accompany statistical tabulations, so that the latter are not left to 'speak for themselves', or become open to multiple (or manipulative) interpretations by others, which leads us to the third category of critique – the political.

Politics

All research findings are potentially subject to political manipulation. The argument is that this is especially the case for questionnaires, first because they tend to be larger-scale numerically, and second, because statistics are more prone to manipulation either by the researcher and by 'others' who wish to take various 'readings' from such research for their own end purposes (or include readers who do not understand the statistical findings as reported and/or their implications). Because of this, researchers in education (see Pole and Morrison, 2003, for example) are frequently enjoined to undertake rigorous secondary analysis of large-scale data-sets derived from questionnaires that are already in the public domain. These can be studied as documents for research scrutiny in order to provide contexts, conceptual frameworks and research 'pieces' that contribute to the holistic enterprise of research in and about educational settings. Meanwhile, some of the obvious misinterpretations of statistical findings can be obviated by careful presentation of results.

In recent years, the number and range of formats for questionnaires has increased considerably to include computer-assisted personal interviewing (CAPI) and a range of formats for computer-assisted self-interviewing (CASI). Dependent upon respondents having access to, and the skills necessary to use, computer technology, CASI includes sending would-be respondents disks by mail (DSM), asking them to attend a location where computers would be set up, and/or respond by email or website (discussed in Burton, 2000: Chapter 23).

See also:
Correlational Research (18); Empiricism (36); Objectivity (70); Paradigm (72); Positivism (75); Power (77); Qualitative Research (80); Quantitative Research (81); Sampling (98); Statistics (100); Survey (105); Telephone Interviews (108); Variable Analysis (116); Virtual Research (117).

83 Realism

The question of a real world existing independently from our conceptions of it has exercised the minds of theorists and philosophers for the last two millennia. It hinges on the types of relationships that we can envisage between the way we describe that world and reality itself. A correspondence view of reality, sometimes described as naïve realism, suggests that there is a mirror image between language and its referents. This is now generally acknowledged to be a misleading image, and a number of arguments have been suggested to support this contention. First, observations are conceptually mediated, that is, the researcher cannot observe anything in the world without a prior theory about what it might mean. Social phenomena are concept-dependent. Second, it is difficult to argue that competing views of the world can be resolved by reference to the facts of the case, as what constitutes a fact rests on some prior belief about the nature of reality. Third, to suggest that reality can be mediated in some uncomplicated fashion implies a strict set of criteria being applied to the study of the social world that can be interpreted unequivocally. This again demands not just agreement about this set of criteria because this leads back to a form of conventionalism, but also a certainty that these criteria are the correct ones, and this is impossible to ascertain. In short, there is no Archimedean point of reference outside of language to determine the truth of the matter.

The alternatives to naïve forms of realism are numerous, though three stand out: conventionalism, critical realism and radical relativism. Conventionalists would want to argue that reality is mind-independent, but that the way it is described does not depend in any absolute sense on the nature of the thing-in-itself. Though it exerts an influence on discourse, there are a number of ways of describing it, which are incommensurable and equally valid. They would also want to posit a two-way relationship between reality and conceptual framework, so that reality influences framework, and in like fashion, framework influences reality. Conventionalists are opposed to solipsistic and idealist views of reality, which essentially argue that the individual can understand reality in any way they want, and indeed reality changes if they change their worldview. Conventionalists argue that the network of concepts that mediate reality are the result of power struggles that took place in the past and are presently being conducted, and their resolution, partial but never complete, results in conventions about how reality is mediated. Individuals cannot operate outside of these conventions.

Radical relativists, usually of a postmodern persuasion, move outside the relationship discussed above. The principal relationship that concerns them is between the signifier and the signified, where the former refers to words or images and the latter refers to concepts or groups of concepts. What radical relativists frequently ignore is the referent, that to which the signifier and the signified refer and which is independent of both. In short, they are anti-realist, and this means that any one account of reality cannot be privileged over any other.

Critical realists would want to make a number of claims which are in opposition to naïve realist and radical relativist accounts of reality. First, both material and discursive phenomena have a real existence. Second, observations cannot be theory-independent, but this does not mean that they are theory-determined. Third, there is a two-way relationship between discourse and reality; discourse never simply describes an independent reality. Fourth, they argue for a depth ontology where the collection of sense data about the world is never adequately constitutive of that world, and this means that the observer or researcher has to intervene in the world in order to understand it. Fifth, social phenomena have an emergent quality, which means that notions of reality are determined by both current and evolving ways of understanding the world.

The importance of this discussion about different versions of realism and anti-realism for educational researchers is that methodologies are in part framed, implicitly or explicitly, by different positions on this matter. So, for example, variable analysis is underpinned by an empiricist view of reality, which gives a privileged status to sense data and marginalizes the need for a depth ontology. Radical relativists in turn, committed as they are to the possibility of multiple perspectives about reality, would argue that no one set of methods for bridging the divide between discourse and reality is either possible or feasible. Both these examples suggest that methodologies which purport to operate at the strategy and methods levels are always underpinned by epistemological and ontological assumptions, even if these are not acknowledged. The debate about realism may seem abstruse, but arguments about appropriate method and strategy cannot be resolved without reference to them.

See also:
Critical Realism (21); Discourse (31); Empiricism (36); Epistemology/ Ontology (38); Interpretivism (56); Method (64); Observation (71); Positivism (75); Postmodernism (76); Power (77); Social Constructionism (99); Strategy (101); Variable Analysis (116).

84 Reductionism

Reductionist explanations of human behaviour conceive of an object exclusively in terms of one constituent part of its make-up, or, as Sayer (2000: 89) argues, this constitutes: 'the practice of explaining the behaviour of concrete (that is, many-sided) objects by reducing them wholly to (or reading them off from) just one of their abstract (that is, one-sided) constituents'. A black person is understood as having all the attributes that society has designated belong to a black person, so the categories of difference and sameness apply across, and in a uniform pattern, all the activities, beliefs, attributes and characteristics of the black person, *qua* their blackness. Some characteristics pertain to their blackness, such as a tendency to be discriminated against; other characteristics such as the exercise of certain virtues or even some embodied knowledge do not have a relation to their skin colour though they may be construed as having a connection. Thus in every way they are deemed to behave as a black person, whereas there are many decisions they make and activities they perform that are not influenced by the colour of their skin. Likewise, women are understood as behaving and acting as women regardless of the activity they are performing.

A further variant is where the characteristics given to a group are assumed to apply to individuals in that group. The identification of a group, and the further identification of behaviours which attach to members of that group, mean that boundaries of either a strong or weak nature are established between the group of people and others or other groups. The designation of these boundaries always has the effect of including certain people and excluding others. Furthermore, the designation of these boundaries means that characteristics are given to members of the group, and reductionism occurs when those members are deemed to have in equal measure those characteristics. Frequently, one or more of those characteristics are given priority to the effect that the designated member of the group is understood in terms of the totality of those characteristics that define the group.

The issue is complicated by the looping nature of the relationship between discourse and object. Though a reductionist explanation may in itself misrepresent social life, it may in time come to represent it adequately because the categorization involved has real effects, and individuals then understand themselves and behave in accord with the original reductionist explanation. However, it is important not to assume that it will necessarily change reality. The relationship between the cultural and the ontological is dependent on a range of factors, such as the means of dissemination of ideas in society, and the privileged, or otherwise, status of these ideas. However, reductionism comprises in its initial manifestation a misdescribing of the social relation that it wishes to explain.

Some methodological strategies have built-in reductionist tendencies. For example, mathematical modellers of educational processes and systems argue that it is important to identify discrete characteristics of individuals so that comparisons can be made between types, and so that these variables can be either eliminated as causal factors or implicated in the causal explanation. These reductionist tendencies are best expressed as the marginalization of the intensional dimension of human behaviour and the subsequent translation of those intensional elements into extensional properties. As a result, mathematical modellers are engaged in a process that effectively leads to reductionist and essentialized descriptions of social life. As Wilson (1990: 398–9) argues:

> It is crucially important to note explicitly that use of a mathematical model does not imply that descriptions are untainted by intension. Rather, when we develop and apply such a model we arrange to package intensional idioms in such a way that, for the purposes at hand, we can proceed with formal calculations.

Because variables have to be able to be expressed quantitatively, they have to adhere to the principle of equivalence. The category system that is used, for example, racial classification, has to ignore the many complications that inhere in the production of such lists, not least that the social actors concerned may refuse to accept the criteria that underpin the category system or may be coerced into accepting it (as in the census). Thus for the sake of the modelling exercise, the intensional idiom is reduced or packaged so that it can be expressed as an extensional property.

See also:
Agency (4); Anti-racism (6); Causation (11); Coding (14); Culture (23); Dissemination (32); Epistemology/Ontology (38); Fallacies (45); Feminist Research (47); Hermeneutics (52); Mathematical Modelling (62); Power (77); Quantitative Research (81); Realism (83); Variable Analysis (116).

85 Refereeing

This is a system used by the educational research community to ensure the quality of articles/books before publication. If an article is submitted to a refereed journal or a book proposal is submitted to a publisher, then editors will set in motion a variety of refereeing procedures. In the case of a refereed journal article, the editor of the journal chooses between two and five referees, who he/she adjudges to be capable of examining the piece. These referees are asked to provide a commentary about the piece and to recommend that it:

- should be published without amendments;
- should be published after minor amendments have been made;
- should be published after a major rewrite;
- should be rejected.

The editor then receives back the referees' reports and, if there is a discrepancy between their judgements, may resolve it him/herself or seek a further referee's judgement. In the case of a proposal for a book, each publisher issues their own proforma for completion by the putative author(s). These proformas comprise a series of questions asking for information about the following:

- the rationale and format of the book;
- the contents;
- an outline of the various chapters;
- the intended market;
- competitor products;
- curriculum vitae of the authors.

The editor may also ask for an exemplar chapter, to allow them to make a judgement about the capabilities of the author(s). In turn, they will send this material to a number of referees who will be asked their opinion of the quality of the proposed book, and its marketability.

Peer examination therefore has a number of functions:

- *Quality assurance*, where the piece is judged to be of sufficient quality, and conforming to the specifications and criteria laid down for publication.
- *Product improvement*, in that the referees provide formative advice for the author(s) for the purposes of making it ready for publication.
- *Competitive rationing*, in that where the demand for publication by putative authors exceeds the amount of available publication slots, peer examination allows selection of the best pieces.
- *Improving capacity*, where the ability of the research community and its capacity to judge quality is enhanced.

This brief examination of the process, however, ignores the many implications of such a system. Editors have a two-fold function: to determine which referees should be approached and to interpret their comments in order to make a final judgement concerning publication. Their role in the process is therefore crucial as the choice of referees is central to the judgements that are produced in evidence. The educational research community, from which referees are chosen, is divided about what would be considered to be acceptable research and methodological frames. Two referees drawn from different methodological schools are likely to make different judgements about the worth of a piece. However, the alternative is that editors take on the responsibility of creating the standard and judging the worth of educational products by themselves.

Peer review, because it involves a greater number of people in the process, deepens and clarifies the judgement that is eventually made. It is not, however, free from those power relations that characterize the life of a community of practice. Furthermore, because the noviate's work is required to undergo peer examination, this has the effect of embedding new work in the canon, and at the same time limiting the ability of new researchers to innovate, and operate through new perspectives and new ways of working. The thrust and perhaps the intention of peer reviewing therefore may be to reify the work of the community.

See also:
Assessment (7); Power (77); Publishing (79); Research Community (95).

86   Referencing Systems

There are several systems used for referencing a piece of academic writing. The most widely used are: Harvard (or author/date); Vancouver; Modern Language Association (MLA); Chicago/Turabian Documentation; and American Psychological Association (APA). There are no logical reasons for choosing one method over another, though in the course of time some methods have acquired a higher status than others, and particular subject disciplines have adopted or developed distinctive approaches in their published outputs. Education journals and books have adopted a variety of styles with some high-status publishers insisting on a historical or chronological approach, where numbers are used (in ordinary brackets, or as superscripts or subscripts) within the text of the essay, article or book. The numbers then refer to notes at the bottom of the page or at the end of the chapter or at the end of the book/article/essay. The advantage of this method is that ordinary referencing can be combined with the inclusion of extra information or comment that is not considered to be central to the argument being developed in the text. However, most education journals and books adopt styles of referencing that cite the author(s), date of publication and, if it refers to a quotation, page number, in the text, and then provide a fuller bibliographic reference in a reference or bibliographic list at the end of the chapter/article or book.

The principal reason for the development of referencing systems is to acknowledge through citation the work of others, and to prevent plagiarism of other writers' ideas. They are therefore used in part as a way of structuring the discipline or school of thought, so that new ideas, models and ways of understanding phenomena build on the cumulative work of other writers working in the same area. New knowledge is therefore understood as incremental rather than revolutionary. This incremental process may take a number of forms: a critical appraisal of previously developed models and ideas and their replacement with more adequate ways of understanding phenomena; or the application of previously developed ideas to new situations or settings; or the further development of these ideas so that they explain a greater range of phenomena than they did previously.

The most commonly used of these systems is the Harvard or author/date system. The underlying principle of this method is that the entry in the text (the author and the year) is the key, or marker, for a full entry in the bibliography. Footnotes are rarely used and any extra information about the topic is incorporated into the text itself. An example of this method would be:

Scott and Usher (1999) [in the text]; and Scott, David and Usher, Robin (1999), *Researching Education: Data, Methods and Theory in Educational Enquiry*, London, Cassell [in the bibliographic section].

The Vancouver System is a style of referencing which uses Arabic numerals within parentheses in the text; and the number in parentheses is then linked directly to the reference list at the end of the piece of work. References are numbered consecutively in the order in which they appear in the text, and they are not listed alphabetically by author or title or in date order. An example of this method would be:

(31) [in the text]; and 31. Archer M. Morphogenesis versus Structuration. British Journal of Sociology. 1982; 33.4: 455-85 [in the reference list].

The Modern Language System (MLA) format follows the author/page method of citation, so the author's name (or title of the work) and the page (or paragraph) number is placed in a parenthetical citation. Full citation information is then provided in a Works Cited List. An example of this method would be:

[In the text] As Norris (134) suggests, the ideal speech situation is 'A regulative idea (in the Kantian sense) which manifestly cannot be realized under present conditions, but which hold out the prospect of a genuine dialogue – an uncoerced exchange of differing arguments and viewpoints – from which truth might yet emerge at the end of the enquiry'. [In the Works Cited List] Norris, Nigel. *Understanding Educational Evaluation.* London: Heinemann, 1995.

The Chicago/Turabian system uses numbers consecutively ordered at the end of a line and these refer to a footnote or an endnote where the reference is provided.

The American Psychological Association (APA) referencing style has some similarities with the Harvard System. The reference or quotation is cited in the text with a page number, if relevant, provided in the following way:

Usher (1997, p. 36) suggests a number of important ways of understanding this. Each text has a context 'in the sense of that which is with the text. What is "with" the text in this sense is the situated autobiography of the researcher/reader.'

This is cited in the bibliography as follows:

Usher, R. (1997). Telling a story about research and research as story-telling: Post modern approaches to social research. In G.McKenzie, J.Powell and R.Usher (Eds.), *Understanding Social Research: Perspectives on Methodology and Practice* (pp. 34–52). London: Falmer Press.

These are examples of referencing systems. However, there are many more such systems, though all of them are either constructed as page/end notes or as author/date systems.

See also:
Literature Review (60); Power (77); Research Community (95).

87   Reflexivity

Reflexivity is a key notion for most post-positivist researchers. This is because they do not believe that a clear separation exists between the observer and what they are observing, and therefore the values and frameworks through which they operate are implicated in the research account they produce. Reflexivity, therefore, may be defined as the process by which the researcher comes to understand how they are positioned in relation to the knowledge they are producing, and indeed, is an essential part of that knowledge-producing activity. This immediately places this form of research at odds with traditional forms of research, including those forms that emphasize disinterested observation, objective assessment and a technicist role for the researcher. However, the insertion of a notion of reflexivity into research is a statement about what research is, and therefore it implies that research that is not reflexive offers a less truthful account of the world.

Three types of reflexivity have been suggested.

- *Personal reflexivity.* This type foregrounds the personal characteristics and values of the researcher both in the conduct of the research and in the way it is written up. Thus, if the researcher is white, middle class and university educated, these characteristics are considered to be fundamental to the type of knowledge that is eventually produced, and it is incumbent on the researcher to write this autobiographical account into their research report. The authorial 'I' is privileged and a confessional approach is adopted. This type of writing can be clearly distinguished from a traditional form of academic writing, where no reference is made to the autobiography of the writer, or to the personal context within which the research is positioned. Furthermore, the insertion of the self into these accounts reflects a view that a clear separation between researcher and those being researched is neither feasible nor truthful.

- *Disciplinary reflexivity.* The insertion of a personal reflexive account into the research report is considered by some researchers to be a useful adjunct, but not fully constitutive, to the role of reflexivity in research. These researchers would want to extend the notion of reflexivity to include the way research accounts are also embedded in certain ways of conceiving knowledge. Thus research is more than just a personal account, it is also a social and political account. It is positioned within a community's disciplinary matrix, which is a network of power relations that determine which types of research are acceptable and which are not. Thirty years ago ethnographic research approaches were not considered to constitute real knowledge-making activities. They have now achieved a limited form of respectability within the academy. Disciplinary reflexivity comprises a belief that knowledge-making has political, social and cultural implications.

- *Epistemic reflexivity.* A further type of reflexivity relates to the way research texts are epistemological products. Thus each research text has a context 'in the sense of that which is with the text. What is with the text in this sense is the situated autobiography of the researcher/reader' (Usher, 1997: 37). Each research text also has a pre-text, in that it is embedded within particular forms of language, specific ways of organizing meaning and textual strategies that shape the way it is received. Finally, the research text has both a subtext and an inter-text, where in the first case it is located within certain types of power arrangements, and in the second case has relations to other texts; it refers to them.

These forms of epistemic reflexivity require the researcher to, as best they can, understand the nature of their knowledge-producing activities and write them into their accounts. Reflexivity, in whatever guise, indicates a particular approach to research, and one that is characteristic of post-positivist research perspectives, where subject and object are not clearly separated.

See also:
Biography/Autobiography (8); Culture (23); Epistemology/Ontology (38); Ethnography (40); Observation (71); Positivism (75); Power (77); Research Community (95); Social Constructionism (99); Textuality (110); Values (115); Writing (118).

88 Regression Analysis

Quantitative researchers may in certain circumstances want to move beyond simple descriptions of the distribution of scores, and examine the relationship between two or more variables. In the first place, this involves calculating the correlation coefficient between two measurement sets. For example, it may be of interest to the researcher to try to understand the relationship between the scores of a sample of students on mathematics and English tests taken by those students during a similar time period. It cannot be assumed that each child is equally adept in mathematics and English; however, it is unlikely that a perfectly negative correlation would be obtained, where the child with the best score in mathematics records the lowest score on the English test, the child with the highest score on the English test records the lowest score on the mathematics test, and indeed the rank order is reversed between the two tests. However, a measure of how closely the two rank orders are in agreement can be obtained by calculating the correlation coefficient. Correlational coefficient values range from +1 to

– 1, where +1 indicates a perfect positive correlation and − 1 indicates a perfect negative correlation. Care has to be taken with interpreting the results of correlation coefficient exercises, as they do not necessarily indicate a causal relationship.

A number of different types of correlation coefficients are available to the statistician. A *product moment calculation* compares parametric scores from the same sample. A *rank order correlation* is used when the same test is marked by two different markers to determine the degree of fit between their scores. A *tetrachoric correlation coefficient* is used to assess the relationship between a wide range of scores on one variable and a restricted range of scores on another, where both are normally distributed. Finally, a *bi-serial correlation coefficient* can be calculated when with both variables a simple pass or fail grade is recorded.

A further statistical operation that can be performed is to show the *regression line* between two or more variables. This indicates a best fit between the two sets of scores. These are usually plotted on a graph, with one variable placed on the y axis and the other on the x axis. The scores are then inserted and a line of best fit is drawn. This line of best fit may be linear or curved. It allows predictions to be made about the relationship between the two variables. If the researcher is interested in the relationship between more than two variables, then either a factor analysis calculation can be made or a multiple regression equation is used.

The use of correlation coefficients and regression lines are ways of displaying and calculating the relationships between a number of variables. They are therefore tools used by statisticians in various forms of variable analysis, and are underpinned by a number of beliefs about how the social world should and can be investigated. Mathematical modelling of educational processes and activities depends on the accuracy of the data that is inputted into the model for how successful it is in describing the setting. Scores from tests, questionnaires and other similar types of instruments are invariably approximations or quasi-indicators of the variable that they seek to represent.

See also:
Causation (11); Distribution (33); Mathematical Modelling (62); Questionnaire (82); Statistics (100); Tests (109); Variable Analysis (116).

89 Relativism

In the philosophical literature, four types of relativism are discussed.

Moral relativism

There are no universal grounds for suggesting that one version of morality is superior to another. This is supported by the fact that moral systems vary across cultures, historical periods and different people within the same culture. It would be false to infer from this fact that there are no moral absolutes, as one of those systems might be right and all the others wrong. However, in the absence of other arguments to the contrary, this would suggest, but not prove conclusively, that there are no moral absolutes. Again, there is no suggestion here that moral relativists should be entirely sceptical about the existence of moral absolutes, though perhaps this gives them good grounds for being sceptical about identifying what they might be. Even if most, or indeed every society, shared some moral belief, this in turn would not prove the existence of moral absolutes, since all of them might be wrong. Furthermore, moral relativists might claim an allegiance to a moral system that is embedded in the society to which they belong, without at the same time subscribing to any absolute or universal system of morality.

Conceptual relativism

Different people in different cultures and in different time periods vary in the way they organize experience. They therefore operate with different conceptual frameworks. As with moral relativism, the argument of variety does not disprove the existence of some universal conceptual system by which reality can best be known. However, it is more difficult to believe in conceptual relativism than it is to believe in moral relativism, because whereas the one is concerned with behaviours and right actions, the other is concerned with accessing the world. A conceptual relativist would argue that thought, belief and knowledge systems are embedded in particular social arrangements, which cannot be changed through individual willpower, but nevertheless do not persist over time and are different in different cultures. Immersion in one culture means that it is only with the greatest effort that a person can access another culture, if at all, and even then, they are stepping outside their native culture and entering a new one. The two cultures are still incommensurable.

Perceptual relativism

A subset of conceptual relativism is perceptual relativism, and the same dilemma applies here as it did with the first two categories. Whorf (1954: 213) defines perceptual relativism in the following way:

> We dissect nature along lines laid down by our native language. The categories and types that we isolate from the world of phenomena we do not find there because they stare every observer in the face; on the contrary, the world is presented in a kaleidoscopic flux of impressions which has to be organised by our minds – and this means largely by the linguistic systems in our minds.

Perceptual or radical relativists argue that there is no grounding in nature that compels us to organize it in one way rather than another.

Truth relativism

Radical relativists would argue that there are no universal absolutes embedded in logic or rationality. Different societies have their own systems of logic, their own sets of criteria for determining the truth of the matter and their own procedures for carrying this out. To understand another culture, therefore, requires a complete reappraisal of how one thinks and, therefore, how one behaves.

All these different forms of relativism are essentially anti-realist, though more moderate relativists suggest that the world can be real even if there are no absolute or universal standards by which it can be judged. Thus reality exerts an influence on the way it is described, which means that it cannot be described in every possible way. Indeed, some philosophers (cf. Strawson, 1959) have even suggested that there are some universals of coherent thought, which would set limits to those forms of life that individuals are embedded within and the way those individuals can process reality. These debates underpin arguments in the field of educational and social research methodology that focus on the realist/anti-realist dilemma. Resolution of this dilemma in whatever way is fundamental to a proper understanding of appropriate methods and strategies in the field.

See also:

Culture (23); Ethics (39); Historical Research (53); Methodology (65); Objectivity (70); Postmodernism (76); Realism (83); Reductionism (84).

90 Relevance

Educational theorists have identified relevance as a criterion for determining the quality of a research product. Hammersley (1992b), for example, suggests a four-fold schema: plausibility/credibility (whether the evidential claims are plausible or credible to the reader of the research); coherence (whether evidence and argument logically cohere); intentionality (whether a study is credible in relation to its stated intentions); and relevance (whether the research findings are relevant to issues of legitimate public concern).

A judgement cannot be made about relevance as a useful concept, unless that judgement is made in terms of what it refers to. For example, a piece of research may not on the surface have any relevance to current educational problems, and thus be of no current legitimate public concern, but it may have relevance to future problems and concerns of educational systems and procedures, and therefore have value. Indeed, it is possible to take this argument one step further and suggest that relevance as a concept is determined by a complex of power networks operating at policy and practice levels that results in some concepts having more relevance than others at particular moments in time.

Furthermore, within these networks of power, and at different levels of the policy cycle, concepts, ideas and the like may be more relevant to some people than others. So, for example, critical research that suggests an unequal or inequitable relationship in education systems may not be relevant to teachers whose concerns are with the provision of solutions to problems that they are encountering in the present. Relevance is therefore determined by the concerns and preoccupations of specific sets of people operating within particular contexts.

Educational researchers in a further sense use the notion of relevance. This is where it is used as a synonym for appropriate association. Thus, experimentalists express their data in a numerical form so that they can make more precise comparisons between test scores collected at a number of different points in time. Quantitative representations of reality are in this case appropriately associated with experimental procedures. Some educational researchers would want to describe these appropriate associations as logical and therefore as necessary. However, others would suggest that relations between the different parts of a research design have no logical necessity, but are merely conventional. This use of the idea of relevance has little obvious mileage as other words and phrases perform the same function.

However, relevance does have some credibility in relation to the first definition. Recently, educational research has been criticized for not being relevant to the real concerns of practitioners or to the development of the practice (Tooley with Darby, 1998; Hargreaves, 1996; Hillage *et al.*, 1998). These criticisms have been couched in a language which suggests that what is relevant can be defined unequivocally. Frequently, the concept of relevance is used stripped of any ideological import, and as a rhetorical device. The research findings are deemed to be irrelevant if they do not fit with the immediate concerns of particular educational stakeholders, or if their base is different from that held by the stakeholder. Relevance is therefore one of those educational words that is frequently used to disguise the contested nature of the discourse being used.

See also:

Correlational Research (18); Critical Theory (22); Experiment (44); Power (77); Quantitative Research (81); Research Community (95); Statistics (100); Tests (109); Values (115).

91 Reliability

Traditionally, reliability is used as a measure of quality and the term means repeatability or consistency. A measure is reliable if it provides the same results on two or more separate occasions, when the assumption is made that the object being measured has not changed. Thus, for quantitative educational researchers, if a measure or indeed series of measures when repeated give a similar result, it is possible to say that it has high reliability. However, a finding from a research project may be reliable, and yet not be valid, and thus of no worth to the researcher. Qualitative researchers may wish to replicate their research to determine how reliable their findings are; however, they would not want to use a quantitative instrument, arguing that reliability can best be determined qualitatively. Whether quantitative or qualitative measures are used, the key to successfully applying a notion of reliability is that the object being measured remains stable.

There are four general classes of reliability estimates. The instrument being used may be a test or a questionnaire; however, it must be capable of producing quantitative data.

- *Inter-rater or inter-observer reliability.* If in a research project, a structured observation schedule is being used to determine the levels and types of teacher–pupil interaction in classrooms, then this form of reliability is used to test the degree of convergence or divergence between their different observations. If there is a reasonable degree of convergence, then the instrument can be said to be reliable.

- *Test–retest reliability*. This measure is used by educational researchers to determine the consistency of a property being assessed by a test over time. Thus, if similar results are obtained at both the testing and retesting stages, the instrument can be said to be reliable.
- *Parallel forms of reliability*. This is used to determine the consistency of the results from two tests from the same content domain.
- *Internal consistency reliability*. This is used as an internal measure within a test to assess consistency between items in a test.

Quantitative researchers have developed systems for determining the degree of reliability error – these involve random or systematic forms of error.

Qualitative researchers have suggested different procedures to determine the reliability of their results, and these do not involve quantification. Guba and Lincoln (1985) developed an alternative to traditional forms of reliability, and this is encapsulated in their notions of dependability and confirmability. To ameliorate the problem of the invasive nature of the researcher in the collection and analysis of data, they proposed an auditor, who would work alongside the researcher or research team. The auditor's role is to confirm that the researcher(s) has followed the most appropriate procedures, made the most rational choices of strategies and methods, and drawn the most sensible conclusions from the data that they collected. The auditor has the task of ascertaining 'whether the findings are grounded in the data ... whether inferences based on the data are logical, whether the utility of the category system: its clarity, explanatory power and fit to the data are realistic, and the degree and incidence of observer bias' (ibid.: 323). A more conventional method would be to replicate the project, and compare the results from the two investigations. An assumption is still being made with either quantitative or qualitative strategies that the object under investigation has not changed its constituent nature between the two investigations.

See also:
Observation (71); Qualitative Research (80); Quantitative Research (81); Questionnaire (82); Replication (92); Statistics (100); Tests (109); Validity (113); Variable Analysis (116).

92 Replication

Positivist/empiricist researchers use designs that in theory can be replicated and still produce similar types of data. If a set of conclusions can be confirmed through replication, then the researcher may feel more secure about their results. Replication is a measure of reliability, so, for example, differently phrased questions requiring similar answers are used in a test (placed at different points in the test), and comparisons are made between the different answers to these pairs of questions. If the answers positively correlate with each other, this enhances the reliability and validity of the data. Again, this process can be applied to whole research studies, either constructed with different types of instruments but focusing on the same area, or with precisely similar instruments and analysis protocols focusing on the same area in order to determine confidence levels in the findings.

Post-positivist researchers understand the importance of replication differently, and this is because they ascribe a different role to the researcher in the construction of knowledge and in the collection and analysis of data. Positivist researchers designate a clear separation between researcher and participants in their research. The researcher's values and preconceptions do not act as influencing variables in the collection and analysis of the data. Positivist researchers, therefore, in general favour methods and instruments, i.e. questionnaires, structured observations, tests, etc., that seem to allow a distancing between researcher and participant. The instrument that is chosen is designed so that it can be used in one way only, and the researcher is reduced to a technician. Replication of method is therefore possible and feasible. If dissimilar results are obtained, then it has to be concluded that either one of the two or both sets of data are unreliable and therefore invalid. If results are similar, then the obverse is true: the results of the investigation are sound.

However, with certain types of data-collection instrument, i.e. semi-structured interviews and observations, it is not possible to have this same degree of confidence in their ability to be replicated. This is because the researcher and the way they operate are essential parts of the data-collection process. Their presence contributes to the type of data collected. This, however, should not be seen as a reason for abandoning the use of such instruments as there are methodological justifications for their use, such as probing for the reasons individuals give for their actions and trying to understand the way they construct meanings in the world, and these are central to any proper under-standing of reality. Replication in this case is therefore neither possible nor desirable. This has certain implications. First, complete replication is not possible, because a different researcher will bring a different set of resources to the research setting and this will influence the type of data that is subsequently collected. Even if the same researcher at a later point in time followed the same procedures as they did in the first instance, precise replication would not be forthcoming, because both the researcher and the setting that they are researching will have changed. Second, implicit within post-positivist perspectives is the idea that the researcher does not just collect data in a disinterested way, but also by their very presence change the setting that they are researching.

A further issue is foregrounded by this discussion, and this is that though both positivist and post-positivist perspectives argue for transparency, the rationale for such an argument is different in the two cases. In the first case, it is to allow replication and thus enhance the reliability of the study. In the second case, reliability is not considered to be a desirable attribute; however, it is still considered to be desirable that the reader of the research report is fully informed about the values that inform the construction of knowledge which has taken place, and this above all else comprises the values of the researcher themselves.

See also:
Correlational Research (18); Interview (57); Longitudinal Observation Studies (61); Observation (71); Positivism (75); Questionnaire (82); Reliability (91); Social Constructionism (99); Statistics (100); Tests (109); Validity (113); Values (115); Variable Analysis (116).

93 Representativeness

Using data from a sampling frame to draw conclusions about a total population is a key aspect of generalization. Who or what becomes part of a researcher's sample for research investigation is a vital component in determining the validity of outcomes. In statistical research the emphasis is upon the extent to which the sample can be said to be representative of the total population. Representativeness is, therefore, a key aspect of research that is based on probability sampling, where researchers make use of a variety of statistical means to make decisions about the composition and size of the sample that will enable estimates of representativeness and allow hypotheses to be tested.

The statistical means used by quantitative researchers to estimate the representativeness of their sample are unlikely to be applied by qualitative researchers. However, the notion being less central to qualitative researchers' concerns does not mean that it is of no interest at all, since the characteristics of the phenomena selected for qualitative investigation will contribute towards determining the concepts, theories and/or typologies that derive from the data. As critical commentators (Bryman, 1988: 77; Silverman, 2001: 222–3) have pointed out, the hallmark of qualitative research has been seen as both its strength and weakness, and ethnographic field studies, in particular, have been subject to accusations of anecdotalism. This is especially so where the rationale for selecting some instances of phenomena rather than others is unclear, as is the extent to which such instances are typical or representative of other instances. The concern is that interview and/or observation extracts may be used to fit preconceived notions, and other data bits avoided or ignored if they do not. This is not to deny the strengths of qualitative research but rather to reinforce the importance of transparent and systematic qualitative data analysis procedures and audit trails in order to confirm the authenticity and credibility of research findings. Elsewhere, document research is subject to similar concerns about the representativeness of selected documents compared with other documents that might exist but are unavailable or unknown to the researcher, or pertain to a specific category of people rather than to other categories (Scott, 1990).

In such ways, the interdependence between representativeness, sampling procedures and epistemological dispositions towards research is clear, even if, as Brown and Dowling (1998: 31) suggest 'the extent to which theoretical considerations *explicitly* operate in the construction of the sample does vary', as does, we might add, the ways such concerns are explained in final research reports.

See also:
Epistemology/Ontology (38); Sampling (98); Statistics (100); Survey (105); Tests (109); Validity (113).

94 Research Assessment Exercise

Though the Research Assessment Exercise (RAE) is peculiar to the UK, other countries around the world have developed funding mechanisms for research which are similar in nature. The RAE is a device for allocating research funds to universities, and at the same time avoids direct bidding for particular research projects. UK university research is funded through both types of mechanisms. The RAE takes place at regular intervals, and has changed its format over the last 20 years. It has, however, retained two elements: a commentary on the research activity within the unit being assessed, and a judgement made about four pieces of work submitted by each research active participant from each unit. Previous to the forthcoming 2008 exercise, an overall grade was awarded to each submitting unit, and these grades ranged from 1 to 5*. Funding was allocated using a different mechanism at each RAE via this grading system, with the more successful receiving the largest amounts of money. The 2008 exercise requires each RAE panel to indicate proportions of excellence in research, and thus it is likely that funding for each submitted unit will be proportionately allocated.

There are some major problems with allocating funding for research in this way. *First*, the judgements that are made by panels representing the various interests involved may be unreliable, especially as with some of the panels in previous exercises all the submitted work is not read properly. *Second*, potential RAE results become the principal criterion by which the work of units and departments in universities is judged; and thus vice-chancellors are more and more inclined to decide the fate of whole departments or units on the basis of their potential to be awarded a high-funded grade some years before the census date. *Third*, the definition of research, and more importantly good research, is a contested matter; and this therefore gives an inordinate amount of power to the panel members to define what is good or bad research and even what should be submitted as research (philosophical, historical and other types of work which do not conform to a relatively simple model of empirical research have an ambivalent position in the RAE). *Fourth*, exercises such as these are generally designed to concentrate research within a small group of universities; and the overall effect is to widen the gap between the traditional universities in the UK and the new universities. *Fifth*, RAEs set university against university; and this direct competition may not contribute to the core business of the university sector – the development and dissemination of knowledge.

On the other hand, allocating research monies to units and universities is a contentious business. Two other allocation systems have been identified. The first is direct bidding for particular research projects by individuals; the second is fair and equal allocation of the available monies to registered individual researchers or groups of researchers. In the first case, funding is already extensively allocated in this way; and in the second case, there is a problem with identifying and then licensing individuals or groups of individuals. As with any system that is assessment-driven and performativity-orientated, research activity through the RAE is not evaluative-neutral, since the evaluation itself sanctions certain types of research activity and marginalizes other types.

See also:
Assessment (7); Dissemination (32); Publishing (79); Research Community (95).

95 Research Community

Research communities are discipline-based and provide the contexts in which members of that community work. Research communities operate in different ways and can be described as regionalized (Bernstein, 1996). Bernstein further identified different types of symbolic systems which underpin research communities. He distinguished between horizontal and vertical forms of discourse, and with the latter hierarchical and horizontal knowledge forms. Horizontal forms of discourse are described by Bernstein (1996: 170–1) as 'the form of knowledge usually typified as everyday, oral or common-sense knowledge [which] has a group of features: local, segmental, context dependent, tacit, multi-layered, often contradictory across contexts but not within contexts'.

Vertical discourses, by contrast, are defined in terms of two characteristics: verticality and grammaticality. Verticality denotes the way theory is developed and it can take two forms. The first of these is hierarchical where the constructs that form the mode of knowledge can be arranged in a hierarchical fashion, starting at the bottom of the pyramidal structure with more concrete propositions and moving up the hierarchy towards more general and abstract principles, which are effectively integrated within the hierarchical structure. An example of this would be the physical sciences. However, some knowledge forms have a horizontal structure which consists of the proliferation of more and more specialized types or languages which are incommensurable with each other. An example of this might be educational studies. For Bernstein (1977: 167), this weak horizontal structure has certain consequences, principally that, 'every new approach becomes a social movement or sect which immediately defines the nature of the subject by re-defining what is to be admitted, and what is beyond the pale, so that with every new approach the subject almost starts from scratch'.

Whereas this type of knowledge form is concerned with internality – the relations between the parts of the discourse that are internal to itself – Bernstein developed a further relation which attempts to connect it to the empirical world – grammaticality. Some knowledge bases then have a weak capacity to 'generate empirical correlates' (Muller, 2004: 3) and therefore a weak capacity to progress as a form of knowledge; whereas others have a strong relationship with the empirical world, have developed a strong language for confirming or disconfirming theory, and therefore have a greater capacity for progression. Thus some research communities have a strong integral form, whereas others are weakly organized. This profusion of specialized languages best characterizes the discipline of education and thus the work of the educational research community may be described as fragmented, disputed and, in Bernstein's terms, having a weak grammar.

See also:
Ideal Speech Situation (54); Paradigm (72); Power (77); Publishing (79); Research Assessment Exercise (94).

96 Respondent Validation

Qualitative researchers use a number of devices to check on the validity of their conclusions. One such device is respondent validation. Here, the researcher, having kept a detailed record of his/her observation notes or having made a verbatim transcript of interviews that he/she conducted, then sends these data-sets back to the respondents to check for accuracy. A further use of respondent validation is where the research report itself, or sections of it, are sent back to participants for confirmation or amendment. At either of these two stages, respondents are being asked to:

- confirm that the data they provided may be used in the research report, even if various anonymity devices are used to protect their interests;
- confirm that the data they provided is an accurate representation of their beliefs, attitudes and constructs;
- confirm that the interpretations and data reduction made by the researcher are fair and have not distorted the data.

Democratic evaluators (cf. Simons, 1984) engage in lengthy processes of negotiation and renegotiation to reach agreement with respondents before the research report is released to the general public. However, other types of researchers/evaluators would limit this process to one opportunity for the respondent to check and amend the data, and possibly a further opportunity to check the research report itself.

A number of problems with these processes are apparent. The first of these concerns the capability of the respondent to make the most appropriate judgement about whether their data and subsequent interpretations by the researcher should be amended. If the purpose of the exercise is to protect the interests of participants, then the researcher may be in a better position to make this judgement, as he/she is likely to have a greater knowledge of research processes and how the general public receives research reports. He/she may therefore be in a better position to protect the interests of respondents than those respondents themselves. Likewise, if the respondent validation process is designed as a series of negotiations and renegotiations with respondents before the report is released, then respondents may be at a disadvantage in comparison with the researcher/negotiator, since the latter may have more experience and understanding of the negotiation process.

The second concern focuses on the notion of authenticity. One of the problems with collecting interview data from respondents is that the presentational dimension to the data they provide is reinforced and extended if respondents are given the opportunity to reformulate their data-set. Since the purpose of the exercise is to collect authentic data, uncontaminated by presentation, this may have the effect of making the data less authentic. Related to this is the problem of time. Individuals do not just present themselves during interviews and other research encounters, they respond in terms of context. One of these contexts is that each interview session is positioned in time. Given the opportunity to amend their data, respondents may not be giving a better or more authentic version of their beliefs and constructs, but one that has been changed by time. Since interviews are partly designed to collect data about past events, the further away from the original event being described, the less meaningful is the description. What respondent validation is doing here is increasing the artificiality of the data-collection process, and therefore decreasing the authenticity of the data. However, it can be argued that this time-distancing allows a fuller and more complete version of events to be formulated, especially as the researcher has intervened in the process, allowing greater reflexivity.

Many educational researchers apply some forms of respondent validation and not others. So, they will seek confirmation and validation from their respondents, but will not allow them a veto over what and how data are incorporated into the research report. This allows a measure of validation and therefore a greater faith in the authenticity of the data, without the researcher being embroiled in lengthy processes of checking and rechecking. However, if the researcher or evaluator is not particularly concerned with descriptive authenticity, but they understand their purpose as intervening in a naturally occurring educational setting in order to effect some beneficial change to that setting, i.e. for the purposes of empowerment, then respondent validation is being used in a different way and has a different purpose.

See also:
Access (2); Data Reduction (25); Dissemination (32); Empowerment (37); Ethics (39); Evaluation (42); Historical Research (53); Interpretivism (56); Interview (57); Observation (71); Qualitative Research (80); Realism (83); Reflexivity (87); Validity (113); Values (115).

97 Retroduction

Retroduction is a mode of thinking used by educational researchers where social relations are understood as stratified and emergent, and can be contrasted with *empiricism* where it is believed that only sense data (usually expressed as regular occurrences) have a real existence, and *actualism* where it is believed that reality can be adequately accounted for by examining occurrences and events. Though actualists suggest that reality operates at two levels, *critical realists* posit a third and deeper level of social relations, that of mechanisms, which may be activated, but also may lie dormant. Reality is therefore stratified and this calls for approaches to thinking about and conceptualizing realia that are qualitatively different from induction, deduction and even abduction. Bhaskar (1979: 4) suggests that only careful experimentation, where the three levels of social life are aligned, allows access to these deeper-lying structures or mechanisms, and he argues that:

> We have in science a three-phase schema of development, in which in a continuing dialectic, science identifies a phenomenon (or range of phenomena), constructs explanations for it and empirically tests its explanations, leading to the identification of the generative mechanisms at work, which now becomes the phenomena to be explained, and so on. On this view of science, its essence lies in the move at any one level from manifest phenomena to the structures that generate them.

A retroductive research strategy might take the following form:

1. The purpose of research is to explain regularities between phenomena that have been observed and plotted; and it is only possible to do this by discovering the underlying mechanisms

and relations between mechanisms and structures that cause events in the real world.

2. The focus is therefore on structures and mechanisms that are not immediately available to consciousness and cannot therefore be observed in any straightforward way. The retroductive researcher's first move is, therefore, to construct a possible model that might explain both the events and the observable regularities. This can only be achieved by qualitative investigation, drawing on evidence that is either observational or discursive.

3. This modelling is an attempt to infer the existence of underlying causal mechanisms, with the understanding that these mechanisms or structures may not be activated.

4. The next stage is to test the model in real-life settings. However, this cannot involve straightforward experimentation, because the events that are being investigated are taking place in open social systems. To assume that these causal mechanisms can be identified using closed-systems procedures is to misunderstand the nature of social life. The testing process is therefore about seeking confirmation of the existence of unobservable entities that cause observable events and occurrences.

5. If the testing is successful, then the retroductive researcher has good grounds for believing in the existence of these mechanisms and a causal relationship or explanation about cause and effect can be formulated.

The method itself is complicated, can only produce speculative results, and depends on a belief in critical realism, where objects exist in the world whether they are known or not, and indeed may still be real without appearing so. The existence of these mechanisms and structures is inferred from a complicated process of modelling, experimentation and testing.

See also:
Causation (11); Closed and Open Systems (13); Critical Realism (21); Discourse (31); Empiricism (36); Experiment (44); Qualitative Research (80); Realism (83); Structure (103).

98 Sampling

Social scientists have neither the time nor resources to carry out a study of a whole population, or *census*. Neither can they assume that any one element of the social world is identical to another and, therefore, that census studies are unnecessary. It follows that all research investigations involve *selection*. Sampling refers to the activities involved in selecting a subset of persons or things from a larger population. This is also known as a *sampling frame*. Methods used to select the sample will determine the nature and validity of the findings that are generated from the study of that sample. Different approaches yield different kinds of data and, therefore, different constructions of knowledge. Who or what is included in the sample is dependent upon the core research problem and the methodological approach taken. These are most commonly distinguishable in terms of qualitative and quantitative approaches, and various combinations of both.

Education researchers will often want to use data obtained from the study of a sample in order to say or write something about the larger population. Their capacity to do so will, as above, depend upon the key research questions, their underlying purpose, and the methodological route considered most appropriate to address the question(s) set. *Sample generalizability* is the ability to generalize from the sample to the larger population and rests on the basis that the selected sample *is* representative of the larger population. This means that the character-istics of the sample are the same as the distribution of those characteristics in the larger population. Such a subset is known as a *representative sample*.

Selecting a representative sample is a key element of research design and requires pre-planning in terms of knowledge of the population to be sampled and rigorous selection procedures. In statistical approaches, rigour takes the form of calculations in order to ascertain the degree of confidence that can be placed in the sample statistic. More important in qualitative approaches are careful audit trails that are systematic and reflexive records of how samples are drawn. Audit trails provide the bases for explanations about how and why researchers' selection of, access to, and relations with the sample population have affected data collection, analysis and, as appropriate, theory formation.

The most common types of sampling are *probability* (or *random*) sampling and *non-probability* sampling.

Probability sampling

Probability sampling relies on selection procedures to ensure there is no systematic *bias* in the selection of the subset, and that the odds of selecting people or things are known in advance and carefully controlled. Probability sampling is a feature of all quantitative approaches and the statistical analyses of subsets. A random or probability sample is one where every element (person or thing) has an equal chance of being included. *Systematic* probability (or random) sampling occurs when people or things are selected from a list, with every *nth* element selected. *Stratified* probability (or random) sampling uses knowledge already known about the population to divide that population into strata; elements are then selected from those strata in accordance with the procedures identified above.

The likely degree of error in a probability sample decreases with the size of the sample and the homogeneity of the larger population. Statistical formulae are used to calculate the minimum sample size needed for a researcher to be 95 per cent confident that estimates are within given levels of accuracy. *Sampling error* affecting a sample statistic can be estimated from the characteristics of the sample and knowledge about *sampling distributions*. The tool for calculating sampling error is known as inferential statistics. The effect of sample design on sampling error can be quantified in the form of *design effects*, also known as *Deffs*.

Significance testing allows the researcher to compare an observed pattern or relationship in a sample with the pattern that would have been expected in the sample given a hypothesis that no such relationship exists in the population (*the null hypothesis*). A significant relationship is therefore one that the researcher is prepared to infer exists in the larger population as well as in the sample. Statistical *generalizations* arise from such forms of sampling, and include the claim that there is an *x* per cent chance that what was found in the sample population will also be found in the larger population.

Probability sampling can be affected by *non-response*, either its magnitude, or the *distinctiveness of non-respondents*. In probability sampling, having an equal chance of being selected does not eliminate entirely the issue of bias. For example, one solution to the probability of under-sampling or over-sampling among certain sub-groups within a sample is to weight the findings at the analysis stage and this process is called *weighting*. The process can be used to compensate for non-response, albeit with attendant risks of increasing bias.

Non-probability sampling

Non-probability sampling takes a variety of forms and occurs when a person or thing to be sampled from a larger population does *not* have an equal chance of being selected. Non-probability sampling is commonly associated with qualitative approaches and aims to be both systematic and principled. (Delamont (1992: 70) applies the term *principled sampling*.) The intention may be to use the sample for exploratory research, in order to develop *typologies* or *hypotheses*, or to *pilot* research questions that might be used in a range of research instruments.

Availability or *convenience* sampling occurs when people and things are selected as a subset because they are available or convenient to access. *Snowball* sampling involves getting research participants to direct the researcher to other potential participants. *Quota* sampling is meant to overcome some of the perceived shortcomings of convenience sampling, and occurs when researchers select individuals or things from quotas that are set to ensure that the sample represents people or things in proportion to their prevalence in the larger population. Quota sampling assumes that information about prevalence is known in advance. *Purposive, focused* and *judgement* sampling are all terms that apply to researchers who make theoretically informed decisions about whom or what to include in their sample.

Generalizing from such samples is usually speculative, or considered inappropriate, or inapplicable to the main research purposes. Bassey (1999) goes further. He argues that generalizations of the scientific kind (following Popper, 1963) are impossible as well as inappropriate in education research, arguing instead the case for 'fuzzy generalizations', or propositions – which show how the discovery (as summarized in a research report) '*may* apply' more widely (Bassey, 1999: 54, his emphasis). Where sampling decisions are not made on statistical grounds, writers (like Guba and Lincoln (1985), for example) have preferred to use the term *transferability* of findings rather than generalizability. Transferability refers to applying the findings of the research study in contexts similar to the contexts in which they were first derived. So far, our discussion has centred on the selection of people or things from wider populations. We now turn to another form of sampling.

Theoretical sampling

More than the collection of data about the characteristics of people and things, theoretical sampling is concerned with the identification of concepts and their constituents, a key focus being the generation of theory from an examination of the relationship between those concepts. Using Glaser and Strauss's (1967: 45) words: 'Theoretical sampling is the process of data collection for generating theory whereby the analyst jointly collects, codes, and analyses his [sic] data and decides what to collect next, and where to find them, in order to develop his [sic] theory as it emerges.' It follows that only first-stage decisions can be reached about who or what to include in the sample before fieldwork begins. The researcher selects his/her sample on the basis of relevance to his/her developing theory, and then collects data to the point described by Glaser and Strauss as *theoretical saturation*. This occurs when data collected becomes familiar rather than novel, and ceases to generate new concepts or relationships between them. This does not preclude the exploration of instances that do not fit an emerging conceptual framework since 'atypical' instances serve as devices to challenge, modify and expand such frameworks.

Elsewhere, Strauss and Corbin (1990) have described the initial stages of theoretical sampling as *open* or *relational* or *variational* sampling; the purpose is to maximize sample diversity for theoretical development. Earlier, Denzin (1970) described theoretical sampling as a form of *interactive* sampling (cf. statistical sampling as *non-interactive*). Perhaps a key point of difference is that the judgements made about theoretical sampling are based on the 'quality' (however defined) of the theory, whereas statistical forms of sampling are judged in terms of the appropriate application of statistical procedures (ibid.).

Fundamental to all forms and applications of sampling lies the key importance for researchers to make public and transparent the means by which the selection of people and phenomena for study takes place. These will include the mechanisms for inferring the quantitative and/or qualitative significance of such selections, and is a prerequisite for all forms of research report, whether underpinned by statistical or qualitative methods, or a mix of both.

See also:
Generalization (50); Grounded Theory (51); Methodology (65); Mixed Methods (66); Prediction (78); Qualitative Research (80); Quantitative Research (81); Statistics (100); Transferability (111); Validity (113).

99   Social Constructionism

This term refers to an influential epistemology in educational research and can be contrasted with objectivism and subjectivism. Objectivists separate out reality from consciousness, and suggest that the meaning of an object resides in the object itself. Consciousness therefore has the role of recognizing that meaning, rather than constructing or creating it. Subjectivists, on the other hand, argue that there is nothing in the object or referent that allows meaningful interaction with it, consciousness imposes meaning on it, and this suggests that different types of meanings could be imposed on the same object. Constructionists, however, argue that meaning is not created but constructed out of the interplay between consciousness and the object. The object therefore exerts an influence on the meaning individuals give to it. This does not invoke a solipsistic or individualistic viewpoint, because construction-ism always has a social dimension to it, and thus the term usually used to denote this epistemology is social constructionism.

The social element is therefore foregrounded, as human beings are born into cultures with their own symbolic systems that always underpin individual meaning-making activities. These symbolic sys-tems therefore precede and are not the creation of determinate human beings. This image invokes the idea of a homogeneous culture with agreed and shared meaning systems, but this would be misleading. Culture is always contested, and it is perhaps more appropriate to consider it as a resource from which social actors draw, which comes before and not after action, reflection and thought, but then in turn influences the formation of new cultural constructions.

Objectivists claim that certain properties are attached to the social object regardless of place and time. There are a number of problems with this. The first of these is that it is clear that some elements of social life are specific to particular societies and the way those societies are constructed. This might include language systems, social behaviours, institutional arrangements and the like. It might further be suggested that individual subjectivities are specific to particular social arrange-ments – certainly gendered, classed and sexualized elements are of this type. Strong anti-essentialism or strong social constructivism implies a view of the human condition where all the attributes of human beings are literally constructed by the discourses, institutional mores and traditions of the society of which the individual is a member. Furthermore, this would suggest that knowledge of those institutions and how they work is also socially mediated and relative to the society of which they are a part.

However, social constructionists do not have to make such extra-vagant claims. Moderate social constructivists would claim that discourses, power networks and social arrangements do not have any natural legitimacy, but are inventions of groups of people in society and these groups of people are stratified so that those who have greater control of resources in society are in a better position to determine future arrangements for social life. This version of social construction-ism emphasizes the socially constructed nature of human institutions. For example, Young's (1999) designation of the curriculum as socially constructed involves three modes: high or low stratification; broad or narrow degrees of specialization; and insulated or connective relations between knowledge areas. Whether a curriculum is highly or lowly stratified, broadly or narrowly specialized or strongly or weakly classified is determined by social arrangements, or to put it another way, power enters into deliberations about the curriculum which a society adopts and different arrangements of power could have resulted in different types of curricula. Social constructionism is a highly influential epistemology that underpins the use of certain types of educational research strategies, such as some forms of case study, autobiographical studies and action research.

See also:
Action Research (3); Biography/Autobiography (8); Case Study (9); Culture (23); Epistemology/Ontology (38); Gender (49); Interpretivism (56); Objectivity (70); Power (77); Realism (83); Reductionism (84); Relativism (89); Subjectivity (104).

100 Statistics

Statisticians deal with numeric data and properties of individuals and educational units that can be quantified. They are concerned with the relationships between different quantifiable items. Statistical procedures can be categorized in two ways: descriptively and inferentially. *Descriptive statistics* are used where the intention is to summarize the numerical data or present them. *Inferential statistics* allow the researcher to go beyond presentational description of the data. Bryant and Jones (1995) give four reasons for using inferential statistics.

- To draw conclusions from the data obtained from a given sample of research subjects about the population from which the sample has been drawn.
- To determine whether the statistical results produced by the research could or could not have been achieved by chance. If not, then the results can be said to be significant; if they could then the results can be said to be non-significant.
- To determine the level of confidence in the significance of research results.
- To test hypotheses about relationships between variables.

Statisticians then differentiate between a *population* of cases which have similar properties and about which the researcher wishes to generalize, and a *sample*, which is a subset of the population and from which data are collected. There are two principal types of sampling: probability and non-probability. In the first case, criteria for selecting respondents are known, and in the second case the criteria are unknown. *Probability sampling* allows probabilistic generalizations, which are always expressed with indices of error. Error is more likely to occur with smaller samples. However, increasing the sample size does not necessarily produce exponential gains in accuracy. Furthermore, the greater variability in a population and the more complicated the analysis that is made, the larger the sample size has to be. *Non-probability sampling* is used where it is not known in advance what the relevant characteristics of the population are. Generalization from the sample to the population is therefore more difficult to make, except where the researcher is confident that the whole population has been included in the sample.

Statisticians also distinguish between *constants*, where the same value applies to all the members of a sample or population and *variables*, where the property has more than one value, and thus members of the population or sample can be placed on a scale of values. Scales can be at *nominal*, *ordinal*, *interval* or *ratio* levels. A major component of inferential statistics is the use of statistical tests, and the type of test that is used may take two forms: *parametric* and *non-parametric*. Parametric tests assume a number of characteristics about the parameters of the population to which the sample refers, use interval or ratio-level data, involve independent or random sampling and, more fundamentally, reflect a normal distribution of scores in the population. Non-parametric tests are based on fewer assumptions about the population and can be used with nominal or ordinal data. They also reflect a skewed distribution of scores. Inferential statistics use more complicated techniques than those referred to above, such as regression analyses and multi-level modelling.

See also:
Distribution (33); Experiment (44); Generalization (50); Mathematical Modelling (62); Quantitative Research (81); Regression Analysis (88); Sampling (98); Variable Analysis (116).

101 Strategy

Examples of research strategies in education are: case study, experimentation, action research, survey and ethnography. They are therefore commonly distinguished from methods such as observations or questionnaires; and from epistemological and ontological concerns such as relativism, objectivity and reflexivity. Distinguishing between ontology, epistemology, strategy and method (or instrumentation) at an analytical level allows proper relations to be established between them, and also suggests that decisions about each can only be made with reference to the other three.

The idea that there is a necessary relationship between ontology, epistemology, strategy and method has been disputed by Bryman (1988: 125), among others, on the grounds that: '(t)he problem with the "ought" view [the identification of ontological and epistemological positions which precede and influence the identification of strategies and methods] is that it fails to recognize that a whole cluster of considerations are likely to impinge on decisions about methods of data collection'. Empirical research is therefore a pragmatic matter, and issues to do with the respective relations between data collected in different ways or the appropriate relationship between the researcher and who and what they are researching can be resolved by reference to whether satisfactory answers are provided to the original questions of the researcher. This view provides no resolution at all, as the issue of whether the eventual description of reality which emerges is valid, truthful and generalizable, or even satisfactory is bypassed. The contested nature of much empirical research can therefore only be resolved by reference to meta-theoretical considerations such as objectivity, realism and reflexivity, though debates about these are of course resolved in different ways by researchers committed to different ontological and epistemological theories. Since the researcher by definition engages with the world and provides a description of it, then philosophical issues, even if they are not explicitly acknowledged, underpin methodological decisions that are made.

Even if this is accepted, this doesn't solve all the methodological problems that confront educational researchers; since they still have to identify the most appropriate ontological and epistemological theory, given the nature of the world and potentially how we can know it, in order to develop strategies and methods at the data collection and analysis phases. Furthermore, those philosophical dilemmas are not easy to resolve, and philosophers and theorists from different schools of thought have found it difficult to reach agreement about many of these important matters. One of the consequences of this is that educational researchers operate pragmatically, as Bryman (1988) suggests they should. This may result in a trivializing of knowledge, and an inability to resolve disputes between different researchers researching the same area, especially when they draw conclusions that are diametrically opposed.

See also:

Case Study (9); Correlational Research (18); Critical Realism (21); Design (28); Empiricism (36); Epistemology/Ontology (38); Ethnography (40);

Experiment (44); Hermeneutics (52); Interpretivism (56); Method (64); Methodology (65); Objectivity (70); Positivism (75); Reflexivity (87); Survey (105).

102 Structuralism/Poststructuralism

Structuralism and poststructuralism are theories about the social world that give emphasis to deep-lying structures that are not directly visible, but influence the way social actors think and behave. This school of thought is opposed to empiricism with its focus on experience, and in particular the constant conjunction of those experiences, as it seeks to identify these underlying structures that are prior to, and indeed cause, human behaviours. The most prominent form of structuralism is the linguistic variant, exemplified by the work of Ferdinand de Saussure and Claude Levi-Strauss. For them, it is the hidden and underlying structures of language that condition the behaviours and forms of thinking adopted by human beings. This therefore lays it open to the charge that it embraces a deterministic dimension, in which human beings are so imprisoned by linguistic structures that they cannot operate outside their bounds.

Saussure distinguishes between *langue* and *parole*. Langue is the formal structure of the language we speak, and determines the relations between the different parts. Parole is the way this is translated into everyday speech. Saussure was more concerned with the former than the latter, and he described langue as a system of signs where the meaning of each sign does not reside in each individual part but in the relationship between these parts. So, we cannot understand a word like 'formal' without also relating it to its binary opposite, 'informal'. Furthermore, these binary systems which structure our language are a function of the way language has evolved. Meanings that people give to events in their lives are therefore shaped by these structures. This linguistic turn in social theory came to incorporate other social phenomena and regard them as representations or signs, such as fashion, sporting contests and the like. Indeed, a version of structuralism, known as *anthropological structuralism*, popularized by Levi-Strauss, sought to extend this basic means of analysis to all forms of relations between human beings. His most famous example was the way he used the underlying structures of language to inform his study of kinship systems. Ultimately, he sought to extend structural analysis to the mind and in particular claimed to have identified unconscious structures that through careful analysis could be described as general laws.

Various forms of poststructuralism were invented, notably structural Marxism and Foucault's early work on the archaeology of knowledge. These rapidly gave way to forms of postmodernist thinking, which are informed by a rejection of foundational principles (structuralists sought to develop such principles, in particular, by emphasizing language structures), and indeed, by a desire to decentre human existence, to move away from a logo-centric viewpoint.

Educational researchers were greatly influenced by the linguistic turn in social theory, and the emphasis it placed on meaning residing in language structures. However, the weaknesses in structuralist analysis (the marginalization of agency, and the deterministic dimension) have meant that social and educational theorists have begun to move towards dualistic (embracing structure and agency) ways of understanding social life. However, certain forms of mathematical modelling of educational systems still retain elements of structural determinism, even if they are not located in systems of language.

See also:
Agency (4); Causation (11); Critical Realism (21); Determinism (29); Empiricism (36); Interpretivism (56); Postmodernism (76); Structure (103).

103 Structure

The notion of structure in educational research is a contested concept, and is used in different ways by researchers. It is also frequently used in opposition to agency, and this has resulted in research perspectives that prioritize one of these at the expense of the other. So, for example, interpretivism, ethnomethodology and phenomenology are approaches that focus on and prioritize the intentional and active role of the individual in social life, whereas variable analysis, correlational research and mathematical modelling are strategies that focus on persistent patterns of human relations, and may as a result marginalize agency. However, though structure and agency refer to different aspects of social life, this does not mean that they cannot be understood as in a relation to each other. The nature of this relation has been the subject of much discussion over the last 20 years, with two competing theories taking centre stage.

The first, popularized by Anthony Giddens (1984), is the theory of structuration. This comprises four interrelated propositions (Clark, 1990). The first of these is that social theory needs to focus on social practices, and not on individual action (for example, methodological individualism) or social determinism (for example, structural functionalism or neo-Marxism). The second proposition is that human beings are knowledgeable agents with powers to make a difference. Furthermore, they have the capacity to monitor their own actions and thus change the practical setting of action. The third of these propositions suggests that these social practices are ordered across space and time. Social actors draw on these structural properties, but are never absolutely constrained by them. Finally, what follows from this is the fourth of his propositions, which is that structure is both the medium and outcome of human interaction and thus human agency is responsible for both the production and reproduction of society.

The second theory, popularized by Margaret Archer (1982), is a morphogenetic/morphostatic framework, which again comprises four interrelated propositions. The first of these is that agency and structure cannot be so tightly integrated that they cannot be examined separately. The second proposition, and indeed an implication of this, is that action or complex interchanges (agency) may lead to changes in structures, but these do not immediately change the conditions in which individuals and collectivities of individuals make decisions and act with each other. This is because there are emergent properties that are separable from the actions and interactions that ultimately produced them. The third proposition is that this process results in endless sequences of action and interaction, structural change and then structural elaboration. Finally, the fourth proposition is that this results in a dualism between structure and agency and not a duality, as in the theory of structuration.

Both these then are attempts to reconcile structure and agency, and in the process move beyond those educational strategies and methods that prioritize the one over the other. The question still remains as to what these structures are, and this is more contentious. There are a number of possibilities.

1. Structures are constraints on human action. So, for example, language or discourse acts to only allow particular ways of thinking about and understanding the world. Or, to give another example, laws compel attendance at school for children between certain ages – there is a penalty attached to the breaking of this law.

2. Structures are rules and resources in society that both constrain and enable social actors in what they do. So, for example, affluent parents can choose to send their children to either fee-paying or maintained schools, whereas less affluent parents do not have this choice. The arrangement of resources in society therefore acts as an organizing and conditioning (both enabling and constraining) device for action and interaction.

3. Structures refer to persistent relations between human beings, so, for example, children between certain ages go to school – schooling can therefore be defined as an institutional structure because it persists over time and because it refers to relations between social actors.
4. Material structures refer to the character of the physical world and the corporality of the body. Again, this type of structure may be understood as enabling or constraining. It would be a mistake to limit understanding of structure to the material or physical alone; structure also refers to non-material phenomena, such as discourses, as these operate on human beings and indeed act as the condition for action.

Structures or structural phenomena, therefore, play an important part in discussions of educational research methodology, because educational researchers seek to describe a real world, consisting of both agency and structures.

See also:
Agency (4); Correlational Research (18); Critical Realism (21); Determinism (29); Discourse (31); Ethnomethodology (41); Interpretivism (56); Mathematical Modelling (62); Phenomenology (73); Power (77); Reflexivity (87); Variable Analysis (116).

104   Subjectivity

The concept of subjectivity is used by educational researchers to refer to different aspects of the research process. The first of these is the researcher's relations with the subjects of their research, and it is contrasted with a notion of objectivity, where the researcher's biases, preconceptions and values are eliminated from their descriptions of reality because they are deemed to be subjective. The second aspect refers to the emphasis that should be given by the researcher to their research subjects' desires, projects or intentions. Different paradigms or approaches to research adopt different positions in relation to this. So, for example, behaviourism, located within a natural science model of explanation, seeks to eliminate any references to beliefs, purposes and meaning. On the other hand, a phenomenological approach to educational research foregrounds these subjective elements, and indeed would not want to attach any pejorative meaning to them.

In relation to the researcher's relations with participants, some theorists would understand their task as the elimination of bias from the act of doing research, with the effect that subjective elements, including political, social and ethical preferences for one version of reality over another, play no part in the eventual descriptions that are made of the educational setting. The difficult question that has to be answered by researchers is whether it is both possible and desirable to eliminate such subjective preferences. Weber (1974) suggested that the research act comprises three phases: orientation, data collection and analysis, and dissemination. The first and last of these phases, he argued, are value-relevant activities. The middle phase, for him, should, however, be value-free. The major problem with his approach is that even here it is difficult to see how all traces of value can be eliminated, especially in so far as observation involves a theory about what it means. It is not literally possible to observe anything in the world without a theory or definition that precedes the act of observation. Definitions are fundamentally belief-orientated. In short, language cannot be neutral and it involves us in using pre-judgements about what we observe.

The second aspect of subjectivity, though related to the first, refers to the subject matter of research. Individuals in society have preferences, desires and intentions. The question that has concerned theorists is whether an authentic science of society is possible without proper reference being made to these inner states of being. Are they irrelevant to descriptions of human life or are they central? Those theorists who would argue for their centrality suggest that reasons can be causes, and this enjoins the researcher to seek out and incorporate into their research texts the self-reported reasons for individual actions. However, those taking up this position do not then want to conclude that social actors can give a complete and accurate picture of what is going on, only that these self-descriptions are central to a proper understanding of social life. What this also implies is that a purely phenomenological perspective is inadequate, and this is so for four reasons. First, social actors operate through acknowledged conditions, that is, social structures within which the actor is positioned. Second, individuals immersed in society operate under the assumption that there are unintended consequences to their actions, because of the collective nature of human life. Third, social actors operate through tacit knowledge structures, of which they may only have a bare inkling. Finally, individuals may be influenced by unconscious motivations. Behaviourist desires to marginalize these states of consciousness are therefore, despite the caveats suggested above, likely to lead to impoverished descriptions of human activity.

The final question that needs to be addressed by educational researchers is the epistemological one of how we can know and describe these subjective states, and this is where the two meanings given to the notion of subjectivity are connected. If it is accepted that educational research is not value-free, but comprises, at least in part, the imposition of one set of values on another, then describing another person's subjectivity is always an act of power; and furthermore, one in which the researcher does not just describe those subjective states but contributes to their formation. Research is therefore active in the sense that it both paints a picture of what is and, in part, adds to the discursive resources in society that contribute to individual actions. Researchers in turn have to make difficult decisions about how they understand and focus on subjectivity, both in terms of researcher relations with subjects and the subjective states of those being researched.

See also:
Causation (11); Coding (14); Dissemination (32); Objectivity (70); Paradigm (72); Phenomenology (73); Positivism (75); Power (77); Realism (83); Structure (103); Values (115).

105   Survey

In education much research is carried out in the name of survey, or a survey approach, and the published literature reflects eclectic definitions, some of which are particularly inclusive. Consider Denscombe's (1998: 7) definition of survey as 'an approach in which there is empirical research pertaining to a given point of time which aims to incorporate as wide and inclusive data as possible': perhaps the broadest definition in circulation. The key point being made, however, is that survey is an approach or strategy rather than a single method or technique and draws upon a range of methods that include questionnaire, interview and document survey, for example. A less inclusive definition comes from Cohen *et al.* (2000: 169):

> Typically, surveys gather data at a particular point in time with the intention of describing the nature of existing conditions, or identifying standards against which existing conditions can be compared, or determining the relationship between specific events.

Perhaps its most familiar usage can be identified in terms of a rather narrower definition in which its most commonly identifiable characteristics are to collect information:

- from a group of people in order to *describe* characteristics such as attitudes, opinions, beliefs, aptitudes, abilities, or knowledge;
- by *asking questions* in which the responses or answers to those questions constitute the data of the survey;
- from a *sample* rather than every member of the population. (Adapted from Fraenkel and Wallen 2003: 396.)

Survey research has had a somewhat chequered history in education and the social sciences. As Pole and Lampard (2002: 89) point out, this has varied from 'uncritical acceptance to irrational distaste' to the extent that more than 20 years ago, Marsh (1982) felt it important to defend the survey against its critics in the social sciences. Today, this is unnecessary, but as Pole and Lampard suggest, Marsh's (1982: 7) definition of a social survey still provides us with a very good starting point, especially her identification of three key features. These also allow us to build on the definitions shown above.

In her view, a survey takes place when:

- systematic measurements are made of the same set of properties or *variables*, for each of a number of cases;
- the resulting data can be laid out in a form of a rectangle, or *matrix*, in which the rows correspond to the cases and the columns respond to the properties or variables;
- the intention is to look at patterns in the variables by aggregating information from the cases. (ibid.)

Five general points can be made. First, it can be seen that the primary interest of the survey researcher is in *description*. Second, the emphasis is very much upon the collection of *standardized* information. Third, implicit in this standardization is what Pole and Lampard (2002: 90, their emphasis) describe as the '*counting process* implicit in the aggregation of information across cases'. Fourth, 'the validity of this counting process depends upon the *equivalence* of the information collected from the various cases' (ibid., our emphasis) or instances. Fifth, as the definition from Cohen *et al.* (2000) indicates, surveys can also be *relational* or *analytical*, that is, designed specifically to explore the relationship between variables. Where this occurs, researchers are commonly interested in examining the relationship between one set of responses and another and apply the techniques of correlational research. In summary, then, a survey approach is the most appropriate when systematic and comparable data are needed, usually from a relatively large number of individuals.

There are two main types of survey, *cross-sectional* and *longitudinal*. In the former information is collected at one point in time from a predefined sample population. If an entire population is sampled, it is commonly known as a census. In a longitudinal survey, data is collected at more than one point in time in order to study changes over time. These are generally known as *trend, cohort* and *panel* studies, and following Fraenkel and Wallen (2003: 396–7), can be summarized as follows.

- In a trend survey, different samples from a population whose members may change are surveyed at different points in time.
- In a cohort survey, the researcher samples a particular population which does not change over time, and a different sample from the same population would be sampled at different times.
- In a panel survey, the researcher surveys the same sample at different points of time during the survey.

Surveys may differ widely on a range of dimensions.

- *Scale and Scope.* Some surveys are small, and may be taken, for example, from a case study of an individual education institution where a survey is used with all teaching staff. This is quite a common approach in small-scale research for doctoral studies. Other studies are large like the National Child Development Study (Fogelman, 1985) or very large like Elley's (1994) study of literacy across more than thirty school systems worldwide.
- *Structure.* Types of surveys vary. Moreover, some large-scale surveys combine different types at different stages, for example, cross-sectional in one part with longitudinal in another.
- *Purpose.* Surveys can be used to answer many different kinds of questions. De Vaus (1996) identifies four types of survey to reflect purpose: factual, attitudinal, socio-psychological and explanatory. Each draws upon different levels of statistical complexity, from head counts, to two-way tables or correlations, to more complex, multivariate analyses.
- *Insrumentation.* Most commonly used is the questionnaire, and also interviews. Recently, both have drawn upon methods other than face-to-face approaches, such as telephone and, increasingly, email and the Internet. These bring particular challenges (see below).

The most common types of instrument are the questionnaire and the interview survey. Obvious differences between them lie in the absence or presence of the researcher as questioner. With regard to interviews, the researcher conducts face-to-face interviews, using pre-scheduled questions. There are rather obvious advantages and disadvantages. Positively, the researcher as interviewer may be able to gain rapport and get full responses, which can be clarified and developed. Less positively, this approach can be expensive, especially of time resource, and at the largest scale, requires many trained interviewers. And there are some topics in education that may be sufficiently sensitive *not* to be surveyed face-to-face.

For such reasons, questionnaire-type surveys are more common, and can be variously administered. Face-to-face administration of questionnaires to a group who are available to the researcher at the same time is cost-effective and offers prospects for a 100 per cent response rate. However, not all surveys of a 'captive audience' are appropriate and may raise issues about the likely truthfulness of 'quick' response and about the relationship between the researcher and the researched. Postal surveys can be relatively cost-effective but their appearance is crucial to maximize interest and likelihood of response. They may also minimize survey-interviewer bias but they can take time to complete and this may be a deterrent to completion. Telephone surveys are a relatively fast way of gaining data, and rarely last more than 10 to 15 minutes; they also allow a breadth of response from a large number of participants, who, in addition, can be probed further in ways that are not possible in a postal survey. They do, of course, depend upon participants having access to a telephone. Good general accounts of the field are available (e.g. Lavrakas, 1993). Because there are numerous texts devoted to the survey approach, these are not repeated here. However, specific mention is given to more recent forms – web-based surveys, mixed-mode surveys and recent developments in cross-cultural surveys.

With regard to the first, Dillman (2000) provides very useful principles in relation to the design of questionnaires for *web surveys*. Some principles, of course, pertain for all surveys that are adapted for web-based use: for example, the importance of beginning with a welcome screen that is motivational and gives clear guidance for actions needed for the website respondent to proceed, and providing a PIN number that is available for access only to those people in the survey. Advice is also given to present each question in a conventional format but to provide clear and specific on-screen guidance on how to proceed through 'drop-down' responses, 'skip questions' and the like. Access and representativeness issues magnify in relation to email and Internet surveys; technological proficiency on the part of researchers and participants is strongly implicated, as is the latter's affinity with regular web use. Web-based surveys are becoming more popular. In Internet surveys, both email and HTML form-based surveys can be used. Web-based surveys may be reserved for HTML form-based surveys or alternatively, web-type surveys can be sent to participants on disk.

Advantages accrue in terms of time, cost and ease of distributable post-survey feedback to participants. Not surprisingly, disadvantages are also apparent. The first relates both to participant access and willingness to use the Internet; second, it may be difficult to access appropriate sampling frames; third, response rates to Internet surveys still remain lower than for other forms of survey, although this is changing; fourth, it is more difficult to meet the needs for anonymity and confidentiality and may therefore raise particular ethical issues; fifth, the appearance of the survey, especially where would-be participants have different kinds and levels of access can have significant effects. Finally, the immediacy of being able to log off 'instantly' can act as a deterrent to completion and return.

Increasingly popular are *mixed-mode surveys* that combine the use of telephone, postal, web-based and face-to-face procedures to collect data for a single study. Dillman (2000) provides a summary of factors in favour and against. Particularly, to counter the high economic cost of surveys and low-response rates, three main advantages are cited: first, mixed modes may enhance survey participation if participants are able to switch methods (though this may not always be the case); second, mixed sequential methods can also decrease costs, for example, sending a postal survey first, and then following up non-respondents by telephone; third, mixed modes can be used in a survey where the data being collected has particularly sensitive components, for example, in the use of computer-assisted self-interviewing (CASI). Disadvantages centre on the need to minimize mode effects, i.e. the issue of whether the respondent's answer in one mode is the same as it might have been if answered in another. According to Dillman, three factors would appear to contribute to mode differences: the presence or absence of the survey interviewer, the use of communication that is aural rather than visual, and whether control of the question stimulus is by the survey interviewer or by the respondent.

The conditions under which survey research is carried out in different parts of the world may differ widely. When research methods texts are transposed internationally, it can be argued that insufficient attention is often given to particular national, regional and local conditions. Writing more than 30 years ago, Frey (1970: 184) argues that the differences are one of degree rather than kind:

> There are no fundamental differences in principle or in logic between cross-cultural survey research and within-cultural survey research ... important 'sub-cultural' variations between classes, educational groups, regional populations and other social echelons plague the domestic survey researcher in a manner quite

analogous to the more pronounced full-cultural variations that loom before the cross-cultural survey researcher ... [Nonetheless] differences in degree ... have weighty implications for cross-cultural survey research. Not only are the problems more severe, but their existence is more conspicuous.

It could be argued that the criticisms levelled against *cross-cultural surveys*, in terms of reliability and validity, are no more serious than for other forms of research, such as observational studies, where distortion and lack of understanding might be manifest in different forms. It would be important not to exaggerate the cross-cultural survey effect, although it is suggested that surveys are, in particular, prone to different interpretations of what, how and why responses should be given (or not), and in various relation to truthfulness. Meanwhile, advocacy of cross-cultural research approaches to educational leadership and management, for example, continues to grow. For recent examples and rationale, see Walker and Dimmock (2004).

Regardless of whether the researcher is using more traditional approaches to surveys or is drawing upon the most recent application of ICT within-cultures or cross-cultures, a number of key issues pertain to survey design and these can be summarized as follows.

- The nature of the question asked and the way it is asked is extremely important.
- Most questionnaire surveys use some form of closed-ended question. Here, the emphasis is upon the short, the simple (as possible) and the unambiguous, and avoidance of leading questions, bias in use of language and 'double negatives'.
- Some questionnaires use open-ended questions. These allow more individualized responses, but may be more difficult to measure in a quantitative way. Some would-be respondents avoid them, and this can encourage item non-response.
- All questionnaire surveys should be piloted or pre-tested.
- The appearance of a survey may determine whether an informant responds.
- Well-organized contingency questions (a question whose response depends on how the informant responded to a previous question) are very important.
- Cover letters are crucial.
- Using survey instruments requires skill and training. These requirements are amplified in large-scale surveys.
- Total non-response and individual item non-response are major problems for survey research. This tendency has increased in recent years.

- Analysing surveys requires skill and competence.
- In addition to defects in instrument design, there are a number of threats to the internal validity of the survey instrument: mortality (in the case of longitudinal surveys); location (where the survey takes place); and instrumentation (when the interviewer is untrained, tired, rude, biased ...). (Adapted from Fraenkel and Wallen, 2003: 410–11.)

Researchers in education tend to have rather polarized views about the importance of surveys. Debates link not only to the construction and design of surveys as technically satisfying aspects of survey design but also to issues of theory construction and analysis. As Pole and Lampard (2002: 90–1, their emphasis), comment:

The choice of concepts to be covered within a research instrument [like the survey] inevitably reflects the researcher's substantive and theoretical agenda, as does the ways in which the questions designed to measure those concepts are constructed. The process of *operationalisation* i.e. the generation of measurable forms of indicators of concepts, is fundamental both to the form of the research instrument and its validity. In survey research the most important elements ... need to be predetermined, and the concepts deemed to be important dictate which data are collected.

Variables are constructed to measure 'effects' (dependent variables); explanations or 'causes' (independent variables); the relationship between the independent and the dependent; and the effect of context (or 'background' variables).

The multi-purpose and complex nature of the task has, in part, made survey research vulnerable to two different kinds of criticism. On the one hand, survey research is seen as a 'real world' strategy or set of tools for hypothesis testing for the verification of theory and, on the other hand, a falsely prestigious form of research 'dangerously presenting itself as a source of findings whose meaning can be understood without theoretical explanation' (Pole and Lampard, 2002: 91). The status of survey research has also, in important respects, been associated with the criticisms levelled at positivism (albeit understood in myriad forms) and quantitative approaches to research. In response to such critiques, Pole and Lampard (2002: 95) acknowledge that some survey research has been 'scientistic' (in ignoring the importance of the agency of its subjects), sexist and/or manipulative, but that it does not have to be. Historically, most large-scale research was done by men, and mostly by the powerful 'on' the powerless. Advocating a healthy scepticism of its outcomes, they argue, does not negate the usefulness of surveys. In such ways, researchers in education can be as reflexive about surveys, it is argued, as they are about other forms of research, especially when such scepticism generates a number of helpful questions.

1. Can the educational phenomena of interest be quantified in such a way as to produce values which are valid measures of respondents' characteristics?
2. Are these values comparable and hence the aggregation inherent in counting them legitimate?
3. Are the variables generated by a survey theoretically meaningful and relevant, and are their assumed meanings consistent with the respondent's perspective on the phenomenon?
4. Can the data collected by a survey be used to answer theoretically interesting questions, or do they pose interesting substantive questions which require further theorizing or data collection? (Adapted from Pole and Lampard, ibid.)

Elsewhere, Oppenheim (1992: 17–18) warns against the tendency to give 'strong' (by statistical calculation) associations between variables the status of 'causes':

The reason ... is that we do not know their place in the complex network of causality ... In choosing our research strategy, our research design, and statistical analysis, we should therefore remain aware that they contain implicit assumptions about causal links and causal processes in people ... Whilst we can make good use of existing research methods in the service of replicability, data disaggregation, and representativeness ... human lives are not composed of layers of regression coefficients.

See also:
Causation (11); Correlational Research (18); Design (28); Questionnaire (82); Method (64); Methodology (65); Objectivity (70); Quantitative Research (81); Questionnaire (82); Reflexivity (87); Reliability (91); Representativeness (93); Sampling (98); Statistics (100); Telephone Interviews (108); Validity (113); Variable Analysis (116).

106 Symbolic Interactionism

Symbolic interactionism has provided a framework for investigating education that was especially popular in the UK from the 1960s onwards when a considerable number of school ethnographies were considered to derive from symbolic interactionism. Within such frameworks or paradigms, there is a central focus upon the symbolic meanings that human beings attach to interpersonal relations. In the example of Burgess (1983), this was to focus attention on the ways that various members of Bishop McGregor School, as it was called, defined the situations in which they worked and studied, by giving detailed attention to the various ways in which such definitions were re-worked and reinterpreted as everyday school practice. For Burgess, then, school was seen as a 'social creation' (ibid.: 3) in which relations among teachers, among pupils, and between teachers and pupils were negotiated (and renegotiated), defined (and redefined) in and as everyday action.

The issue of the *situated* nature of individuals' accounts is of particular note, as it was in relation to the now seminal works of the genre that emerged from the social sciences in the USA, specifically the work of the Chicago School in the first half of the twentieth century. As Silverman (2001: 288) comments:

> Using their eyes as well as listening to what people were saying, these sociologists invariably located 'consciousness' in specific forms of social organization. As we saw, Whyte (1949) showed how the behaviour of barman and waitresses was a response to the imperatives of status and the organization of work routines. The experiences of such staff needed to be contexted by knowledge of such features and by precise observation of the territorial organization of restaurants.

From the above, participant observation is of key importance in order to gain knowledge about participants' perspectives. Other methods have become increasingly commonplace as evidenced in diary, document and interview research.

A second important aspect of symbolic interactionism is the focus upon the *social self*, and is a distinctive aspect of the work of one of the most influential symbolic interactionists of the twentieth century, namely G.H. Mead (1984), and before him Cooley (1902). As Bryman (1988: 54-5) explains:

> The idea of the social self draws attention to the individual as a complex mixture of biological instincts and internalized social constraints. These two facets of the self are captured in the distinction between respectively the 'I' and the 'Me' ... The 'Me' contains our view of ourselves as others see us, an idea neatly captured in Cooley's (1902) notion of 'the looking-glass self'.

Whereas the 'I' comprises the untrammelled urges of the individual, the 'Me' is a source of reflection about how we should act in particular situations.

Combining the central ideas constituted by 'definition of the situation' and 'the social self', symbolic interactionists' key interests derive from the way that human beings do not 'just' act but do so on the basis of how they define a particular situation and how they think others will interpret such actions. In which case, research participants are 'actors' in education *par excellence* and this is further evidenced in symbolic interactionists' determination, through the research process, to capture the 'interpretative process used by the person in dealing with the things he [sic] encounters' (Blumer 1969: 2).

A number of debates have emerged from the interactionist perspective, in particular 'whether the epistemology was closer to the natural science model' (Bryman, 1988: 56) than writers like Blumer might have allowed. Notwithstanding such debates, the significance of symbolic interactionism is in its emphasis upon detailed and deep investigation of the meanings that people (usually in micro-contexts) give to their experiences in educational settings, and this has continued to locate it as the epitome of qualitative research.

See also:
Agency (4); Diaries (30); Interpretivism (56); Interview (57); Naturalistic Observation (68); Qualitative Research (80).

107 Systematic Observation

In quantitative approaches, an essential element is the description and interpretation of educational experiences and activities in numerical terms, with a particular emphasis upon regularities, patterns, frequency and duration. Key proponents of what is sometimes called *systematic* or *structured observation* have been Croll (1986), Flanders (1970) and Galton *et al.* (1980) and such observations have been commonly applied to classroom observations in school. Notwithstanding attendant dangers in describing quantitative approaches *only* as 'systematic' (qualitative approaches to observation also require careful and systematic data management and analysis), a key feature of systematic observation lies in the careful definition and explication of the phenomena to be observed which are also measurable. As Croll (1986: ix, our emphases) explained:

Systematic observations in classrooms is a research method which uses a system of *highly structured* observation procedures applied by *trained* observers to gather data on *patterns of behaviour* and interaction in classrooms. Its key elements are, first that the observational procedures are carefully *defined* and *highly explicit* so that it is clear how descriptions are arrived at and the *idiosyncrasies* in an individual's selection and perception of events *are eliminated*. Second, variables are expressed in *quantitative terms*. The careful *definition of variables and categories* ... make it suitable for large-scale, comparative studies, in a way that is not generally true of other approaches to the study of classrooms. However, the methodology is also appropriate for small-scale research and case studies.

A number of implications derive from the above.

- An idea has to be translated into a variable and that variable has to be observable.
- Variables can be made up of elements or categories of behaviour.
- The observer knows beforehand what will be relevant. What is relevant is linked to the answer to the research question being addressed. It follows that there is an answer or answers.
- Observations are precise. Each category for observation is demarcated beforehand, agreed and understood.
- Observations require the minimum of interpretation although Croll (1986) distinguishes between *high-inference* and *low-inference* categories.
- Once observers have been trained, observations are relatively easy to record, and will be precise and complete.
- Observations are counted and analysed statistically for associations and correlation between variables.

We have suggested that the key elements of both naturalistic and systematic, qualitative and quantitative approaches to observation can be seen in terms of their epistemological underpinnings. Debates have often revolved around the perceived strengths and weaknesses of each method. More recently, approaches have been increasingly combined rather than competing, and a late-twentieth-century development was to add practitioner and action research as additional streams to observational approaches previously derived from, or separated into, more positivist or interpretivist traditions. In such ways, the advocacy of 'systematic self-critical enquiry' (first advocated by Stenhouse, 1985) draws upon peer observation, frequently in classrooms and more recently across schools, to encourage educators to work reflexively and in collaboration with each other as researchers, or with other researchers, to inform, develop and evaluate their own practice.

See also:
Action Research (3); Correlational Research (18); Epistemology/Ontology (38); Ethics (39); Ethnography (40); Interpretivism (56); Longitudinal Observation Studies (61); Mixed Methods (66); Naturalistic Observation (68); Observation (71); Positivism (75); Qualitative Research (80); Quantitative Research (81); Reflexivity (87); Variable Analysis (116).

108 Telephone Interviews

Telephone interviews are most often discussed either as an alternative to face-to-face interviewing or as an aspect of large-scale questionnaires in which the telephone is used as an alternative to the postal questionnaire or to the face-to-face interview survey or most recently, to email surveys. Historically, much of the negative criticism about telephone interviewing centred upon accusations of bias or the difficulty in obtaining a representative research sample of the population. Some of that criticism can now be countered. Most of the population in the UK has direct access to a telephone and, applying most recent technologies, a would-be random sample of respondents can be contacted using a random digit-dialling technique. However, criticism of this kind cannot be discounted altogether. The argument still pertains strongly to developing countries. Moreover, there is a growing trend for more domestic telephone numbers to be ex-directory, and for those who are to be ex-directory to share certain characteristics, for example, living in cities or living alone. Those who remain without a telephone are also most likely to be unemployed, on low incomes and single parents.

Criticisms that telephone interviews are less likely to yield 'honest' answers have also been levelled. This is not just because would-be respondents might be telephoned 'cold' and, therefore, researcher–informant rapport is less likely to develop across a short time interval, but there is also a tendency for telephone interviews, in any case, to be shorter, with a related tendency for answers to be briefer or more brusque. Again, such arguments have also been countered, for example by Thomas and Purdon (1995: 4) who argue not only that responses by telephone are as valid as by face-to-face interviewing, but that they might be more valid, with the tendency towards a willingness to respond to sensitive issues more frankly when *not* face-to-face. They may also remove the necessity of cluster sampling (Pole and Lampard, 2002: 113).

For all the arguments, it is difficult to avoid the conclusion that telephone interviewing is becoming more popular *mainly* because it is relatively cheaper than other forms of interview, allowing researchers in education to interview large numbers of respondents in different geographical locations and over a short timescale. Resource gains, therefore, are in terms of researcher time, less travel and breadth of coverage. Moreover, telephone interviews have the potential to share some of the advantages of face-to-face interviews. Questions or queries can be cleared up by the interviewer as the interview proceeds and, in common with the face-to-face interview, interview schedules can be customized to prompt answers to previous questions and use complicated skip patterns. For most respondents, it is considered that verbal responses to verbal cues are 'easier' than written ones. And a central interviewing centre may make the task of supervising a team of interviewers, as well as standardizing the approach taken, more straightforward.

A familiar aspect of telephone interviewing is its 'cold calling' technique which has the advantage of wide coverage and the means of moving from one potential interviewee to the next when the would-be respondent is not at home or unavailable or refuses to respond. However, response rates can be seriously affected when 'calling cold'. As Gillham (2000: 86) points out: 'In a society where unsolicited telephone sales approaches are a contemporary nuisance, you have to be particularly skilled, or particularly thick-skinned, to overcome the initial confusion or resistance of the person you are calling.' To this we might add, particularly resilient given the proliferation of telephone answering machines that make it more challenging to have direct voice-to-voice contact.

For ethical reasons, as well as those to do with the effects of non-contacts and refusals upon the validity of the instrument, increasing numbers of researchers use telephone interviews once they have negotiated access with the respondent beforehand. While this is not dissimilar to other forms of interviewing, it does decrease the resource savings noted above. So, times may be 'booked' in advance for the telephone interview and/or questions can be sent to the interviewee in advance. If the telephone interview is to be recorded, then permission of the respondent might also be confirmed (or denied).

A disadvantage of the telephone interview is the absence of non-verbal cues and a heightened awareness by the researcher as well as the respondent of the sound and intonation of his/her own voice. Given rapid advances in telephone technology, such absence may be short-lived as visual telecommunications become more commonplace and/or when the respondent has received the questions in writing beforehand. Meanwhile, given the concentration required by both parties and the respondent's willingness or not to remain on the telephone, it is unusual for telephone interviews to last longer than 20 minutes (see also Lavrakas, 1993).

For the reasons given above it seems likely that, in the short term at least, telephone interviewing as a substitute for the postal questionnaire or a face-to-face survey is likely to be more widespread than its use to replace in-depth qualitative approaches to interviewing, other than when the absence of a face-to-face encounter is judged to be the more ethical approach to researching sensitive subject matter.

See also:
Access (2); Ethics (39); Interview (57); Questionnaire (82); Sampling (98); Survey (105).

109   Tests

Various types of standardized and non-standardized tests have been developed and these aim to measure a wide range of individuals' skills, aptitudes, traits and behaviours. For example, tests have been developed to measure: self-esteem, intelligence, stress, manual dexterity, musicality, creativity, political orientation, mathematical aptitude, reading ability, hyperactivity/distractability and aggressiveness. Standardized tests allow researchers to compare the results from their own tests given to a small sample of respondents with the results from a national population. Tests are of two types: *norm-referenced* and *criterion-referenced*. Norm-referenced tests determine a fixed level of passes at particular grades regardless of the yearly intake. They thus follow a normal distribution curve, which is determined beforehand. Criterion-referenced tests do not operate through the setting of quotas for particular grades, but assess an individual's work against a set of indicator descriptors. In theory if a test has five levels of passing and one level of failing, then if the test was criterion-referenced, everyone taking the test could pass at the highest grade level. If the test was norm-referenced, then individuals would be distributed in line with a normal or standardized distribution curve, and this means that not everyone could pass at the highest grade. In practice, especially with high-stakes examinations such as the GCSE, though they purport to be criterion-referenced, adjustments are frequently made so that they conform to previously established norms.

Tests are required to be reliable and valid. Reliability refers to the degree of accuracy of a test in relation to what it purports to measure. A common method of determining the reliability of a test is to test the same group of people on two separate occasions over a short period of time. Results are then compared and if they correlate, the test is said to be reliable. Three assumptions are being made here: first, that the time gap between the two testing occasions is short enough so that it can be assumed that their skills have not naturally improved; second, that the taking of the first test does not improve the ability of the students to take the second test; and third, that both testing occasions accurately measure the capability of the individuals taking the tests. This is a form of *test–retest reliability*. Another way of determining the reliability of a test is the *split-half method*, where scores obtained from comparable halves of a test or from odd and even questions are compared and correlated. If the correlation is a high one, then the researcher is entitled to conclude that the test is reliable. However, even here, there are problems, as an assumption is made that items in a test that are being compared are alike in all their essential aspects, and it is not always possible to make this assumption.

Tests also have to be valid and in this context, a number of types of validity have been suggested (Borg and Gall, 1983).

- *Content validity.* This is a measure of whether the items in a test measure the content that they were intended to measure.
- *Predictive validity.* This is a measure of whether the scores from a test are able to predict a score on a test conducted at a later time point where the same constructs but at a different level of difficulty are being used.
- *Concurrent validity.* This is a measure of whether results from the testing instrument correlate with other results where both sets of data are collected at the same time point.
- *Construct validity.* This is a measure of whether items in a test measure hypothetical constructs or concepts.
- *Face validity.* This is a measure of whether the items in a test appear at face value to measure what they intend to measure.

The use of tests in educational research has been criticized for a number of reasons. First, as we have suggested above, reliability and validity devices are not always easy to apply and may give misleading results. Second, the construct being measured has to be tightly enough defined so that it can be measured and, unless this is done, it may lead to the measurement of an impoverished or incoherent construct. An example is IQ tests where it is very difficult to establish and reach agreement about a general construct of intelligence. Third, test-takers do not always perform to the best of their ability when being tested, and thus the test results reflect performance in a test and not actual competence. Finally, some attributes, traits or behaviours may be of the type that is not amenable to being tested for. Attitude inventories are frequently thought of as misrepresenting the distribution of that attitude among a defined population for two reasons: first, respondents are not sure about their beliefs and frequently change their minds; second, in order for the distribution of an attitude to be tested it has to be reduced and instrumentalized so that in the end the results of the tests are unable to capture a true understanding of the construct purportedly being measured.

See also:
Assessment (7); Distribution (33); Prediction (78); Reliability (91); Sampling (98); Validity (113); Variable Analysis (116).

110 Textuality

The notion of textuality refers to the way the educational research text or report is constructed. The *academic realist text* is a traditional form of academic writing in which the writer of the research report writes himself or herself out of the text. No reference is made to the autobiography of the writer, or to the context in which the data was collected. There is generally some methodological discussion that explains the way the data was collected and analysed. The assumption is made that the writer's own preferences, understandings of the world and ways of conceiving method can be put to one side during the data collection and analysis stages and do not contribute to the type of data collected. The text is linear, again usually presented as a series of stages: hypothesis formation, operationalizing of concepts, presentation of data, data analysis and conclusions/recommendations. All traces of the constructed nature of the text are erased thus giving the impression that the text stands in some unproblematic way for the reality it purports to describe.

A *broken text*, on the other hand, does not exhibit a linear form, but is broken up, discontinuous, comes to sudden endings and does not have a recognizable coherence to it. It is difficult to read as most readers are inducted into traditional forms of writing and therefore look for coherence where none is intended. Indeed, texts such as these are sometimes judged by conventional standards and usually found wanting. The rationale for such a textual form is that it seeks to convey the impression that the sequence of events it is attempting to describe does not take the form that the realist textual approach would suggest. If reality is unstructured, messy, serendipitous, then the text should convey this in the way it is written.

Van Maanen (1988) identifies another form of textuality, which can be distinguished from the academic realist form, where the authorial 'I' is privileged. The *traditional academic text* excludes the confessional or refers to it separately from the research report itself. Recently ethnographers have sought to provide confessional accounts of the research process and within these accounts justify the choices they made during the fieldwork period. This has by necessity included biographical data, though it is of course biographical data expressed in a traditional academic form. Some researchers would go beyond the merely attached confessional account and argue that the textually mediated reflexive stance needs to be more fundamental than this: 'Rather it is the effect of sociality and the inscription of the self in social practices, language and discourses which constitute the research process' (Usher 1996: 9).

The *transparent text* can be contrasted with opaque writing that seeks to conceal the reflexivity of the writer. Furthermore, the opaque text seeks to present itself as authoritative by using devices such as extensive but uncritical referencing, polemic, assertion, decontextualization both of data collection and analysis and a desire to conceal its epistemological and ontological frameworks with the intention of suggesting that these are unproblematic. The transparent text, on the other hand, shows its hand at every point and allows the reader to make a proper judgement about how the data were collected and how the conclusions the researcher came to were reached. It is transparent in that it does not (though this is rarely possible) seek to conceal its genesis as knowledge.

The *dialogic text* can be contrasted with the monologic text where the voice that is always privileged and given most emphasis is the voice of the researcher. The dialogic form refers to the disprivileging of the author's voice; equal standing being given to a multitude of voices. This may represent an aspiration rather than a reality since the authority of the author is always sustained in any text through the researcher's selection of voices, their central role in the data-collection process and their choice of focus. However, the dialogic author attempts to minimize the extent of their role in the research and give expression to a large number of voices through quotation and minimal comment and analysis.

The distinction between '*readerly*' and '*writerly*' texts is one developed by Barthes (1975). He was concerned to suggest that a text may be deliberately constructed so that it allows the reader to write their own agenda into it during their reading of it. This is a 'writerly' text and can be contrasted with a 'readerly' text, which attempts to rule out or signal as incorrect alternative interpretations. No text is able absolutely to sustain itself as a prescriptive or 'readerly' text, not least in that the reader may simply ignore it altogether. However, the distinction here is intended to suggest that texts are constructed differently in terms of how much space is allowed to the reader to incorporate their own understandings of events and activities referred to in the text into the way they read those texts.

The *polemical text* seeks to persuade its audience that they should think in one way and not in another. It therefore does not engage in any form of internal debate. Evidence is presented selectively to support a particular case, and indeed if it is thought that persuasion is possible without reference to evidence, and even that reference to evidence may weaken the polemical message, then the rhetorical message is deemed to be sufficient. Furthermore, no attempt is made to describe what is and then argue that this is where one should be, because accurate depictions of reality are not necessary if one is trying to persuade the reader to believe that this is what should be.

The *report as a text* is characterized differently. Here the purpose is technical, uni-dimensional, sparse, bereft of references to past work and to wider concerns. An argument is sustained by reiteration so that each point is made a number of times at different moments in the text. Above all, the report is recommendatory so that the purpose is to suggest a plan of action, which, if the report is accepted, will lead to changes to working practices, usually set out in terms of a number of definite steps. Bullet points are common, reflective writing is avoided and practical action is the main rationale for its production. Furthermore, audience receptivity is paramount so that it might include an executive summary for busy readers who cannot find the time to read the report in full; or the vocabulary and constructional devices are such that they are in tune with those used by the readership. For example, a report to parents from a school is written differently from one to the governors of that school. Here assumptions are being made about the discourse community for which the report is designed. Forms of textuality are numerous, some of which have been suggested above.

See also:
Biography/Autobiography (8); Discourse (31); Ethnography (40); Power (77); Realism (83); Reflexivity (87); Research Community (95); Writing (118).

111 Transferability

As an alternative to empirical generalizability, Guba and Lincoln (1985) proposed the notion of transferability. With generalization or external validity, the relationship between a sample of cases and the population to which it refers is established. This can be established prior to the investigation or after the data has been collected. If the method chosen for the research study is experimental, then the generalizability of the results to the whole population is in part determined by the degree of randomness achieved in the selection of the control and experimental groups. Random allocation of subjects to these groups allows the researcher some measure of certainty that the effects they record as a result of their experiment can be applied outside the bounds of the experiment itself and to the larger population. Quasi-experimental groups, where it is not possible to randomly control the selection of subjects, therefore have weak external validity. Survey researchers, on the other hand, in order to establish whether their results can be generalized from the sample to the population, have to make some initial decisions about the type of sampling that they employ. Probability sampling, whether random, systematic or stratified, is determined both by size and sampling error. The purpose is to represent adequately the population and to determine a confidence level in the external validity of the results. Clearly if sampling error is detected, then the researcher is less entitled to claim that their results can be generalized to the wider population to which they refer. Various statistical tests can be applied to the results to determine if a sampling error has been made. Non-probability sampling procedures, though easier to set up by the researcher, have weak external validity, though if the purpose is not empirical generalizability, this may not be a significant consideration.

There are, however, a number of problems with empirical generalizability. First, in order to determine sample composition, size and error in relation to the general population, the case has to be tightly defined and alike in all essential respects to the other cases that make up both the sample and the population. A reductive process of variable analysis, therefore, is a precondition of establishing empirical generalizability. The effects of different variables either have to be pre-controlled, as in a randomized experimental design, or controlled after the data has been collected, as in some forms of correlational research. These processes are difficult to operationalize. Second, there is the problem of induction, where on a strictly logical basis, it is not possible to make universal claims from a finite number of cases (Popper, 1976). Third, as critical realists would argue, empirical generalizability operates at the level of experiences and seeks to describe their constant, or otherwise, conjunctions, and is therefore not concerned with a depth ontology, which suggests the existence of underlying mechanisms that may or may not be activated.

In response to these and a number of other concerns, Guba and Lincoln (1985) proposed an alternative to generalizability or external validity. Instead of seeking to determine the relationship between the sample and the population to enable claims at different levels of statistical significance to be made about the results of a research project, here the burden of proof is left in the hands of readers and users of research. As one of their four trustworthiness criteria for a constructivist inquiry process (the others are credibility, dependability and confirmability), transferability demands of the researcher a thick description of the setting in which the research is being carried out. 'The final judgement [about the transferability of the findings]' then, '... is vested in the person seeking to make the transfer' (Guba and Lincoln, 1985: 217). Its usefulness depends on the merits or demerits of a constructivist epistemology, and whether the weaknesses implicit in variable analysis are accepted.

See also:
Critical Realism (21); Experiment (44); Generalization (50); Induction (55); Prediction (78); Sampling (98); Statistics (100); Survey (105); Validity (113); Variable Analysis (116).

112 Triangulation

The importance of validity and reliability in educational research is seen in terms of increasing the replicability of research design and the verifiability of research outcomes. In experimental approaches to research, replicability is a key issue and in quantitative approaches a number of judgments (content validation) or standardized tests (construct validation) are applied. In qualitative approaches, where the focus for investigation is one or a small number of cases, the application of such measures is difficult. Cross-checking the evidence by collecting different kinds of data about the same phenomenon makes validation possible and is known as triangulation.

Triangulation uses different methods (either qualitative or quantitative or both) to look at the 'same' phenomenon. It is argued, for example, that the use of multiple methods allows researchers to investigate different facets of a phenomenon in order to provide a more holistic and rich account of that phenomenon. As importantly, triangulation provides key pathways for comparing the data collected by different methods, allowing findings to be corroborated. The skills of the researcher are then in the weighting or prioritizing of the various 'truths' revealed through multiple methods.

The term 'same' is contentious. Multiple data-collection methods are not without challenges, not least of which is the issue of whether it *is* the 'same' or a different phenomenon that is being researched; this foregrounds a possible dilemma in deciding which revealed 'truth' to prioritize when, for example, the evidence obtained by different methods produces contradictory findings (Bryman, 1988). Yet, proponents of triangulation, like Denzin (1970) for example, argue that the partial or selective perspectives that individual methods provide can be summated to give a 'whole' picture. Critics of this approach (Fielding and Fielding, 1986; Silverman, 2001) dispute whether 'the inaccuracies [or partiality] of one approach to the data [can or does] complement the inaccuracies of another' (Fielding and Fielding, 1986: 35). In which case, Silverman (2001: 234), following Fielding and Fielding, proposes two key 'ground rules' for the triangulation of data from multiple methods. These are to:

1. Begin from a specific theoretical perspective or model. Then:
2. Choose methods and data which will give an account of structure and meaning from within that perspective. (ibid.: 234–5)

Elsewhere, alternatives to triangulation have been suggested, notably respondent validation in which either the researcher's analysis of the data or the transcribed interview account, for example, or both are returned to research participants who are asked to confirm the factual accuracy of the account, or record their feelings about it, or both. While triangulation is advocated as long as it is not used naïvely to produce a 'whole' from the sum of complex parts, respondent validation similarly demands of researchers that participants' post-data perspectives are used as additional and valuable data for further reflection by researchers rather than as validation *per se* (Fielding and Fielding 1986: 43).

Not all researchers follow one theoretical approach. The application of different theoretical perspectives to study single phenomena has been described as another form of triangulation, as has the investigation of the same by different researchers.

See also:
Method (64); Methodology (65); Qualitative Research (80); Quantitative Research (81); Reliability (91); Replication (92); Respondent Validation (96); Statistics (100); Validity (113).

113   Validity

Two types of validity have been developed: internal and external, where the former refers to the accuracy or authenticity of the description being made, and the latter refers to its application to other cases, across place and time. Internal validity is therefore a measure of accuracy and whether it matches reality; external validity, on the other hand, is a measure of generalizability.

Positivist/empiricist researchers understand the notion of validity in a different way from interpretivist researchers. For example, experimentalists identify a number of threats to internal validity, and these refer to whether the effects that they ascribe to their interventions are in fact caused by those interventions and not by other factors (Campbell and Stanley, 1963).

- *History*. Participants in the experiment have other experiences during the time span of the experiment, and the researcher may as a consequence mistakenly attribute such effects to the intervention.
- *Maturation*. Participants may naturally develop certain attributes or dispositions during the lifespan of the experiment, and the researcher may as a consequence mistakenly attribute these to the experiment itself.
- *Pre-test sensitization*. Participants respond to the intervention itself or its testing in abnormal ways, i.e. they are better motivated than they would normally have been than if they were not taking part in the experiment. Experimentalists therefore do not take account of this added factor and greater benefits are ascribed to the intervention than is justified.
- *Test reliability*. Tests used in experimental designs may not be reliable instruments for measuring capability. Test indicators need to be precisely formulated. If they are not, it is difficult to be sure that the findings of the experiment actually show what they purport to.
- *Selection*. Experimental researchers who operate with control groups have to be certain that both the experimental and the control groups have similar characteristics. Furthermore, both groups should remain intact throughout the duration of the project, especially if they have been chosen randomly. Both effects – selection problems and experimental mortality – may have the consequence of decreasing the researcher's certainty about the validity of their findings.

In a similar fashion, Campbell and Stanley (1963) identify a number of threats to external validity in experimental settings.

- The researcher's inability to conceptualize performance indicators so that other researchers can replicate the experiment.
- The researcher's inability to ensure that their experimental and control groups are representative of larger populations.
- The researcher's lack of confidence that the way they operationalize variables in the experimental setting can be replicated in real-life situations.
- The researcher's inability to be certain that threats to internal validity will not detrimentally effect external validity.

Interpretivist researchers, on the other hand, understand the notion of validity differently from positivist/empiricist researchers. Guba and Lincoln (1985), for example, suggested the following as criteria for determining the validity of their findings:

- *credibility* (whether respondents agreed that the researcher had adequately represented their constructions of reality);
- *transferability* (whether the readers of the research agreed that the conclusions reached related usefully to settings which they themselves were immersed in);
- *dependability* (whether the researcher had been able to identify his/her effects during fieldwork and discount them);
- *confirmability* ('the key question here is whether the data are qualitatively confirmable; in other words, whether the analysis is grounded in the data and whether inferences based on the data are logical and of high utility' (Guba and Lincoln 1985: 323)).

Guba and Lincoln were criticized for suggesting that there was a correct method, which, if properly applied, would lead to a correct account of reality. In an attempt to rebut this criticism, Guba and Lincoln (1989) developed a further set of criteria:

- *fairness* (equal consideration should be given to all the various perspectives of participants in the research);
- *educative authenticity* (good research involves participants in the process of educating themselves);
- *catalytic authenticity* (this is where the research process has stimulated activity and decision-making);
- *empowerment* (participants are now in a better position to make real choices about their professional activity).

The debate between positivist and non-positivist researchers about the nature of validity is complicated by how each of them understands the relationship between language, or description, and reality. Radical relativists, for example, would suggest that a measure or measures to determine the fit between data and what it refers to assumes a simple correspondence view of reality, which they would not accept.

See also:
Empiricism (36); Empowerment (37); Experiment (44); Generalization (50); Interpretivism (56); Positivism (75); Postmodernism (76); Realism (83); Reliability (91); Replication (92); Sampling (98); Tests (109); Transferability (111).

114 Value-added

Value-added data analysis mathematically models the input of particular institutions or systems, such as schools, on the development of individuals that belong to those institutions or systems. Schagen and Hutchinson (2004) suggest that there are three current meanings given to the term. The first of these is a measure of progress made by the individual where the prior attainment of that individual is controlled. The second is a measure of progress where prior attainment as well as a range of other pupil and school factors outside the control of the school is controlled. The third is a measure of progress where these background factors are controlled but no control is exercised over prior attainment. Measurements such as these produce different results if different factors are taken into account.

Most acceptable value-added analyses use a form of multi-level modelling, and this involves initial decisions being made about: a) background factors to be included in the modelling exercise; b) interaction factors for the model; c) the levels of hierarchy in the model; and d) the coefficients that it is assumed will be random at each level (ibid.). Statistical relationships can as a result be calculated for relationships between different variables within the model.

Some of the problems with value-added data analysis are as follows.

- The outcome measures used may not be reliable and may not represent the actual competence of each pupil.
- An assumption is made that the pupil will respond in the specific way to the socio-economic category that they have been placed within, i.e. if the measure is free school meals, then it is assumed that all pupils who receive this benefit will display in their behaviours attributes that are associated with poverty.

- A further assumption is made that the pupil will consistently display these behavioural attributes between the two measurement stages.
- Pupils may not progress in a linear pattern although this modelling assumes that they will.
- An assumption is made that there is no communication of the results achieved at the earlier stage to the pupil or their parents, or that their teacher does not behave in terms of this knowledge. If it is not possible to make this assumption, then the process becomes a self-fulfilling prophecy.

As a result of these processes, a value can be attached to the input of the educational institution as it has impacted on the progress of the individual who has attended it. Indeed, because multi-level modelling is sophisticated enough to operate at different levels within the system, a value can be attached to the input of the LEA, school, department or class. Thus the modelling involved requires the researcher to make a number of decisions about which inputs to include and which relations to determine. This means that value-added systems of collecting and analysing data will be used in different ways by different stakeholders, so that politicians may implement a different system from an independent researcher because they have different purposes. The accuracy of such modelling depends on the belief that the educational researcher has in the reliability and validity of the data that is used, in the decisions they make about which variables to use in the modelling process, and also in the ability of the researcher to develop appropriate indicators or quasi-properties to reflect the actual properties of individuals and educational institutions and their covariance in real-life settings.

See also:
Assessment (7); Correlational Research (18); Mathematical Modelling (62); Reliability (91); Statistics (100); Validity (113); Values (115); Variable Analysis (116).

115   Values

The issues of whether, how and what type of values play a part in educational research are highly contentious ones. Positions about the influence of values range on a continuum, with at the one end, a view that values are present at and influence most stages of research projects, but can and should be made explicit for the readers of the research report, *to* a view that though values tend to influence the activities of researchers, they should be eliminated from such activities and thus it is possible to develop a value-free science of education.

The most forceful distinction between facts and values was made by David Hume in his *Treatise on Human Nature*. For him, an 'ought' cannot be derived from an 'is'. This radical separation of the two ideas is now generally accepted to be unsustainable. This is because it is difficult to identify facts about the world that are not informed by some system of value, though different types of values may inform different types of facts.

A number of different types of value may be relevant to educational research.

- *Personal values.* These comprise those ethical beliefs that a researcher has and they involve placing a positive value on certain types of behaviours, and correspondingly a negative value on other types of behaviours. Such values are frequently attached to religious and political systems of belief. An example might be a Catholic researcher examining capital punishment, and therefore, because of his or her belief system, not being able to take a dispassionate view on the matter. The value that they hold in respect of the sanctity of life informs all the stages of their research project: the research questions, the focus of the investigation, the collection of data, the analysis of the data and the way the results are disseminated.
- *Procedural values.* These types of values are different from personal values in that they refer to the process of doing research. Thus it would be difficult to carry out a research project, where the intention is to find something out about the world, without also wanting to say about the findings that they are true or truer because of the research that has just been conducted. Another example of a procedural value might be objectivity, where it is considered that a research study is better if the methods used were objectively applied. Though objectivity is a disputed value, it is difficult to see how one could dispense with a notion of truth, even if the researcher meant something differently from it having a simple correspondence relationship with reality.
- *Collective values.* These types of values relate to the idea that research is a public affair and thus sponsors, policy-makers, readers of research and other stakeholders seek to influence the way the research is conducted and the conclusions that the researcher draws. Thus a sponsor might insist on the use of certain

types of data-collection methods to the exclusion of others because it is more likely that the data that is subsequently collected will confirm the views that they already hold. These collective values can in theory be eliminated.

- *Observational values.* These types of values need to be differentiated from ethical or personal ones because they refer to those theories that inform perception and are always prior to observations of the world. Thus, in the sense that we cannot make theory-free observations of the world, it is possible to understand research as theory- or value-rich. A further distinction is made here between observations being concept-dependent and concept-determined. If the latter is adopted as a belief, then there is little point in observing the world because the prior theory one has already accounts for what one is likely to see.
- *Epistemic values.* Finally, there is a set of values that inform the activities of the researcher that relate to ontological, epistemological and methodological viewpoints. If the researcher believes that the world is constructed in a certain way, then that belief will influence the type of methodology chosen and the results that are obtained.

Thus, it is difficult to see how research can be value-free when all these different types of values are taken into account. What is sometimes meant by value-freedom is that personal and collective values are eliminated from the data-collection activities, and that procedural, observational and epistemic values are brought to the attention of the reader in some form or another.

See also:
Dissemination (32); Empiricism (36); Epistemology/Ontology (38); Ethics (39); Interpretivism (56); Methodology (65); Objectivity (70); Observation (71); Positivism (75); Realism (83); Research Community (95).

116   Variable Analysis

The idea behind this influential mode of educational research is that social phenomena can be measured in the same way as certain physical properties, such as height or breadth. This requires a measuring device, and a scale of values to position the property. A variable therefore is defined as any attribute of a person or unit that can vary in its value. An example of a variable is social class, a commonly used construct in educational research, where this property of an individual can be scaled. Furthermore, members of a defined population may be positioned differently on this scale, and it is therefore possible to identify the frequency of these values as they occur in that population at a certain point in time. This, in turn, allows a measure of the distribution of that property to be described. If a further property, such as gender, could then be identified for the population, this allows the examination of the covariance of these two properties, social class and gender, in order to determine how they relate to each other.

Some properties are already quantified because of their constituent make-up, i.e. the amount of financial support received from central government for schools in the maintained sector. Other properties are either pre-quantified because of agreement among members of a society, i.e. occupational type, or can be quantified for the purposes of the research project. Further to this, the scale may be *nominal*, where the points on the scale indicate simple classification and no other relationship; *ordinal*, where the scale is a measure of rank order; at *interval-level*, where there is a known interval between the points on the scale; or at *ratio-level*, where equal intervals and a true zero point are constituents of the scale.

An example of a nominal scale is: Asian, Caribbean, English/Scottish/Welsh/Irish, as in the following table.

Table 5: Differences between schools in the ethnic composition of first-year pupil intakes

	Asian	Caribbean	English/Scottish Welsh/Irish
Average % all schools	6.8	11.8	59.0
Max. % pupils any school	37.5	52.6	95.6
Min. % pupils any school	0.0	0.0	22.0

(From Mortimore et al., 1988: 177, Table 9.1)

An example of an ordinal scale is schools ranked in a league table in terms of performance in examinations at a set point in time. It is not assumed with ordinal scales that absolute quantities or equal intervals between points on the scale are present. An interval-level scale, contrastingly, has equal and standard intervals between the various points, and an example of this type of scale is result statuses in an examination where an assumption is made that they are equally distributed. Finally, ratio-level scales build in a specified number of equal points from zero, as in an IQ test.

A further process is required in variable analysis, and this is that for each variable, an indicator has to be identified. The analysis is therefore of the covariance between these indicators and not the covariance between the properties themselves. The relationship between the property and the indicator can in most instances only be poorly defined and is therefore probabilistic. However, the parameters of that probabilistic relationship cannot be identified because the property to which they make reference can never be directly inspected. If it could, then there would be no need for indicators or quasi-properties because direct access to the phenomena would be possible. Variable analysts, aware of this problem, usually point to the way a number of different studies using the same indicators show consistently strong correlations with other variables, and this allows them to claim that the indicator is reasonably effective.

From this base, a number of other mathematical processes have been developed, i.e. regression analysis and multilevel modelling. The problems of such an approach have already been alluded to, and to reiterate, these involve the difficulties of providing indicators that represent the properties of the individual and/or the educational institution; the assumptions that are inevitably made concerning the relationship between the individual or institution and those properties; the reductionist and essentializing nature of the packaging that is required when intensional properties are reduced to their extensional form in order to make mathematical calculations; and the assertion that is frequently made that causal relations can be inferred from descriptions of associations or correlations between variables.

See also:
Causation (11); Correlational Research (18); Distribution (33); Gender (49); Mathematical Modelling (62); Prediction (78); Quantitative Research (81); Regression Analysis (88); Values (115).

117 Virtual Research

Virtual research is used here to describe educational research that focuses mainly or entirely on research interaction between and among researchers and research participants that is provided mainly or entirely by a computer network. In one sense, the phrase is a misnomer since the term virtual is not used as if in opposition to the term 'real': virtual research is no more or less 'real' than research that has described and explained educational experience either directly though face-to-face encounter with the researcher subject(s) or indirectly through questionnaire and document surveys, based on accounts by the living (or the deceased).

For researchers working in contexts of late modernity and major developments in ICT, especially the use of the Internet and web-based communications, ICT and, specifically, computer mediated communication (CMC) provides the latest in a long line of modernist devices to extend and develop science as the rational basis for understanding education and pursuing educational research. Viewed in this light, positivist approaches to educational research absorb the new technologies as 'advanced' tools for conducting research. An example would be email and web-based surveys discussed elsewhere in this book. This is not to ignore that such use brings specific challenges to both researchers and research participants, but to note that these are seen mainly (though not entirely) as technical problems of computer 'know-how' or access or training for use (or lack of some or all of these), and less as the epitome of increased surveillance and control. These, in turn, present ethical issues, that are deemed resolvable, it is argued, by revision of existing codes to accommodate computer-focused research. The subject matter of such research, of course, does not necessarily focus upon electronic forms of teaching and learning or upon ICT and CMC as educational leadership and management aids although, not surprisingly, computer-focused evaluation research about such topics is not uncommon.

For postmodern researchers, web-based research casts further doubts about research that is framed in terms of singular rather than multiple representations of reality. As Hine (2000: 7) declares: 'In the Internet postmodernity seems to have found its object, in an "anything goes" world where people and machines, truth and fiction, self and other seem to merge in a glorious blurring of boundaries'. Such 'glories' are often highly problematic for both new and experienced researchers engaged in critical literature reviews, for example, that, of necessity, extend beyond the relative 'safety' of authoritative texts published as books.

If either or both of the above positions tend to emphasize the importance of structure rather than agency in terms of technology impacting upon research design and process, other commentators have noted the complexities of the interrelations between computers and the ways in which we conduct, receive and participate in research, viewing 'impact' as the result of iterative and multi-directional social processes (Grint and Woolgar, 1997) that depend variously on the users and designers of such technology, and the different ways technology is understood, used or avoided.

Applying a specific example, Pole and Morrison (2003: 121–6) examine the potential of virtual ethnography. In doing so, they draw attention to some of the key debates which surround its use, specifically in qualitative and interpretive approaches to research, and its commonalities and distinctiveness in relation to other forms of ethnography. Conventionally, ethnographic research in education has focused on face-to-face interactions between and among individuals and groups, usually in educational settings. Using the Internet, not only is close physical contact unnecessary but the narrowly confined locales that have been key features of case studies, for example, can be expanded to the extent that researchers and research participants can converse 'globally' in ways that would have been unthinkable even a few years ago. In asking what would happen if all the research that constituted an ethnography took place on-line, a number of issues arise, some common to all ethnographies, and others distinctive to virtual ethnography (ibid. and see also Hine, 2000: Chapters 1 and 2).

> Some features of virtual ethnography – how much to record, how many lecturers to sample, the scope of the 'snapshot' – might be considered to be common for all ethnographic research. Issues for virtual and traditional ethnography might also include physical limits to a researcher's stamina, concentration, and access to resources ... the issue in a virtual environment might be how long to stay logged on ... Like traditional ethnographers, virtual ethnographers would still prioritize access to and engagement with participants but the focus of that engagement might shift.
> (Pole and Morrison, 2003: 124)

Ethical issues, it is argued, remain but need to be framed rather differently. Issues of anonymity and confidentiality retain their importance, but require attention to issues such as passwords for entry to conferencing and chat rooms, for example.

Distinctiveness is also evident, though its extent could be exaggerated. For example, researchers working in virtual environments do not need to share the same time frames as their informants, but this may also be the case when researchers draw upon archival and documentary evidence. However, with the possibility of working in synchronous and asynchronous time frames, researchers might be less likely to engage in selectivity of data during collection (such as writing notes during an interview) and selection of text could take place after on-line engagement. Other tendencies are noted like, for example, a tendency among researchers and participants to spend longer composing a 'considered' written conversation on-line than might occur face-to-face.

Hine (2000: 42–65) identifies three specific issues pertaining to virtual ethnography. The first relates to face-to-face interaction. Distinctively, virtual ethnographers do not get 'the seats of their pants dirty ... Internet ethnographers keep their seats very firmly on the University's upholstery' (ibid.: 45). Yet, like all ethnographers, they are actively engaged in the sifting, sorting and interpretation of a 'story' that is told holistically, except that the processes occur in cyberspace. The second relates to the relationship between texts, technology and reflexivity. In traditional ethnography, oral interactions predominate. In virtual ethnography, far more attention is given to written texts. This does not just mean more emphasis on the technical skills involved, but as for all ethnographies, there are, it is argued, equivalent dangers in 'going native' in cyberspace, which need to be countered by specific attention to written articulation as one form of reflexivity. The third point is to signal the potential importance of virtual environments in opening up new configurations for educational study in time and space.

As Pole and Morrison (2003: 126) conclude:

> Previously the ethnographer has acted as the intermediary between his or her world (mostly but not always of the academy) and the world of subjects (teacher or pupil participation in [a] ... school, for example, in which the ethnographer is physically present in each setting).

In such ways, using the virtual as a research tool, as well as studying Internet connectivity and connections as research topics in their own right, may have a specific appeal. In a changing local–global nexus, virtual research reminds readers of the extent to which researchers in education may need to re-think their approaches, and of why and how.

See also:
Access (2); Case Study (9); Culture (23); Design (28); Ethics (39); Ethnography (40); Interpretivism (56); Positivism (75); Postmodernism (76); Qualitative Research (80); Quantitative Research (81); Subjectivity (104); Textuality (110); Writing as Representation (120).

118 Writing

Advice on how to write for academic purposes has become almost a publishing industry in recent years. Some bewilderment about the array of guidance on offer is understandable, and, on occasion, exacerbated by international diversity in expectations about writing for academic purposes, in understandings about writing in a range of genres and research frameworks, and an almost implicit acceptance that the best way to learn about writing is 'to write'. For academics, 'what', 'how', 'how often' and 'how much' they write overwhelmingly determines career success or failure. For doctoral students, several years of effort is assessed mainly through a single extended piece of writing.

Challenges are occasionally reinforced by assumptions that instruction in essential writing skills is somehow more appropriate for students or colleagues who are writing in a language that is not their first (thereby mistaking linguistic skills for writing skills). There is also a lack of consensus about which approaches to writing work best. In education research, the reporting and dissemination of most funded research remains overwhelmingly text-based, although practice *is* changing, albeit slowly, as researchers and sponsoring bodies move towards on-line reporting for specific audiences, often professional practitioners, and sound-bite summaries for media or policy consumption.

Kinds of writers

It might be presumed that 'craftspersons' achieve writing success using similar techniques. This is not so. Writers are productive from a range of starting points. Grant (2002) (cited in Morrison and Watling (2002)) suggests that there are four types of writers.

The organizer

- The organizer has a clear desk and sharpened pen and pencils at the ready.
- Empty computer disks are carefully labelled in preparation for writing under appropriate topic and section headings.
- Organizers often start writing at the same time each day, they write almost every day and often set a specific target or number of words which they must produce before doing anything else.
- Organizers can be 'put off' writing when things disturb their routine.

The anxious motivator

- Anxious motivators can only produce text when a deadline is almost upon them.
- They work rapidly and are able to be very single-minded.
- They often experience a lot of stress in the process of completing a piece of writing.
- It is difficult for anxious motivators to produce writing unless someone else provides the motivation.

The inspired creator
- Inspired creators have to feel 'switched on' in order to be able to write.
- They don't plan ahead or organize very much.
- They would hate to write at the same time every day.
- When they are writing they can concentrate for a long time.
- Sometimes they have too many projects going on at the same time.
- Some inspired creators find it hard to finish things.

The planner
- Planners need to have a thorough understanding of the material they are going to write about.
- They like to get the words right at the first 'shot' and don't like re-drafting.
- They must have a plan before they begin to write.
- Once they have a plan, they can write rapidly. (Grant (2002), University of Leicester, cited in Morrison and Watling (2002))

Research presentation
Earlier, we noted that writing varies in accordance with the epistemological and methodological frameworks that underpin writers' understandings about research and the priority areas for research investigation and report. Style and content is also increasingly prescribed by external sponsors of research writing and publication.

Format
For presenting work that is predominantly quantitative or qualitative in research design writing formats are fairly well established, if less so in mixed methods approaches. Cresswell (1994: 13–14) summarizes these succinctly. For predominantly quantitative research, formats include:

An introduction
- Context [or statement of the problem]
- Purposes of the study
- Research questions or hypotheses
- Theoretical perspectives
- Definition of terms
- Delimitations and limitations of the study
- Significance of the study

Literature review

Research design

- Sample, population or subjects
- Instrumentation and materials

Data analysis

Summary, Conclusions, Ways forward . . .

Appendices: Instruments

For predominantly qualitative research, formats are less standardized, although the following is not uncommon:

Introduction

- Statement of the problem
- Purposes of the study
- The 'grand tour' question and the sub-questions
- Definitions
- Delimitations and limitations
- Significance of the study

Informing critical literature

Procedure

- Assumptions and rationale for a qualitative design
- The type of design used
- The role of the researcher
- Data collection procedures
- Data analysis procedures
- Methods for verification

Outcomes of the study in relation to theory and to the literature

Summary, Conclusions, ways forward . . . .

Appendices: Research tools, audit trail . . .

Writing traps

There are a number of stylistic traps that await all writers. These have been described by Fairburn and Winch (1996: 142–59) and include:

- *longwindedness, gobbledegook,* and *pomposity*: in other words, long words and long sentences used inappropriately.
- *frozen language*: this is a tendency to write in clichés.
- *word limits*: one of the most challenging aspects of independent writing is having to be responsible for 'what you leave in and what you leave out of your written work' (Cresswell, 1994: 158). Learning to edit out irrelevancies and duplication described

unflatteringly as 'Christmas stocking fillers' and 'verbal junk' (ibid.), is a time-consuming skill for even the most experienced writer.

Not everyone agrees that taking a value stance in writing is a writing 'trap', although some do. Sometimes referred to as 'commitment', this is a point of view that is expressed in writing. For some writers, an explicit value stance is fundamental to all research writing. Others actively discourage commitment in writing, arguing instead for a balanced and neutral view of a range of epistemological or methodological positions. The former view holds that:

> It is of course a sign of competence when someone writing academically is able to describe and to handle the arguments in his [sic] field of study, and area of controversy. But this does not, or should not preclude him [sic] from being committed to a position, whether this is one he [sic] has described that derives from others or one that is completely different. What he [sic] does have the responsibility for is the presentation of evidence and/or arguments for the point of view that he [sic] holds himself [sic] and of which he [sic] is trying to persuade others ... This is as true of the undergraduate as it is for the international scholar ... Commitment injects tension into the processes of writing. It forces the writer to engage more fully with the positions he [sic] is adopting, opposing or describing. (Fairburn and Winch, 1996: 160)

The style as much as the content of the above quotation helps direct readers to other important issues.

Language forms: non-sexist, non-racist and non-disablist

Writing is a powerful tool for communicating writers' values – explicit and implicit. Many disciplines now issue guidelines that encourage writers to apply language in ways that are neither patronizing nor offensive. Examples can be found on the websites of the British Sociological Association (1996), the British Educational Research Association (2004), the British Psychological Society, and others.

At fundamental levels of philosophical thinking about the many different forms of racism and sexism, is writing emanating from anti-racist and feminist perspectives, for example. Such writing has challenged and disrupted technicist and essentialist forms of knowledge construction and representation, and continues to do so. In relation to feminist methodology, the 'stronger' form of this position is that patriarchal domination of knowledge construction and publication has effectively included some forms of (patriarchal) writing which becomes published and public knowledge, and has excluded others. Such exclusions have effectively 'silenced' many people's lives, notably accounts of and by women. In its looser or 'weaker' form, readers of research are enjoined to 'distrust ... [as partial, unfinished, or dishonest] research reports which include no statement about the researcher's experience' (Webb, 2000: 48), notwithstanding a view among other writers that to do so may risk violating 'an expectation that a researcher be detached, objective, and value free' (ibid.).

Writing for publication

Writing for academic purposes often begins during doctoral studies. (Many others forms of publication – for professional purposes – may, of course, precede or follow this, and purposes are not necessarily exclusive.) Delamont *et al.* (1997: 170) argue that:

> Graduate students and their supervisors have joint interests and responsibilities towards publication in the promotion of the research itself and sponsorship of the student.

They site possible outlets for written dissemination, which include:

- university department-based occasional and working papers;
- refereed journals;
- professional or popular journals;
- conference papers, which may lead to publication;
- chapters in books;
- national media;
- newspaper reports;
- electronic publishing;
- monographs and scientific papers;
- books.

Following Delamont *et al.* (1997: 174) some useful general questions for potential writers for publication are:

- Who publishes in your topic area?
- Do any publishers have special lists covering your topic area?
- Have any publishers published similar studies to yours?
- What specialized journals exist in your area?
- Are there general journals that might welcome your sort of approach?

- What sort of audience are you trying to reach?
- Are there any new outlets coming on-stream?
- Are there any special editions in general journals planned in your area of study?
- What genre or writing style are you intending to apply/use?
- Which journals might have a specific interest in your methodological approach?

Writing blocks

Failure to write can be caused by a number of factors: lack of confidence, a sense of insecurity, or reluctance to take risks in 'exposing' ideas by committing them to computer screen or paper. Sometimes failing to write can be caused by stress; failure to write can also cause stress and panic. Cottrell (1999: 136-7) offers a list of activities to help writers overcome blocks when they occur. Activities come 'tried and tested' at various levels of sophistication and combination. Finally, it is perhaps worth reminding ourselves that temporary writing blocks can have more to do with life events than with the research endeavour or writing task. Again, Cottrell offers some helpful advice on managing stress. These include pointers to:

- staying relaxed (sleeping properly, taking breaks);
- monitoring your state of mind (controlling panic, questioning ways of thinking, celebrating success);
- managing your time (setting priorities, being organized);
- taking care of the your body (exercise, diet);
- relaxation (what works for you – sport, music, taking a relaxing bath, doing 'absolutely nothing');
- apply the 'drawer treatment' (or computer equivalent) to writing already done. Put it away in a drawer and go back to it several days later. This is refreshing for the writer and the writing.

See also:
Anti-racism (6); Coding (14); Design (28); Feminist Research (47); Literature Review (60); Media (63); Publishing (79); Qualitative Research (80); Quantitative Research (81); Refereeing (85); Sampling (98); Values (115); Writing for Academic Purposes (119); Writing as Representation (120).

119 Writing for Academic Purposes

Essentially, all writers need to ask three questions:

- Why am I writing?
- Who am I writing for?
- What will my readers expect to see and read?

Burton (2000), for example, notes differences between writing for taught undergraduate and postgraduate (including some Masters) degrees and writing a doctoral thesis. Although some differences might be exaggerated (and less appropriate for professional doctorates like the Doctor of Education (EdD) which combines a mix of taught units and theses), the following table draws some useful distinctions:

Table 6: Writing for different purposes

Taught course	*Thesis*
Short pieces	Chapters or papers
Few drafts	Many drafts
Can work out paper as you write (more relevant to Masters than professional doctorate)	Ideas too complex to write straight off
One-off assignments (again, less applicable to professional doctorates)	Papers all related to building a thesis
Papers contain basic data	Papers contain large amounts of complex data
Writing schedules are imposed	Few writing schedules imposed (but MPhil transfer provides important landmark)
Writing focus is highly structured	Writing focus is self-structured
Feedback from tutor frequently post-submission	Feedback from supervisor (should be) considerable
Not always necessary to word process (although hand-written assignments increasingly rare)	Essential to word process (and in required formats)

(Adapted from Burton, 2000: 425.)

As Burton (2000) also notes, at least four issues are immediately apparent:

1. Most of the responsibility for writing rests with authors who need to find a writing process that works for them.
2. Drafting, re-drafting and editing are essential elements of all writing.
3. Because of its sheer volume, strategies for breaking down a large piece of writing into manageable pieces are essential.
4. Perhaps the most challenging writing skill is that which requires writers to develop a continuous dialogue between the different parts of their work so that the writing flows logically and coherently from section to section, chapter to chapter. 'Moving on' from the point at which writers of extended accounts feel reasonably satisfied, is probably best advice.

Writing for Doctoral theses

Again, adapted from Burton (2000) writing follows well-recognized forms. An *abstract* provides a summary of the research – its focus, content, key features and findings. The *introductory chapter* summarizes what the thesis contains and should provide an overview as well as precise and coherent statements about the scope, context, aims and objectives of the study. The *literature chapter* contains a review of previous research and critical scholarship. However, the role and positioning of the literature review shows variation in accordance with the epistemological and methodological approaches taken by writers, and/or in accordance with the requirements and conventions within the writer's core academic discipline. The *methods chapter* is often one of the most underestimated parts of the thesis and, paradoxically, the chapter that thesis examiners appear to ask most questions about in oral examinations. (One reason for such underestimation by relatively new writers might be the paucity of methodological explanation provided in the published texts of more experienced authors.) For theses, the expectation is that a precise statement of the logic and rationale for the research, as well as the description of methods and methodology, will be given. This would include an explanation of why 'this' approach rather than 'that' approach was taken, and the implications of such decisions for research design and outcomes.

While the requirements of disciplines and departments vary, the *results* or *findings* chapters commonly form the main body of the doctoral thesis. These chapters are variously structured and numbered, often with a basis division between *results* and *analysis* and *discussion*. There is an important emphasis upon the ways in which writers integrate their findings with theoretical debates and previous research findings. The *concluding chapter* provides an overall summary of the findings and a discussion of how the project has advanced academic debate – including knowledge and understanding – in the topic area. It is also likely to raise issues for further research, identify items of professional relevance, and/or make recommendations for further development. Theses of quality will identify areas of possible future study. Finally, the *bibliography* and *appendices* are not infrequently where examiners will turn first as they begin their reading, partly because they give them an important sense of the literature base that (should) inform the thesis, and partly because the appendices frequently includes the research tools, audit trails and policy documents that underpin the work.

All writers for academic purposes are required to follow conventions, whether of the academy or of editorial boards for journals and books. Commonly, these refer to: referencing styles, word lengths, margins, line spacing, fonts, use of footnotes and endnotes, and so on. As Morrison and Watling (2002) point out, writers are also required to give attention to:

- *Type style and emphasis.* Too many emphases will reduce impact; excessive use of underlining is sometimes perceived as rather outdated.
- *Sub-headings.* Use them like signposts. If they become too numerous and convoluted, readers can lose their way!
- *Bullet points.* These can add clarity and succinctness; over-use becomes list-like and, at worst, a poor substitute for careful explanation.
- *Text alignment.* Indented text is very effective for emphasizing a paragraph or quotation; again, over-use reduces impact.
- *The use of paragraphs.* Remember that a paragraph contains a main idea, described by Williams (1996: 35) as a ' "topic sentence" that is expanded into a number of explanatory sentences. These explain, develop, illustrate, or modify the main idea in the topic sentence.'
- *The use of different sentence types.* Effective writing draws on different sentence types. Long sentences do not necessarily feature as part of good academic writing, even though academics themselves do not always appreciate this!
- *The use of full stops, apostrophes, commas, colons and semi-colons.*
- *The use of quotation marks.* Inconsistency in use can drive readers to distraction. The American style is to use double quotation marks for all quoted material in text and dialogue. British English uses single quotations for dialogue or quoted material in text. Double quotation marks are reserved for quotations within quotations, unless the quotation marks are part of the quotation

itself. A rule of thumb is that if the quotation is longer than 30–40 words, separate the quotation from the main text and indent, normally without quotation marks. Some authors reduce font size.

- *The use of exclamation and question marks.*
- *The use of dashes between clauses and hyphens to form compound words.*

Again, a golden rule is consistency in application. This gives a much better effect than randomness.

See also:
Literature Review (60); Method (64); Publishing (79); Writing (118).

120   Writing as Representation

Writing and writing up research signify much more than issues of format and textual convention, being the means by which researchers seek to convince readers about the truthfulness of their work. This is crucial in research where writing is *both* the process and the product of the research. For ethnographers (see Pole and Morrison, 2003, Chapters 4 and 6), for example, writing and representing is central to *analysis*. Yet, amidst a plethora of clear guidance and advice on writing to engage readers and intended audiences (for example, Woods, 1999), debates abound among writers who are divided about the status of their texts.

The most obvious dichotomy is between realists and anti-realists. The former hold the perspective that it is possible to employ an authoritarian style whether it is on the basis of telling it as it is, or through strict adherence to methodological procedures that 'accurately' represent the truth. Anti-realists deny that any one story can be privileged over another. And between these two poles are the post-postmodernists and critical realists in which thick description is mixed with analyst constructed taxonomies. Thus Miles and Huberman (1994) write about a balance in the mix between 'stories' and 'variables', and between thinking derived from 'paradigmatic' and the 'narrative', 'texts' and 'displays'. (Pole and Morrison, 2003: 106)

More recently, 'fiction' has been used to write qualitative, including ethnographic, research.

From this perspective, ethnography ceases to become a representation of 'reality' ... [and is written] as drama or poetry ... or in dialogic forms either as researcher talking to 'self' or another, or where there is a juggling of real text ... in non-linear or non-sequential forms. (Pole and Morrison, 2003: 107)

Notwithstanding experimental approaches to convey the outcomes of qualitative research, the written narrative account remains dominant. In part, this may be a reflection of narrative as the most accessible approach. Such an account also 'has the power of persuasion and rhetoric through which the ethnographer seeks to convince his or her readers that his or her story is authentic and reliable' (ibid.: 142).

Writing in the first or third person

Whether writing is in the first or third person is more than a question of taste or preference. In the natural sciences, the expectation is for writing to be in the third person, and this convention applies to technical and scientific reports. The view is that writing in the third person signifies the kind of objectivity one might expect from research studies in the positivist scientific paradigm (Kirkham, 1992). Moreover, in education and social science the critical literature review is usually written in the third person. Not surprisingly, it has, in some quarters, become synonymous with academic writing. Fairburn and Winch (1996) usefully expand on this by drawing attention to a range of serious (and occasionally amusing) examples of effective as well as poor writing in the third person, with its attendant dangers of 'pomposity' and 'bureaucratic intensity'.

Yet for research with a qualitative orientation, writing in the first person is often used to signify and locate the 'self' or writer as active participant in the study. A careful balance may be required. Using 'I' too often may become obtrusive and render accounts overly 'anecdotal'. Over-use of personal style can also become a source of resentment among some readers; terms like 'forced bonhomie' and 'patronizing' are applied by Fairburn and Winch (1996: 135) to poor first-person usage.

Is it possible to operate using mixed forms of the first and third person? Again, Fairburn and Winch (ibid.: 139) think that, with care, writers can. They cite the opening passage from John Rawls' (1971: 4) book *A Theory of Justice* as a positive example:

These propositions seem to express our intuitive conviction of the primacy of justice. No doubt they are expressed too strongly. In any event I wish to inquire whether these convictions or others similar to them are sound, and if so how they can be accounted for. To this end it is necessary to work out a theory of justice in the light of which these assertions can be interpreted and assessed. I shall begin by considering the role of the principles of justice. Let us assume, to fix ideas, that a society is ...

Writing 'voice'

Clarification of the voice used in writing is also critical. Multiple voices are more prevalent in qualitative research. Van Maanen's (1988) *Tales of the Field* distinguishes several possible 'voices' using examples from his own and others' work:

- *Realist*: a direct, matter-of-fact portrait, with methods left mostly undescribed. Many details. The field worker is invisible and 'interpretively omnipotent'.
- *Confessional*: written from the field worker point of view with personalized authority.
- *Impressionist*: personalized, a-theoretical accounts, often story-like, aiming to link reality and the field worker, and to enable the reader to re-live their experience. (Cited in Miles and Huberman, 1994: 300.)

According to Miles and Huberman (ibid.: 301), such:

voices have profound consequences for what is included in research reporting and what can be learned from it. For example, Van Maanen notes that a 'realist voice' tends to rule out alternative interpretations and/or pretend that the interpretations come straight from the respondents. 'Confessional' tales may over-focus on the field worker ... blurring 'what happened' and may lead to a paralysis of method. An 'impressionistic' account may provide [always provides?] a portrait that is far more coherent than disorderly reality.

So, if writers have a choice, the advice is to choose their voice(s) wittingly. Finally, we note that tense and verbs are often used in writing to signify 'voice'. In doctoral writing, for example, advice is to use verb tense to strengthen and invigorate the writing. So:

a common practice is to use the past tense to review the literature and to report results of the study. The future tense would be appropriate ... in research proposals and plans ... [for example] the use of 'will' in describing the purpose statement. For completed studies use the past tense to add vigour to the study, especially in the Introduction ... And avoid anthropomorphic verbs, giving nouns human-like qualities like 'the Study spoke about the effect of criticisms'. (Cresswell, 1994: 202–3)

See also:
Coding (14); Critical Realism (21); Ethnography (40); Experiment (44); Literature Review (60); Narrative (67); Objectivity (70); Postmodernism (76); Qualitative Research (80); Realism (83); Reliability (91); Textuality (110); Writing (118); Writing for Academic Purposes (119).

References

Acker, S. (1994) *Gendered Education: Sociological Reflections on Women, Teaching, and Feminism*, Buckingham: Open University Press.

Alasuutari, P. (1995) *Researching Culture: Qualitative Method and Cultural Studies*, London: Sage.

Archer, M. (1982) 'Morphogenesis versus Structuration', *British Journal of Sociology*, **33** (4): 455–83.

Archer, M. (1990) 'Human Agency and Social Structure: A Critique of Giddens', in J. Clark, C. Modgil and S. Modgil (eds) *Anthony Giddens: Consensus and Controversy*, London: Falmer Press.

Atkinson, P. (1992) *Understanding Ethnographic Texts*, Qualitative Research Methods Series 25, London: Sage.

Atkinson, P. and Delamont, S. (1985) 'Bread and Dreams or Dreams and Circuses? A critique of "case study" research in education', in M. Shipman (ed.) *Educational Research. Principles, Policies and Practices*, Lewes: Falmer.

Austin, J.L. (1962) *How To Do Things with Words*, Oxford: Clarendon Press.

Ball, S.J. (1987) *The Micropolitics of the School*, London: Methuen.

Barry, A-M. (1993) ' "Women-centred" politics; a concept for exploring women's political perceptions', in J de Groot and M. Maynard (eds) *Women's Studies in the 1990s: Doing Things Differently?* London: Macmillan.

Barthes, R. (1967) *Elements of Semiotics*, London: Jonathan Cape.

Barthes, R. (1975) *S/Z*, London: Jonathon Cape.

Bassey, M. (1999) *Case Study in Educational Settings*, Buckingham: Open University Press.

Becker, H.S. (2000) 'Case, Cases, Conjunctures, Stories, and Imagery', in M. Hammersley, R. Gomm and P. Foster (eds) *Case Study Method*, London: Sage.

Bell, J. (1999) *Doing Your Research Project: A Guide for First-time Researchers in Education and Social Science*, 3rd edn, Buckingham: Open University Press.

Bernstein, B. (1977) *Class, Codes and Control*, Vol. 3, London: Routledge.

Bernstein, B. (1996) *Pedagogy, Symbolic Control and Identity*, London: Taylor and Francis.

Bhaskar, R. (1979) *Possibility of Naturalism*, London: Harvester Wheatsheaf.

Bhaskar, R. (1989) *Reclaiming Reality*, London: Verso.

Blaikie, N. (1993) *Approaches to Social Enquiry*, Cambridge: Polity Press.

Blair, M. (1998) 'The myth of neutrality in educational research', in P. Connolly and B. Troyna (eds) *Researching Racism in Education: Politics, Theory and Practice*, Buckingham: Open University Press.

Blatchford, P. (2003) *The Class Size Debate: Is Small Better?* Buckingham: Open University Press.

Blatchford, P., Edmonds, S. and Martin, C. (2003) 'Classroom contexts: connections between class size and within class grouping', *British Journal of Educational Psychology*, **73**: 15–36.

Blatchford, P., Goldstein, H., Martin, C. and Browne, W. (2002) 'A study of class size effects in English school reception classes', *British Educational Research Journal*, **29**: 691–710.

Blatchford, P., Moriarty, V., Edmonds, S. and Martin, C. (2002) 'Relationships between class size and teaching: a multi-method analysis of English infant schools', *American Educational Research Journal*, **39**: 101–32.

Blumer, H. (1954) 'What is wrong with social theory?', *American Sociological Review*, **19** (1): 3–10.

Blumer, H. (1969) *Symbolic Interactionism*, Englewood Cliffs, NJ: Prentice-Hall.

Bogden, R. and Biklen, S. (1982) *Qualitative Research for Education*, Boston: Allyn and Bacon.

Borg, W. and Gall, M. (1983) *Educational Research: An Introduction*, New York: Longman.

Bourdieu, P. (1977) *Outline of a Theory of Practice*, London: Cambridge University Press.

Bourne, J. (1980) 'Cheerleaders and Ombudsmen: the sociology of race relations in Britain', *Race and Class*, **21**: 331–5.

Brewer, J. (2000) *Ethnography*, Buckingham: Open University Press.

Brice Heath, S. (1983) *Ways with Words: Language, Life and Work in Communities and Classrooms*, Cambridge: Cambridge University Press.

British Educational Research Association (BERA) (2004) *Ethical Guidelines*, Edinburgh: SCRE for BERA.

British Sociological Association (1996) *Guidance Notes on anti-sexist, anti-racist and non-disablist language*, Durham: BSA.

Broadfoot, P. (1996) 'Interviewing in a cross-cultural context: some issues for comparative research', in C. Pole and R.G. Burgess (eds) *Cross-Cultural Case Study, Studies in Qualitative Methodology*, Vol. 6, New York: Elsevier Science for JAI Press.

Brown, A. and Dowling, P. (1998) *Doing Research/Reading Research: A Mode of Interrogation for Education*, London: Falmer Press.

Bryant, I. and Jones, K. (1995) *Quantitative Methods and Statistical Processes in Educational Research*, Southampton: University of Southampton.

Bryman, A. (1988) *Quantity and Quality in Social Research*, London: Routledge.

Bryman, A. and Burgess, R.G. (1994) (eds) *Analysing Qualitative Data*, London: Routledge.

Bulmer, M. (1980) 'Why Don't Sociologists Make More Use of Official Statistics', *Sociology*, **14**: 505–25. (Reprinted in Bulmer, M. (1984) (ed) *Sociological Research Methods*, 2nd edn, London: Macmillan).

Bulmer, M. (1982) *The Uses of Social Research. Social Investigation in Public Policy Making*, London: George Allen and Unwin.

Burbules, N. (1995) 'Postmodern Doubt and Philosophy of Education', unpublished paper, Philosophy of Education Society Annual Conference, San Francisco.

Burgess, R.G. (1983) *Experiencing Comprehensive Education: A Study of Bishop McGregor School*, London: Allen and Unwin.

Burgess, R.G. (1994) 'On diaries and diary keeping', in N. Bennett, R. Glatter and R. Levacic (eds) *Improving Educational Management*, London: George Allen and Unwin.

Burton, D. (2000) 'Design Issues in Survey Research'; 'Data Collection Issues in Survey Research'; 'Questionnaire Design', 'Writing a Thesis', in D. Burton (ed.) *Research Training for Social Scientists*, London: Sage, Chs. 20, 22, 23.

Butler, I. and Williamson, H. (1994) *Children Speak: Children, Trauma, and Social Work*, London: Longman.

Cameron, D. (2001) *Working with Spoken Discourse*, London: Sage.

Cameron, D., Frazer, E., Harvey, P., Rampton, M.B.H. and Richardson, K. (1992) *Researching Language. Issues of Power and Method*, London: Routledge.

Campbell, D. and Stanley, J. (1963) 'Experimental and Quasi-experimental

Designs for Research and Teaching', in N. Gage (ed.) *Handbook of Research on Teaching*, Chicago: Rand McNally.

Carr, W. (1995) *For Education: Towards Critical Educational Inquiry*, Buckingham: Open University Press.

Carr, W. and Kemmis, S. (1986) *Becoming Critical: Education, Knowledge and Action Research*, Lewes: Falmer Press.

Chelimsky, E. (1985) 'Comparing and contrasting auditing and evaluation: some notes on their relationship', *Evaluation Review*, **9** (4): 483–503.

Chen, H.T. (1996) 'A comprehensive typology for program evaluation', *Evaluation Practice*, **17** (2): 121–30.

Clark, J. (1990) 'Anthony Giddens, Sociology and Modern Social Theory', in J. Clark, C. Modgil and S. Modgil (eds) *Anthony Giddens: Consensus and Controversy*, London: Falmer Press.

Clarke, A. and Dawson, R. (1999) *Evaluation Research. An Introduction to Principles, Methods, and Practice*, London: Sage.

Coffey, A. (1999) *The Ethnographic Self: Fieldwork and the Representation of Identity*, London: Sage.

Coffey, A. and Atkinson, P. (2000) 'Hecate's Domain: Ethnography at a cultural crossroads', in C. Pole and R.G. Burgess (eds) *Cross-cultural Case Study*, New York: Elsevier Science for JAI Press.

Coghlan, D. and Branick, T. (2001) *Doing Action Research in Your Own Organisation*, London: Sage.

Cohen, L. and Manion, L. (1984) *Research Methods in Education*, 2nd edn, London: Croom Helm.

Cohen, L., Manion, L. and Morrison, K. (2000) *Research Methods in Education*, London: Routledge Falmer.

Connolly, P. (1998) 'Introduction', in P. Connolly and B. Troyna (eds) *Researching Racism in Education: Politics, Theory and Practice*, Buckingham: Open University Press.

Cooley, C.H. (1902) *Human Nature and the Social Order*, New York: Charles Scribner's Sons.

Cortazzi, M. (1993) *Narrative Analysis*, London: Falmer Press.

Cortazzi, M. (2002) 'Analysing narratives and documents', in M. Coleman and A. Briggs (eds) *Research Methods in Educational Leadership and Management*, London: Paul Chapman Publishing.

Cottrell, S. (1999) *The Study Skills Handbook*, London: MacMillan.

Cresswell, J.W. (1994) *Research Design. Qualitative and Quantitative Approaches*, London: Sage.

Creswell, J.W. (1998) *Qualitative Inquiry and Research Design: Choosing among five traditions*, Thousand Oaks, CA: Sage.

Croll, P. (1986) *Systematic Classroom Observation*, London: Falmer Press.

Cryer, P. (2000) *The Research Student's Guide to Success*, 2nd edn, Buckingham: Open University Press.

Davis, J., Watson, N. and Cunningham Burley, S. (2000) 'Learning the Lives of Disabled Children: Developing a Reflexive Approach', in P. Christensen and A. James (eds) *Research with Children. Perspectives and Practices*, London: Falmer Press.

de Vaus, D. (1996) *Surveys in Social Research*, 4th edn, London: UCL Press.

Delamont, S. (1981) 'All too familiar?', *Educational Analysis*, **3** (1): 69–84.

Delamont, S. (1992) *Fieldwork in Educational Settings. Methods, Pitfalls, and Perspectives*, London: Falmer Press.

Delamont, S., Atkinson, P. and Parry, O. (1997) 'The brave pretence at confidence: launching the student's career', in S. Delamont, P. Atkinson and O. Parry (eds) *Supervising the PhD. A guide to success*, Buckingham: Open University Press.

Denscombe, M. (1998) *The Good Research Guide to Small-Scale Research Projects*, Buckingham: Open University Press.

Denscombe, M. (2002) *Ground Rules for Good Research: A 10-point guide for social researchers*, Buckingham: Open University Press.

Denzin, N.K. (1970) *The Research Act in Sociology: A Theoretical Introduction to Sociological Methods*, London: The Butterworth Group.

Derrida, J. (1978) *Writing and Difference*, Chicago: University of Chicago Press.

Dey, I. (1993) *Qualitative Data Analysis: A User-friendly Guide for Social Scientists*, London: Routledge.

Dillabough, J-A. and Arnot, M. (2001) 'Feminist Sociology of Education: Dynamics, Debates, and Directions', in J. Demaine (ed.) *Sociology of Education Today*, Eastbourne: Palgrave Publishers Ltd.

Dillman, D.A. (2000) *Mail and Internet Surveys: The Tailored Design Method*, New York: Wiley.

Ebbutt, D. (1985) 'Educational Action Research: some general concerns and specific quibbles', in R.G. Burgess (ed.) *Issues in Educational Research: Qualitative Methods*, Lewes: Falmer Press.

Edwards, A. and Talbot, R. (1994) *The Hard-pressed Researcher: a Research Handbook for the Caring Professions*, London: Longman.

Eisenhart, M. (2001) 'Educational Ethnography past, present, and future: ideas to think with', *Educational Researcher*, **30** (8): 16–27.

Elley, W. (1994) *The IEA Study of Reading Literacy: Achievement and Instruction in Thirty-Two School Systems*, Oxford: Pergamon.

Elliott, J. (1991) *Action Research for Educational Change*, Buckingham: Open University Press.

Fairburn, G.J. and Winch, C. (1996) *Reading, Writing, and Reasoning: A Guide for Students*, 2nd edn, Buckingham: Open University Press.

Fay, B. (1993) 'The Elements of Critical Social Science', in M. Hammersley (ed.) *Social Research. Philosophy, Politics and Practice*, London: Sage.

Fetterman, D. (1994a) 'Empowerment Evaluation', *Evaluation Practice*, **15** (1): 1–15.

Fetterman, D. (1994b) 'Steps of Empowerment Evaluation', *Evaluation and Program Planning*, **17** (3): 305–13.

Fielding, N. (1981) *The National Front*, London: Routledge and Kegan Paul.

Fielding, N.G. and Fielding, J.L. (1986) *Linking Data*, London: Sage.

Fine, G. and Sandstrom, K. (1988) *Knowing Children: Participant Observation with Minors*, Newbury Park, CA: Sage.

Flanders, N. (1970) *Analyzing Teacher Behaviour*, Reading, MA: Addison Wesley.

Fogelman, K. (1985) 'Exploiting Longitudinal Data: Examples from the National Child Development Study', in A.R. Nicol (ed.) *Longitudinal Studies in Child Psychology and Psychiatry*, Chichester: Wiley.

Foster, P. (1996) *Observing Schools: A Methodological Guide*, London: Paul Chapman Publishing.

Foucault, M. (1972) *The Archaeology of Knowledge*, London: Routledge.

Foucault, M. (1979) *Discipline and Punish: the Birth of the Prison*, New York: Vintage.

Foucault, M. (1983) 'On the genealogy of ethics: an overview of work in progress', in H. Dreyfus and P. Rainbow (eds) *Michael Foucault: Beyond Structuralism and Hermeneutics*, Chicago, IL: University of Chicago Press.

Fowler, F.G. (1993) *Social Survey Methods*, London: Sage.

Fraenkel, J.R. and Wallen, N. (2003) *How to Design and Evaluate Research in Education*, 5th edn, New York: McGraw Hill Higher Education.

France, A., Bendelow, G. and Williams, S. (2000) 'A "risky" business: researching the health beliefs of children and young people', in A. Lewis and G. Lindsay (eds) *Researching Children's Perspectives*, Buckingham: Open University Press.

Frey, F.W. (1970) 'Cross-cultural survey method in political science', in R.T. Holt and J.E. Turner (eds) *The Methodology of Comparative Research*, New York: Free Press.

Fullan, M. (2003) *Changing Forces: Probing the Depths of Educational Reform*, London: Falmer Press.

Gaber, I. (nd) *Television and radio: a best practice guide*, Swindon: Economic and Social Research Council (ESRC).

Gabriel, Y. (1991) 'Turning facts into stories and stories into facts', *Human Relations*, **44** (8): 857–75.

Gadamer, H-G. (1975) *Truth and Method*, London: Sheed and Ward.

Gage, N.L. (1991) 'The Obviousness of Social and Educational Research Results', *Educational Researcher*, **20** (1): 10–16.

Galton, M., Simon, B. and Croll, P. (1980) *Inside the Primary Classroom*, London: Routledge and Kegan Paul.

Galtung, J. and Ruge, M. (1973) 'Structuring and Selecting News', in S. Cohen and J. Young (eds) *The Manufacture of News: Deviance, Social Problems and the Mass Media*, London: Constable.

Garfinkel, H. (1967) *Studies in Ethnomethodology*, Englewood Cliffs, NJ: Prentice Hall.

Garfinkel, H. (1988) 'Evidence for Locally Produced, Naturally Accountable Phenomena of Order, Logic, Reason, Method, etc. in and as of the Essential Quiddity of Immortal Ordinary Society (I of IV): An Announcement of Studies', *Sociological Theory*, **6**: 103–9.

Gatens, M. (1996) *Imaginary Bodies: Ethics, Power, and Corporeality*, London: Routledge.

Geertz, C. (1973) *The Interpretation of Cultures*, New York: Basic Books.

Gelsthorpe, L. (1992) 'Response to Martyn Hammersley's paper "On Feminist Sociology"', *Sociology*, **26**: 213–18.

Gershuny, J., Miles, I., Jones, S., Mullings, C., Thomas, G. and Wyatt, S. (1986) 'Time budget: preliminary analyses of a national survey', *Journal of Social Affairs*, **2** (1): 13–39.

Gewirtz, S., Ball, S.J. and Bowe, R. (1995) *Markets, Choice and Equity in Education*, Buckingham: Open University Press.

Giddens, A. (1982) *New Rules of Sociological Method*, London: Hutchinson.

Giddens, A. (1984) *The Constitution of Society*, Cambridge: Polity Press.

Gillborn, D. (1998) 'Racism and the politics of qualitative research: learning from controversy and critique', in P. Connolly and B. Troyna (eds) *Researching Racism in Education: Politics, Theory and Practice*, Buckingham: Open University Press.

Gillham, B. (2000) *The Research Interview*, London: Continuum.

Gilroy, P. (1980) 'Managing the Underclass: a further note on the sociology of race relations in Britain', *Race and Class*, **22**: 47–62.

Gipps, C. (1994) *Beyond Testing: Towards a Theory of Educational Assessment*, London: Falmer Press.

Glaser, B.G. and Strauss, A.L. (1967) *The Discovery of Grounded Theory: Strategies for Qualitative Research*, Chicago, IL: Aldine.

Gold, R. (1958) 'Roles in Sociological Field Observation', *Social Forces*, **36** (3): 217–23.

Gomm, R., Hammersley, M. and Foster, P. (2000) (eds) *Case Study Method. Key Issues, Key Texts*, London: Sage.

Goodson, I. (1983) 'The use of life history in the study of schooling', *Interchange*, **11** (4): 62–76.

Goodson, I. and Sikes, P. (2001) *Life History Research in Educational Settings*, Buckingham: Open University Press.

Goudenough, W.H. (1981) *Culture, Language and Society*, Melo Park, CA: Benjamin/Cummings.

Griffiths, M. (1998) *Educational Research for Social Justice: Getting off the fence*, Buckingham: Open University Press.

Grint, K. and Woolgar, S. (1997) *The Machine at Work: Technology, Work, and Organization*, Cambridge: Polity Press.

Guba, E.G. and Lincoln, Y.S. (1981) *Effective Evaluation: Improving the Usefulness of Evaluation Results through Responsiveness and Naturalistic Approaches*, San Francisco, CA: Jossey-Bass.

Guba, E. and Lincoln, Y. (1985) *Naturalistic Enquiry*, London: Sage.

Guba, E. and Lincoln, Y. (1989) *Fourth Generation Evaluation*, Newbury Park, CA: Sage.

Guba, E. and Lincoln, Y. (1994) 'Competing Paradigms in Qualitative Research', in N. Denzin and Y. Lincoln (eds) *Handbook of Qualitative Research*, London: Sage.

Gubrium, J. and Holstein, J. (1997) *The New Language of Qualitative Method*, New York: Oxford University Press.

Habermas, J. (1972) *Knowledge and Human Interests*, London: Heinemann.

Habermas, J. (1974) *Theory and Practice*, London: Heinemann.

Habermas, J. (1987) *The Theory of Communicative Action. Vol. 2: Lifeworld and System: A Critique of Functional Reason* (T. McCarthy, trans.), Boston, MA: Beacon Press.

Habermas, J. (1989) *Theory of Communicative Action*, Boston, MA: Beacon Press.

Hacking, I. (1999) *The Social Construction of What?* Cambridge, MA: Harvard University Press.

Hall, S. (1981) 'Teaching race', in A. James and R. Jeffcoate (eds) *The School in the Multicultural Society: a Reader*, London: Harper and Row.

Hammersley, M. (1992a) 'On Feminist Sociology', *Sociology*, **26**: 187–206.

Hammersley, M. (1992b) *What's Wrong with Ethnography?* London: Routledge.

Hammersley, M. (1997) 'On the foundations of critical discourse analysis', in *Language and Communication*, **17** (3): 237–48.

Hammersley, M. (1998) 'Partisanship and credibility: the case of anti-racist educational research', in P. Connolly and B. Troyna (eds) *Researching Racism in Education: Politics, Theory and Practice*, Buckingham: Open University Press.

Hammersley, M. and Atkinson, P. (1983) *Ethnography: Principles in Practice*, 1st edn, London: Tavistock.

Hammersley, M. and Atkinson, P. (1995) *Ethnography: Principles in Practice*, 2nd edn, London: Routledge.

Hammersley, M. and Gomm, R. (1997) 'Bias in Social Research', in *Sociological Research Online*, **2** (1) www.socresonline.org.uk/2/1/2.html.

Hammersley, M. and Gomm, R. (2000) 'Introduction', in R. Gomm, M. Hammersley and P. Foster (eds) *Case Study Method*, London: Sage.

Hargreaves, D. (1996) 'Educational research and evidence-based educational research: a response to critics', *Research Intelligence*, 58: 12–16.

Harré, R. (1972) *The Philosophies of Science*, Oxford: Oxford University Press.

Haywood, P. and Wragg, E.C. (1994) 'The Literature Review 1', in D. Johnson (ed.) *Research Methods in Educational Management*, London: Pitman Publishing.

Heritage, J. (1984) *Garfinkel and Ethnomethodology*, Cambridge: Polity Press.

Hillage, J., Pearson, R., Anderson, A. and Tamkin, P. (1998) *Excellence in Research on Schools*, London: DfEE.

Hine, C. (2000) *Virtual Ethnography*, London: Sage.

Hitchcock, G. and Hughes, D. (1995) *Research and the Teacher: A Qualitative Introduction to School-based Research*, 2nd edn, London: Routledge.

Hockett, H.C. (1955) *The Critical Method in Historical Research and Writing*, London: Macmillan.

Hockey, J. (1991) *Squaddies*, Exeter: Exeter University Press.

Holly, M.L. (1984) *Keeping a Personal Professional Journal*, Melbourne: Deakin University Press.

Holly, M.L. (1989) *Writing to Grow*, Portsmouth, NH: Heinemann.

Horner, M. (2003) 'Leadership Theory Re-visited', in N. Bennett, M. Crawford and M. Cartwright (eds) *Effective Educational Leadership*, London: Paul Chapman Publishing.

House, E.R. (1993) *Professional Evaluation: Social Impact and Political Consequence*, Newbury Park, CA: Sage.

Hughes, P. (2001) 'Paradigms, methods, and knowledge', in G. Mac Naughton, S. Rolfe, and I. Siraj-Blatchford (eds) *Doing Early Childhood Research. International Perspectives on Theory and Practice*, Buckingham: Open University Press.

Hutchby, I. and Wooffitt, R. (1998) *Conversation Analysis. Principles, Practices, and Applications*, Cambridge: Polity Press.

Jackson, P. (2000) 'Race and Racism', in D. Burton (ed.) *Research Training for Social Scientists*, London: Sage.

James, A. and Prout, A. (1990) (eds) *Constructing and Reconstructing Childhood*, 1st edn, London: Falmer Press.

Janesick, V.J. (1998) 'The Dance of Qualitative Research Design', in N.K. Denzin and Y.S. Lincoln (eds) *Strategies of Qualitative Inquiry*, London: Sage.

Joint Committee on Standards (1994) *Program Evaluation Standards*, 2nd edn, Thousand Oaks, CA: Sage.

Kirkham, J. (1992) *Good Style. Writing for Science and Technology*, London: E&FN Spon.

Kitzinger, J. (1994) 'The methodology of focus groups: the importance of interaction between research participants', *Sociology of Health and Illness*, **16** (1): 103–21.

Klein, G. (2000) 'Improving Inspection for Race Equality', *Improving Schools*, **3** (2): 38–43.

Kress, G. (1990) 'Critical discourse analysis', *Annual Review of Applied Linguistics*, **11**: 84–99.

Krzeslo, E., Rainbird, H. and Vincent, C. (1996) 'Deconstructing the question: reflections on developing a comparative methodology for research union policy towards vocational training', in C. Pole and R.G. Burgess (eds) *Cross-Cultural Case Study, Studies in Qualitative Methodology*, Vol. 6, New York: Elsevier Science for JAI Press.

Kuhn, T. (1971) *The Structure of Scientific Revolutions*, Chicago: University of Chicago Press.

Kumar, R. (1999) *Research Methodology: A step-by-step guide for beginners*, 2nd edn, London: Sage.

Labov, W. (1972) 'The transformation of experience into narrative syntax', in W. Labov (ed.) *Language in the Inner City*, Philadelphia, PA: University of Philadelphia.

Lankshear, C., Peters, M. and Knobel, M. (1996) 'Critical pedagogy and cyberspace', in H. Giroux with C. Lankshear, P. McLaren and M. Peters (eds) *Counternarratives: Critical Studies and Critical Pedagogies in Postmodern Spaces*, New York and London: Routledge.

Lather, P. (1991) *Getting Smart: Feminist Research and Pedagogy with/in the Postmodern*, New York: Routledge.

Lavrakas, P.J. (1993) *Telephone Survey Methods: Sampling, Selection, and Supervision*, 2nd edn, Newbury Park, CA: Sage.

Leithwood, K., Jantzi, D. and Steinbach, R. (2003) 'Fostering teacher leadership', in N. Bennett, M. Crawford and M. Cartwright (eds) *Effective Educational Leadership*, London: Paul Chapman Publishing.

Leonard, D. (2001) *A Woman's Guide to Doctoral Studies*, Buckingham: Open University Press.

Lewis, A. and Lindsay, G. (2000) (eds) *Researching Children's Perspectives*, Buckingham: Open University Press.

Lincoln, Y. and Guba, E.G. (2000) 'The Only Generalization is: There is No Generalisation', in R. Gomm, M. Hammersley and P. Foster (eds) *Case Study Method. Key Issues, Key Texts*, London: Sage.

Lindsay, G. (2000) 'Researching children's perspectives: ethical issues', in A. Lewis and G. Lindsay (eds) *Researching Children's Perspectives*, Buckingham: Open University Press.

Lingard, B. and Douglas, P. (1999) *Men Engaging Feminisms: Pro-feminism, Backlashes, and Schooling*, Maidenhead: Open University Press.

Lloyd-Smith, M. and Davies, J. (1995) (eds) *On the Margins: The Educational Experience of Problem Pupils*, Stoke-on-Trent: Trentham Books.

Lloyd-Smith, M. and Tarr, J. (2000) 'Researching Children's Perspectives: a sociological dimension', in A. Lewis and G. Lindsay (eds) *Researching Children's Perspectives*, Buckingham: Open University Press.

Lofthouse, M.T. and Whiteside, T. (1994) 'The Literature Review 2', in D. Johnson (ed.) *Research Methods in Educational Management*, London: Pitman Publishing.

Lomax, P. (2002) 'Action Research', in M. Coleman and A. Briggs (eds) *Research Methods in Educational Leadership and Management*, London: Paul Chapman Publishing.

Lomax, P. and Whitehead, J. (1998) 'The processes of improving learning in schools and universities through developing research-based professionalism and a dialectic of collaboration in teaching and teacher education 1977–1978', *Journal of In-Service Education*, **24** (3): 447–67.

Luke, A. (1995) 'Text and discourse in education: an introduction to critical discourse analysis', *Review of Research in Education*, **21**: 3–47.

Lyotard, J.F. (1984) *The Postmodern Condition: A Report on Knowledge*, Manchester: Manchester University Press.

Mac an Ghaill, M. (1994) *The Making of Men: Masculinities, Sexualities and Schooling*, Buckingham: Open University Press.

Mac Naughton, G., Rolfe, S. and Siraj-Blatchford, I. (2001) (eds) *Doing Early Childhood Research: International Perspectives on Theory and Practice*, Buckingham: Open University Press.

MacIntyre, A. (1981) *After Virtue*, London: Gerald Duckworth and Co.

MacIntyre, A. (1988) *Whose Justice? Which Rationality?* London: Duckworth.

MacLure, M. (1994) 'Talking in class: rationales for the rise of oracy in the UK', in J. Maybin and B. Stierer (eds) *Languages, Literacy, and Learning in Educational Practice*, Clevedon: Multilingual Matters.

MacLure, M. (2003) *Discourse in Educational and Social Research*, Buckingham: Open University Press.

Malinowski, B. (1922) *Argonauts of the Western Pacific*, London: Routledge and Kegan Paul.

Mandelbaum, D.G. (1982) 'The study of life history', in R.G. Burgess (ed.) *Field Research: A Sourcebook and Field Manual*, London: Allen and Unwin.

Mark, M.M. and Shotland, R.L. (1985) 'Stakeholder-based evaluation and value judgements', *Evaluation Review*, **9** (5): 605–26.

Marsh, C. (1982) *The Survey Method: The Contribution of Surveys to Sociological Explanation*, London: George Allen and Unwin.

May, T. (1993) *Social Research: Issues, Methods, and Process*, Buckingham: St Edmundsbury Press for the Open University.

Mayall, B. (1994) 'Children in action at home and school', in B. Mayall (ed.) *Children's Childhoods Observed and Experienced*, London: Falmer Press.

Mayall, B. (2000) 'Conversations with children; working with generational issues', in P. Christensen and A. James (eds) *Research with Children: Perspectives and Practices*, London: Falmer Press.

Maynard, M. (1994) 'Methods, practice, and epistemology: the debate about feminism and research', in M. Maynard and J. Purvis (eds) *Researching Women's Lives from a Feminist Perspective*, London: Taylor and Francis.

McGrath, C. (nd) *Influencing the UK Policymaking Process*, Swindon: Economic and Social Research Council (ESRC).

Mead, G.H. (1934) *Mind, Self, and Society*, Chicago, IL: University of Chicago Press.

Meloy, J.M. (1994) *Writing the Qualitative Dissertation*, Hove: Lawrence Erlbaum.

Miles, M.B. and Huberman, A.M. (1994) *Qualitative Data Analysis: An Expanded Source Book*, 2nd edn, London: Sage.

Miles, R. (1982) *Racism and Migrant Labour*, London: Routledge and Kegan Paul.

Mitchell, J.C. (2000) 'Case and Situation Analysis', in R. Gomm, M. Hammersley and P. Foster (eds) *Case Study Method. Key Issues, Key Texts*, London: Sage.

Montgomery, M. (1986) 'Language and power: a critical review of Studies in the Theory of Ideology by John B. Thompson', *Media, Culture, and Society*, **8**: 41–64.

Morgan, D. (1988) *Focus Groups as Qualitative Research*, Newbury Park, CA: Sage.

Morgan, D. (ed.) (1993) *Successful Focus Groups*, Newbury Park, CA: Sage.

Morrison, M. (1999) 'Researching public libraries and ethic diversity: some black and white issues', in G. Walford and A. Massey (eds) *Studies in Educational Ethnography*, Vol. 2, England: JAI Press.

Morrison, M. (2002a) 'Using diaries in research', in M. Coleman and A. Briggs (eds) *Research Methods in Educational Leadership and Management*, London: Paul Chapman Publishing.

Morrison, M. (2002b) 'What do we mean by educational research?', in M. Coleman and A. Briggs (eds) *Research Methods in Educational Leadership and Management*, London: Paul Chapman Publishing.

Morrison, M. and Galloway, S. (1996) 'Using diaries to explore supply teachers' lives', in J. Busfield and E.S. Lyons (eds) *Methodological Imaginations*, London: Macmillan in association with the British Sociological Association.

Morrison, M. and Watling, R. (2002) *Introduction to Research Methods for Postgraduate Students in Education and Social Science*, Leicester: University of Leicester for the Graduate School.

Mortimore, P., Sammons, P., Stoll, L., Lewis, D. and Ecob, R. (1988) *School Matters: The Junior Years*, Wells: Open Books.

Mouly, G.J. (1978) *Educational Research: The Art and Science of Investigation.* Boston, MA: Allyn and Bacon.

Muller, J. (2004) 'On the shoulders of giants: a digression on knowledge, curriculum and finally, the teacher', Paper presented at the Third Basil Bernstein Symposium, University of Cambridge, July.

O'Brien, M., Alldred, P. and Jones, D. (1996) 'Children's constructions of family and kinship', in J. Brannen and M. O'Brien (eds) *Children in Families. Research and Policy*, London: Falmer Press.

O'Kane, C. (2000) 'The Development of Participatory Techniques: Facilitating Children's Views about Decisions which Affect Them', in P. Christensen and A. James (eds) *Research with Children. Perspectives and Practice*, London: Falmer Press.

Oates, C. (2000) 'The use of Focus Groups in Social Science Research', in D. Burton (ed.) *Research Training for Social Scientists*, London: Sage.

Oppenheim, A. (1992) *Questionnaire Design, Interviewing, and Attitude Measurement*, New York: Basic Books.

Osler, A. and Morrison, M. (2000) *Inspecting Schools for Race Equality: OFSTED's Strengths and Weaknesses*, Stoke-on Trent: Trentham Books for the Commission for Racial Equality.

Outhwaite, W. (1987) *New Philosophies of Social Science: Realism, Hermeneutics and Critical Theory*, London: Macmillan.

Ozga, J. (2000) *Policy Research in Educational Settings: Contested Terrains*, Buckingham: Open University Press.

Parlett, M. and Hamilton, D. (1976) 'Evaluation as Illumination: a new approach to the study of innovatory programmes', in C. Glass (ed) *Evaluation Studies Review Annual*, Vol. 1, Beverley Hills, CA: Sage.

Patai, D. (1994) 'When Power becomes Method', in A. Gitlin (ed.) *Power and Method*, London: Routledge.

Patton, M.Q. (1982) *Practical Evaluation*, Beverly Hills, CA: Sage.

Patton, M.Q. (1988) 'The evaluator's responsibility for utilization', *Evaluation Practice*, **9** (2): 5–24.

Pawson, R. and Tilley, N. (1997) *Realistic Evaluation*, London: Sage.

Pell, A. and Fogelman, K. (2002) 'Analysing quantitative data', in M. Coleman and A. Briggs (eds) *Research Methods in Educational Leadership and Management*, London: Paul Chapman Publishing.

Pennycook, A. (1994) 'Incommensurable discourses?', *Applied Linguistics*, **15** (2): 115–37.

Pink, S. (2001) *Doing Visual Ethnography*, London: Sage.

Platt, J. (1981) 'Evidence and proof in documentary research. 2: Some shared problems of documentary research', *Sociological Review*, **29** (1): 53–66.

Plummer, C. (1983) *Documents of Life: An Introduction to the Problems and Nature of the Naturalistic Method*, London: George, Allen and Unwin.

Pole, C. (1993) 'Local and national evaluation', in R.G. Burgess (ed.) *Education Research and Evaluation: for Policy and Practice?* London: Falmer Press.

Pole, C. (2001) 'Black teachers: curriculum and career', *Curriculum Journal*, **12** (3): 145–56.

Pole, C. and Lampard, R. (2002) *Practical Social Investigation: Qualitative and Quantitative Methods in Social Research*, Harlow: Pearson Education for Prentice Hall.

Pole, C. and Morrison, M. (2003) *Ethnography for Education*, Buckingham: Open University Press.

Popper, K. (1963) *Conjectures and Refutations*, Oxford: Oxford University Press.

Popper, K. (1976) 'The Logic of the Social Sciences', in T. Adorno, R. Albert, R. Dahrendorf, J. Habermas, H. Pilot and K. Popper (eds) *The Positivist Dispute in German Sociology*, London: Heinemann.

Potter, J. (1997) 'Discourse analysis as a way of analysing naturally occurring talk', in D. Silverman (ed.) *Qualitative Research: Theory, Method, and Practice*. London: Sage.

Powney, J. and Watts, M.D. (1987) *Interviewing in Educational Research*, London: Routledge and Kegan Paul.

Poynton, C. (2000) 'Linguistics and discourse analysis', in A. Lee and C. Poynton (eds) *Culture and Text: Discourse and Methodology in Social Research and Cultural Studies*, Lanham, MD: Rowman and Littlefield.

Purvis, J. (1984) *Understanding Texts*. Open University Course E205, Unit 15, Milton Keynes: Open University Press.

Ramazanoglu, C. (1992) 'On Feminist Methodology: Male Reason versus Female Empowerment', *Sociology* **26**: 207–12.

Rawls, J. (1971) *A Theory of Justice*, Oxford: Oxford University Press.

Richards, T. and Richards, L. (1994) 'From filing cabinet to computer', in A. Bryman and R.G Burgess (eds) *Analysing Qualitative Data*, London: Routledge.

Richards, T. and Richards, L. (1998) 'Using computers in qualitative research', in N. Denzin and Y. Lincoln (eds) *Strategies of Qualitative Inquiry*, London: Sage.

Richardson, L. (1990) 'Narrative and Sociology', *Journal of Contemporary Ethnography*, **19**: 116–35.

Roach, P. and Morrison, M. (1998) *Public Libraries, Ethnic Diversity and Citizenship*, London: British Library Board.

Robson, C. (2000) *Small-Scale Evaluation*, London: Sage.

Rossi, P.H. and Freeman, H.E. (1993) *Evaluation: A Systematic Approach*, 5th edn, Newbury Park, CA: Sage.

Sayer, A. (1992) *Method in Social Science: A Realist Approach*, London: Routledge.

Sayer, A. (2000) *Realism and Social Science*, London: Sage.

Schagen, I. and Hutchinson, D. (2004) 'Adding Value in Educational Research – the marriage of data and analytical power', *British Educational Research Journal*, **29** (5): 749–66.

Schon, D. (1983) *The Reflective Practitioner: how professionals think in action*, New York: Basic Books.

Schutz, A. (1963) 'Common-sense and Scientific Interpretation of Human Action', in M. Natanson (ed.) *Philosophy of the Social Science*, London: Routledge.

Schutz, A. (1972) *The Phenomenology of the Social World*, London: Heinemann.

Scott, D. (1996) 'Methods and data in educational research', in D. Scott and R. Usher (eds) *Understanding Educational Research*, London: Routledge.

Scott, D. (2000) *Realism and Educational Research: New Perspectives and Possibilities*, London: RoutledgeFalmer.

Scott, D. (2000) *Reading Educational Research and Policy*, London: Routledge Falmer.

Scott, D. (2004) 'Four Curriculum Discourses: a Genealogy of the Field', in D. Scott (ed.) *Curriculum Studies: Major Themes in Education*, London: Routledge.

Scott, D. (2004) Introduction, *Curriculum Studies: Major Themes in Education*, London: Routledge Falmer.

Scott, D., Brown, A., Lunt, I. and Thorne, L. (2004) *Professional Doctorates: Integrating Professional and Academic Knowledge*, Maidenhead: Open University Press.

Scott, D. and Usher, R. (1999) *Researching Education: Data, Methods and Theory in Educational Enquiry*, London: Cassell.

Scott, J. (1990) *A Matter of Record: Documentary Sources in Social Research*, Cambridge: Polity Press.

Scriven, M. (1967) 'The methodology of evaluation', in R.W. Tyler, R.M. Gagne and M. Scriven (eds) *Perspectives of Curriculum Evaluation*, Chicago, IL: Rand McNally.

Scriven, M. (1991) *Evaluation Thesaurus*, 4th edn, Newbury Park, CA: Sage.

Sergiovanni, T.J. (2003) 'The Lifeworld at the centre: values and action in educational leadership', in N. Bennett, M. Crawford and M. Cartwright (eds) *Effective Educational Leadership*, London: Paul Chapman Publishing.

Silverman, D. (2001) *Interpreting Qualitative Data: Methods for Analyzing Talk, Texts, and Interaction*, 2nd edn, London: Sage.

Simons, H. (1984) 'Negotiating Conditions for Independent Evaluations', in C. Adelman (ed.) *The Politics and Ethics of Evaluation*, London: Croom Helm.

Sinclair, J.M. and Coulthard, M. (1975) *Towards an Analysis of Discourse: The English used by Teachers and Pupils*, London: Oxford University Press.

Sinclair Taylor, A. (2000) 'The UN Convention on the Rights of the Child: giving children a voice', in A. Lewis and G. Lindsay (eds) *Researching Children's Perspectives*, Buckingham: Open University Press.

Skilbeck, M. (1983) 'Lawrence Stenhouse: research methodology', *British Educational Research Journal*, **9** (1): 11–20.

Smith, L.M. (1978) 'An evolving logic of participant observation, educational ethnography and other case studies', in L. Shulman (ed.) *Review of Educational Research*, Vol. 6. Itsca, IL: F.E. Peacock.

Smith, R. (1993) 'Potentials for empowerment in critical social research', *The Australian Educational Researcher*, **20** (2): 75–94.

Somekh, B. (1995) 'The contribution of action research to development in social endeavours: a position paper on action research methodology', *British Educational Research Journal*, **21** (3): 339–55.

Stake, R. (1978) 'The case study in social inquiry', *Educational Researcher*, **7**, February: 5–8.

Stake, R. (1995) *The Art of Case Study Research*, London: Sage.

Stake, R. (2000) 'The Case Study Method in Social Inquiry', in R. Gomm, M. Hammersley and P. Foster (eds) *Case Study Method. Key Issues, Key Texts*, London: Sage.

Stanley, L. (1993) 'The impact of feminism on sociology in the last 20 years', in C. Kramarae and S. Spender (eds) *The Knowledge Explosion*, New York: Harvester Wheatsheaf.

Stanley, L. (1994) 'The knowing because experiencing subject: narratives, lives, and autobiography', in K. Lennon and M. Whitford (eds) *Knowing the Difference: Feminist Perspectives in Epistemology*, London: Routledge.

Stanley, L. and Wise, S. (1990) 'Method, methodology, and epistemology in feminist research processes', in L. Stanley (ed.) *Feminist Praxis*, London: Routledge.

Stenhouse, L. (1985) 'What counts as research?', in J. Rudduck and D. Hopkins (eds) *Research as a Basis for Teaching: Readings from the Work of Lawrence Stenhouse*, London: Heinemann.

Stewart, D.W. and Shamdasani, P.N. (1990) *Focus Groups: Theory and Practice*, Newbury Park, CA: Sage.

Strauss, A.L. (1987) *Qualitative Analysis for Social Scientists*, Cambridge: Cambridge University Press.

Strauss, A.L. and Corbin, J. (1990) *Basics of Qualitative Research: Grounded Theory Procedures and Techniques*, London: Sage.

Strawson, P. (1959) *Individuals: An Essay in Descriptive Metaphysics*, London: Methuen.

Stronach, I. (1998) 'Vocationalism and economic recovery: the case against witchcraft', in S. Brown and R. Wake (eds) *Education in Transition*, Edinburgh: Scottish Council for Research in Education.

Stronach, I. and MacLure, M. (1997) *Educational Research Undone: The Postmodern Embrace*, Buckingham: Open University Press.

Tesch, R. (1990) *Qualitative Research. Analysis Types and Software Tools*. New York: Falmer Press.

Thomas, R. and Purdon, S. (1995) *Telephone Methods for Social Surveys*, Social Research Update 8, Guildford: University of Surrey.

Tooley, J. with Darby, J. (1998) *Educational Research: A Critique – A Survey of Published Educational Research*, London: Ofsted.

Tripp, D. (1993) *Critical Incidents in Teaching*, London: Routledge.

Troyna, B. (1995) 'Beyond reasonable doubt? Researching "race" in educational settings', *Oxford Review of Education*, **21** (4): 395–408.

Usher, R. (1996) 'A Critique of the Neglected Assumptions of Educational Research', in D. Scott and R. Usher (eds) *Understanding Educational Research*, London, Routledge.

Usher, R. (1997) 'Telling a Story about Research and Research as Story-telling: Postmodern Approaches to Social Research', in G. McKenzie, J. Powell and R. Usher (eds) *Understanding Social Research: Perspectives on Methodology and Practice*, London: Falmer Press.

Usher, R., Bryant, I. and Johnstone, R. (1997) *Adult Education and the Post-modern Challenge: Learning Beyond the Limits*, London: Routledge.

Vaitlingam, R. (nd) *Developing a Media Strategy*, Swindon: Economic and Social Research Council (ESRC).

Van Maanen, J. (1988) *Tales of the Field: On Writing Ethnography*, Chicago, IL Chicago University Press.

Verhoeven, J.C. (2000) 'Some Reflections of Cross-cultural Interviewing', in C. Pole and R.G. Burgess (eds) *Cross-Cultural Case Study, Studies in Qualitative Methodology*, Vol. 6, New York: Elsevier Science for JAI Press.

Walker, A. and Dimmock, C. (2004) 'The International Role of the NCSL: Tourist, Colporteur, or Confrere?' *Educational Management and Leadership*, **32** (3): 269–88.

Walker, D. (nd) *Heroes of Dissemination*, Swindon: Economic and Social Research Council (ESRC).

Walkerdine, V. (1990) *Girl School Fictions*, London: Verso.

Wallace, M. and Poulson, L. (2003) (eds) *Learning to Read Critically in Educational Leadership and Management*, London: Sage.

Ward Schofield, J. (1993) 'Increasing the Generalizability of Qualitative Research', in M. Hammersley (ed.) *Social Research. Philosophy, Policy, and Practice*, London: Sage.

Watling, R. (2002) 'Analysing Qualitative Data', in M. Coleman and A. Briggs (eds) *Research Methods in Educational Leadership and Management*, London: Paul Chapman Publishing.

Watts, H.D. and White, P. (2000) 'Getting Published' and 'Presentation Skills', in D. Burton (ed.) *Research Training for Social Scientists*, London: Sage.

Webb, S. (2000) 'Feminist Methodologies for Social Researching', in D. Burton (ed.) *Research Training for Social Scientists*, London: Sage.

Weber, M. (1964) *The Theory of Social and Economic Organization*, New York: Free Press.

Weber, M. (1974) 'Subjectivity and Determinism', in A. Giddens (ed.) *Positivism and Sociology*, London: Heinemann Educational Books.

Weiler, K., Weiner, G. and Yates, L. (1999) 'Series Editor Preface', in B. Lingard and P. Douglas, *Men Engaging Feminisms, Pro-feminism, Backlashes, and Schooling*, Maidenhead: Open University Press.

Weiner, G., Arnot, M. and David, M. (1997) 'Is the Future Female? Female Success, Male Disadvantage, and Changing Gender Patterns in Education', in A.H. Halsey, H. Lauder, P. Brown and A.S. Wells (eds) *Education. Culture, Economy, Society*, Oxford: Oxford University Press.

Weiss, C.H. (1972) *Evaluation Research*, Englewood Cliffs, NJ: Prentice Hall.

Wetherell, M. and Potter, J. (1994) *Mapping the Language of Racism: Discourse and the Legitimation of Exploitation*, London: Harvester.

Whitehead, J. (1993) *The Growth of Educational Knowledge*, Bournemouth: Hyde Publications.

Whorf, B. (1954) *Language, Thought and Reality*, Boston, MA: MIT Press and New York: Wiley.

Whyte, W.F. (1949) 'The social structure of a restaurant', *American Journal of Sociology*, **54**: 302–10.

Williams, A. (1993) 'Diversity and Agreement in Feminist Ethnography', *Sociology* **27**: 575–89.

Williams, K. (1996) *Essential Writing Skills: Developing Your Writing*, Oxford Brookes University: Oxford Centre for Staff Development.

Wilson, R. (1990) 'Sociology and the Mathematical Method', in A. Giddens and J. Turner (eds) *Social Theory Today*, Cambridge: Polity Press.

Wolcott, H. (1981) 'Confessions of a "trained" observer', in T.S. Popkewitz and B.R. Tabachnick (eds) *The Study of Schooling*, New York: Praeger.

Woods, P. (1985) 'Conversations with Teachers', *British Educational Research Journal*, **11** (1): 13–26.

Woods, P. (1993a) *Critical Events in Teaching and Learning*, London: Falmer Press.

Woods, P. (1993b) 'The Magic of Godspell: The Educational Significance of a Dramatic Event', in R. Gomm and P. Woods (eds) *Educational Research in Action*, London: Paul Chapman Publishing.

Woods, P. (1999) *Successful Writing for Qualitative Researchers*, London: Routledge.

Yates, L. (1999) 'Preface', in B. Lingard and P. Douglas (eds) *Men Engaging Feminisms. Pro-feminism, Backlashes, and Schooling*, Maidenhead: Open University Press.

Yin, R.K. (1994) *Case Study Research: Design and Methods*, 2nd edn, Thousand Oaks, CA: Sage.

Young, M. (1999) *The Curriculum of the Future*, London: RoutledgeFalmer.

Zuber-Skerritt, O. (1996) *New Directions in Action Research*, London: Falmer Press.

Author Index

Subject Index